Women and Science:
The Snark Syndrome

DEDICATION

This book is dedicated to all the male and female mentors without whom the author would never have been encouraged to overcome many barriers to high professional achievement: Elizabeth Halsall, former Sixth Form tutor and later academic adviser and lifelong friend; Hal Puddifoot of the former London County Council, whose early faith in me, expert training and political coaching launched my career; Leslie Jackson of Halifax County Borough Council who taught me how to govern wisely and compassionately; Francis Stuart of Lincoln County Borough Council who filled all the missing gaps in my professional experience to equip me for the highest posts; and all of them for backing an unorthodox pioneer woman.

Women and Science:
The Snark Syndrome

Eileen M. Byrne

 The Falmer Press

(A Member of the Taylor & Francis Group)
London • Washington, D.C.

UK   The Falmer Press, 4 John St., London, WC1N 2ET
USA   The Falmer Press, Taylor & Francis Inc., 1900 Frost Road, 101, Bristol, PA 19007

First published 1993
Reprinted 1995

Library of Congress Cataloging-in-Publication data are available on request

A catalogue record for this book is available from the British Library

ISBN 18500 6547 cased
ISBN 18500 6555 paper

Jacket design by Caroline Archer

Set in 11/13pt Bembo by
Graphicraft Typesetters Ltd., Hong Kong

Printed in Great Britain by Burgess Science Press, Basingtoke on paper which has a specified pH value on final paper manufacture of not less than 7.5 and is therefore 'acid free'.

Contents

Acknowledgments

Acknowledgment is made to the four sponsors whose grants totalling A\$77,264 made the University of Queensland (UQ) Women in Science and Technology in Australia (WISTA) Policy Review research possible: the Australian Research Grants Committee and Australian Research Council; the University of Queensland; the Myer Foundation; and the Commonwealth Tertiary Education Commission. My principal debt is to the research team, Merideth Sadler, Senior Research Assistant, and Marie Keynes, Project Officer and Secretary, without whose constant efficiency, reliability, insights and support, the scale and complexity of the research would have been impossible.

Thanks are due also to Dr Elizabeth Hazel, Senior Lecturer in the School of Microbiology at the University of New South Wales, to whose initiative and energy the overall three-stranded WISTA project owes its original foundation in 1984 and its early funding, before the Policy Review Project moved to the University of Queensland under the direction of Professor Eileen Byrne in 1985. It was renamed the UQ WISTA Policy Review Project and provides the basis for this book. We thank the Vice Chancellors, Directors and Registrars of the ten UQ WISTA survey institutions for their constructive cooperation and their supply of a wide range of institutional data, much of it especially prepared for this project; the Deans, Professors, Heads of Schools and academic and professional staff who attended the group interviews in the ten survey institutions, responded to written discussion papers, and subsequently supplied other relevant data. Their views, experience and evidence have helped to shape both interim and final policy recommendations.

A particular debt is due to the Board of Secondary School Studies, Queensland; the New South Wales Department of Education's Statutory Boards Directorate; the Victorian Curriculum and Assessment

Board; the Senior Secondary Assessment Board of South Australia; the Secondary Education Authority of Western Australia; the Schools Board of Tasmania; and the Australian Capital Territory Schools Authority, for data, much of it unpublished, on Grade 12 enrolments and for further background on curriculum content of Grade 12 subjects.

Dr David Chant, Statistical Adviser to the Social Sciences Group of the University of Queensland, has given much helpful advice and guidance on the statistical analyses and has handled the computerization of the student and staff data.

Chapter 1

Introduction:
Changing the Paradigms

'Just the place for a Snark!' the Bellman cried,
As he landed his crew with care;
Supporting each man on the top of the tide
By a finger entwined in his hair.

'Just the place for a Snark! I have said it twice:
That alone should encourage the crew.
Just the place for a Snark! I have said it thrice:
What I tell you three times is true'.
(Lewis Carroll, *The Hunting of the Snark*)

Two decades ago, in the early 1970s, what I have defined in this book as the 'Snark Syndrome' was particularly evident in the pronouncements of the men who controlled science and technology about the girls and women who were so under-represented in all but the biological sciences. By dint of constant repetition ('what I tell you three times is true'), male academics, engineers, mathematicians and Directors of Education have based their policies on the groundless assertions that girls were innately mathematically more deficient than boys, that male and female minds were different and complementary as such and, that girls did not enrol equally in the physical sciences or in technological disciplines because of a lack of interest or because they had different interests from boys. Soon Snark assertions abounded.

The ideas and research on which this book is based accordingly represent a critical review of current received wisdom on the position of women in (or out of) science and technology, in the context of policy for change. Running through the conceptual framework and the research methodology like the warp and woof of a Gobelin tapestry is an examination of what the author has differentiated as the Snark Syndrome and the Snark effect; that is, 'knowledge' or policy based on assertion rather than on clear, logical or empirical soundness.

When the research on which the main conclusions of this book are based was designed in 1985, it became very evident in the first comprehensive literature search that, despite a decade of scholarly research in the area of women and science, too much of what passed for current received wisdom in educational policymaking and in teaching theory in relation to women and science, had still been based on very imperfect policy theory. By dint of repetition three times (or thirty), the educational community had internalized an oversimplified and often unscholarly selection of beliefs and premises which had descended to the 'everyone knows that . . .' level of slogan-like impact. For example, current in most educational reviews and policy reports were such generalized imprecise assertions as: if only we had more women role models, we would have more women students; single-sex education advantages girls; conversely, coeducation equips girls better; girls can't or don't do maths as well as boys because of maths anxiety, or because of differential teacher attitudes, or because of innate genetically inherited differences in spatial ability, or because they do not have the same childhood practical learning experiences as boys. These statements are at best only partly true, in some cases quite unfounded, and only valid in certain specific circumstances. Many of the asserted 'principles' on which current educational policy is built are also based on assumptions as unfounded as those of the nineteenth-century New Zealand teacher who justified and defended teaching mathematics to his girls not because he saw them as future physicists, but because 'he regarded mathematics for girls not only as useful in everyday life, but also essential to prevent their natural tendency to be birdwitted' (Wallis, 1972, p. 33). One is reminded of the view of the Greek philosopher and mathematician Hypatia (*c.* AD 370–415) that 'men will fight for a superstition quite as quickly as for a living truth — often more so, since a superstition is so intangible you cannot get at it to refute it, but truth is a point of view and so is changeable.'

The Snark Syndrome

Because a great deal of received wisdom in the area of women in science is still based on assumption, belief or prejudices operating at the level of superstition noted by Hypatia, the present writer has coined the term 'the Snark Syndrome' to describe what has occurred as a recurrent phenomenon, as a pattern, as a part of the policymaking scene. That is, the Snark Syndrome is the assertion of an alleged truth or belief or principle as the basis for policymaking or for educational practice, although this proves to have no previous credible base in sound empirical research and proves also to be in no way consonant with accredited substantive or grounded theory in the relevant area of knowledge.

The application of the Snark Syndrome produces the Snark effect. This operates when two things are simultaneously found. Firstly, that the assertion is based merely on the educator, teacher or policymaker having internalized it from hearing it repeated many times ('What I tell you three times is true'), and despite the widely cited ubiquity of the belief or principle it proves to be either unfounded, or only occasionally and contextually true. Secondly, at the same time the internalized belief is used to justify and implement major policies (for example, the creation or retention of single-sex schools or classes, or the use of role-model theory instead of mentorship practice in affirmative action programmes).

In the 1970s and 1980s, significant progress has been made in increasing female enrolments in some scientific and technological disciplines. But when in the mid-1980s one looked behind the macro analyses to patterns and trends, it became evident that progress was more cosmetic than organic. Increased female undergraduate enrolments were not matched by parallel increases in postgraduate research. Women were still in a minority of fewer than 10 per cent in senior academic posts, in industry and in research organizations. Attitudes were still redolent of Snark Syndrome prejudice. Some disciplines remained unchanged.

Much of what follows is based on a five-year policy research project based at the University of Queensland's Department of Education, one of three Australian projects which form the overall Women in Science and Technology in Australia (WISTA) project. This policy research, known as the UQ WISTA Policy Review Project, set out to review research and policy using a major critical review of previous research in the area and a sample of ten major Universities and Institutes of Technology as a catchment area for new data and for generating new grounded theory. Chapter 2 describes the basis of the research for those readers interested in methodology and approach.

Australia's economic future is partly dependent on its developing its own manufacturing technology, information technology, scientific innovation and invention. The wastage of scientific and technological talent from the girls and women who represent 51 per cent of the population must be a matter of social, economic and political concern. In Australia, federally commissioned committees on education, training and employment and on technological change respectively, have both recorded extreme concern at Australia's failure to recruit and develop female talent in science and technology, particularly at tertiary levels (Williams Committee [1979] and Myers Committee [1980]). Half a decade earlier the Kangan Report on technical and further education in Australia had recorded a similar message of failure to invest in and encourage female talent (ACOTAFE, 1974). But in 1984 Australia was seen to be 'well behind comparable countries in national initiatives addressing the problems for girls in these [maths and science] areas of the curriculum' (Commonwealth Schools Commission, 1984, p. 29), while three years later the same Commission recommended that 'schools should provide a challenging learning environment which is *socially and culturally* supportive and physically comfortable for girls and boys' (Commonwealth Schools Commission, 1987, p. 70).

But this issue is not only a matter of the loss of skilled womanpower. It is also a question of general scientific literacy, of the participation of all adult people — not just adult males — in the judgmental process involved in applying the results of science and technology to governmental policy. Twenty-five years ago, the Dainton Committee was saying that 'Those who have no scientific understanding are cut off from a great human activity; and may well feel excluded from intercourse with those who have such understanding' (Council for Scientific Policy, 1968). In 1985 the UK Inspectorate, writing of policies for school science, endorsed a much-repeated view that 'the failure of many girls to acquire a broad education in the main areas of science means that they are deprived of essential skills and knowledge, and the nation loses scientific and technological expertise' (Department of Education and Science, 1985a). Women engineers in France have reasserted their conviction that decisions in science and technology policies also need to be influenced by the experience and insights of women as well as men:

> This responsibility [for the consequences of technology] is of the utmost significance for the women scientists and the women engineers. On the one hand, they are in a better position to convey a knowledge acquired through personal experience to a seldom well-informed public opinion. On the other hand, they have to make womankind realise that they should not remain unconcerned in a world ruled by technique, but that they have a part to play in it. (Cercle des Femmes Ingénieurs, 1978, p. 17)

The UQ WISTA research, therefore, set out to look at the barriers which hinder, and the positive factors which help, women's access to science and technology in higher education. It focussed not only on access to higher education from the schooling system but also on the experiences during the higher education years which affect access to and progression in both undergraduate and postgraduate studies in science and technology. The research focussed particularly on the role of institutional ecology in influencing female access and achievement (or otherwise), and on policy strategies and mechanisms for change.

Access is one thing. Retention and progression are another. Research literature has for over a decade now, across many countries and cultures, recorded the phenomenon of 'cascading losses'. That is, institutions record a cumulative and progressive loss of female enrolments as one moves up the levels of the education systems. Chapter 6 discusses this phenomenon in the context of the cluster effect of related factors which influence it. At this stage one notes that Isabelle Deblé (1980, pp. 20–23), for example, cites an IEA study of 1974 into results of boys and girls in physics, chemistry and biology which shows that at the start of schooling the difference between the sexes is minimal. The gap between the results, however, grows steadily, according to sex, as they get older. Her own study of thirty-nine countries analyses female:male enrolments and wastage and finds that ratios are always higher for boys at the 'third level' (tertiary study), except in some parts of Europe and the then USSR (Deblé, 1980). Women are proportionately fewer at each level and stage of education: relatively fewer in tertiary than in secondary courses, fewer in postgraduate than in undergraduate studies, fewer in PhD enrolments than at masters level (Byrne, 1978; Cass *et al.*, 1983; OECD, 1986). A review of sixty-two studies looking at science and maths education in the UK also notes the 'cascading effect' of progressive losses of female participation in relation to male, throughout the educational system up to the beginning of tertiary study (Kaminski, 1982).

Shifting the Paradigms

As a result of the UQ WISTA research and the concurrent critical review of existing research literature, we conclude that several major paradigm shifts are necessary as a basis for future policy and, indeed, for future research priorities.

From Victim to Cause: from Female to Male

The most substantial body of relevant previous research has focussed on girls themselves as a means of finding out why they drop out or under-achieve, or indeed why they succeed. This has been a useful and necessary first step in order more accurately to identify possible barriers and factors of influence. But the first two rounds of this research exercise have shown clearly that the problem lies mainly not with girls and women, but with boys and men. Like rape, it is a male problem resulting in female disadvantage.

For it has been predominantly the men in schooling, science and industry who have created masculine images and attached them territorially to disciplines and occupations. It is primarily male students who define the presence of women students in a discipline as normal or abnormal, who assert exclusive territoriality, and who dominate hands-on experimentation with equipment and computers to exclude girls and women. It is the men in the leadership of higher education who (albeit often unconsciously) act as mentors to male but not to female students, to the great advantage of the former. In essence, *the problem with girls and women is boys and men*, and these issues are factors which critically affect the learning environment of girls and women. One fundamental approach which has underpinned the UQ WISTA research from its outset, therefore, has been a belief that we need to move away from the blaming-the-victim approach of constantly dissecting the behaviour and attitudes of girls in order to find explanations of their lack of access and progression, towards examining the male behaviours, and the structures in the education systems in which they are located, as a mainstream explanatory theory. We believe that real explanations belong in the 'ecology' of the teaching and learning environments and that this ecology functions at institutional level, not simply at the level of the classroom or discipline (or 'ecological niche'). Male behaviour is an integral part of this ecology. We have therefore investigated the concept of 'institutional ecology' as an explanatory theory. This is developed in chapter 3 and in the final chapter.

From Generic Science to a Discipline-based Model

Some of the value of research in the 1960s and early and mid-1970s is diminished by an inadequately diagnostic approach to science in relation to women's participation. Much research, for example, writes incorrectly of female access to 'science' as if this were a homogeneous, defined phenomenon with precise boundaries and content. The improved statistical analyses of actual female and male enrolments in school and university systems in many countries, which we have seen in the decade 1975–85, both worldwide and in different cultures, has illustrated, however, that diagnosis needs to be focussed on specific and different disciplines and subdisciplines: chemistry as distinct from physics, biochemistry as distinct from chemistry, chemical engineering as distinct from civil or electrical engineering, for example. The most researched discipline has been engineering and this has highlighted differences between subdisciplines. Some school-based work also usefully separates out physics from chemistry and biology in the fieldwork, but still does not adequately distinguish the interpretive results by discipline. Policy work in particular continues to generalize about 'women in science and technology' in unacceptably broad generalizations.

Yet increasing statistical evidence from the international organizations (Byrne, 1989) and analysis of a wide range of work on women and engineering (Byrne, 1985) convinced the present writer that there were highly different patterns of behaviour operating both at student (girl, boy) level and at staff levels, in different disciplines and subdisciplines. It seemed evident that future research should focus increasingly on teasing out the different female enrolment and progression patterns in different disciplines and subdisciplines. The corollary of this is that explanations of these increasingly diversified results are as likely to lie in the institution-based factors (the institutional ecology) and in the nature, structure and ecology of each discipline itself (the ecological niche), as in the girls and women themselves.

From Victim to Cause: from Role Modelling to Mentorship

The shift away from role-model theory as a policy mechanism to more overt and conscious use of mentorship outlined in chapters 4 and 5 is a further example of a paradigm shift from blaming women ('if only we had more women role models, we'd have more women engineers') to making men (who still form over 90 per cent of the leadership and the power structure) responsible for positive action to lift women over attitudinal and other barriers. But the UQ WISTA research did not only shift from the blaming-the-victim approach of re-examining women to looking at those who caused the problems or controlled the processes and the educational environment. It was a conscious shift to what Hess and Ferrée describe as 'pushing the field *beyond* the simple add-women-and-stir approach for incorporating women into existing paradigms of research' (Hess and Ferrée, 1987, p. 9).

In addition to moving to paradigm shifts, we have also reset or clarified some concepts which we see as fundamental to reaching a more holistic approach to women's status in science and technology. These are the concept of critical mass, the concepts of non-traditionality or sex-neutrality, and the image of science.

The Concept of Critical Mass

The concept of critical mass is fundamental both to the aspects of institutional ecology investigated, and to a proper understanding of the influence of some (but not all) of the factors of influence. When a particular group (girls, the working class, ethnically different subgroups) is a minority of a school or college class of students, or a minority in the educational institution as a whole, it is below the threshold of proportion of the whole which would enable the groups of girls (etc.) to be seen as a balanced and integral part of the class or institution. The minority group is not seen as 'normal' recruitment. 'Critical mass' in this context is therefore the proportion which forms the threshold beyond which a minority group needs to move in order to establish (a) a sense of normality, a transcendence of identity beyond 'the rubric of exceptions', and (b) sufficient support to the minority group for its members to continue, not to drop out, and to achieve without constraint. Alma Lantz describes this as a process under which 'once a certain proportion or number (mass) of a population is present, re-cruitment and retention of that population becomes a self-sustaining and self-perpetuating system' (Lantz, 1982, pp. 731–37). Critical mass theory asserts that organic, long-term and sustained change will only occur in institutions, departments or other 'populations' above a thresh-old point. This threshold is the point at which a minority group be-comes a large enough proportion of the whole to form a 'critical mass', that is, a mass of significance. The theory is one of level of influence, of identity, of potency as a change agent, and not one of numbers as such. The threshold for change (even if the change is still from the perceived abnormal to the perceived normal) may well vary from scheme to scheme, issue to issue. Lantz postulates that for success (i.e. self-sustaining and self-perpetuating change), the effect of passing over a threshold into normality (away from untypicality) has to be *evident*, or felt in the relevant community.

When we re-examined the current theory, it seemed evident that it was highly relevant to the much-reported issues of male and female attribution of different disciplines as either normal for males, normal for females, abnormal for either, or sex-neutral. Fairly obviously, there would be a threshold above and below which a minority would be seen as (and would feel) normal or untypical respectively. One question we addressed was whether different levels of critical mass were likely to produce significantly different behaviour patterns in girls who were in a very small minority (say 5 per cent) and girls who had achieved a critical mass over a threshold (to be defined) into alleged sex-normality or sex-neutrality in terms of their peers' and teachers' perceptions of them.

We have concluded that, in terms of enrolment proportions:

- There is a critical threshold in the proportion of female enrolment in the whole class or institution.
- Above this threshold, when women achieve critical mass, their enrolments are seen as normal.
- Above this critical mass threshold, female enrolments continue to be substantial without affirmative action.
- Below the threshold, female enrolments are still seen and imaged as untypical, abnormal or exceptional.
- Below the critical mass threshold, female enrolments do not increase above 5 per cent or 10 per cent unless there is *constant affirmative action.*

There are obvious policy implications which flow from this.

It must be said that evidence is far from decisive on the issue of critical mass, although we remain convinced that critical mass theory provides a logical and valid explanation of the actual reported behaviour of minorities of varying proportions in educational settings. Later work by Lantz reviews work on the possible influence of the male:female ratio in the classroom in the context of a critical review of issues concerning mathematics enrolments, and concludes that it remains a 'fuzzy empirical issue [producing] . . . scanty evidence on the effect of the male-female ratio on attrition or achievement' (Lantz, 1985, pp. 347–54). A little surprisingly, Lantz questions whether 'the male-female ratio of the classroom or the sex of the instructor is important' (*ibid.*, p. 354), although her own review records as many researchers who believed their work did support hypotheses that critical mass affects attrition and performance as those who held the reverse. Where the UQ WISTA research departs from previous stances is in the implications of critical mass theory. The hypothesis that women are intimidated (deprived of equal discourse, receive less teacher attention) if they are less than a secure proportion of a mixed class, has been used, for example, to support policies for the provision of single-sex learning environments for girls in maths and science. We will argue in a later chapter that this is to misinterpret available evidence and theory; the real implication should be to change the character of the male-dominated coeducational learning environments in which girls are effectively in a boys' class and not a sex-neutral one.

Some five decades ago Hawley argued that human ecology was basically a 'population' problem, and that the ways in which a particular developing community (e.g. area or institution) was affected by the size, composition and rate of growth or decline of the population were central to human ecological analysis. Insofar as he saw as equally central 'the *relative numbers* in the various functions composing the communal structure, together with the factors which make for change in the existing equilibrium and the ways in which such change occurs', he foreshadowed some of the elements of what we now call critical mass theory (Hawley, 1944, p. 405).

Non-traditional, Sex-normal, Sex-neutral?
A Policy Issue

Earlier general research on gender and education has highlighted the relationship of adolescent motivation and vocational aspirations in young adults on the one hand, and the perception of subjects, disciplines or areas of knowledge as 'male' or 'female' on the other. Other studies contrast disciplines as non-traditional or traditional for the sex concerned. Definitions, however, as to what is traditional or non-traditional (or allegedly sex-neutral) can vary both according to culture, according to the prevailing dominant social definition of sex roles, and according to the purpose of the definition (e.g. for legislation or special training schemes). This led us to see a need to define more clearly than some previous research what is meant by non-traditionality and by 'sex-normality' in choices and aspirations.

No finite international or national agreements have yet been achieved on how to define a discipline or occupation as 'non-traditional' for one sex or another. Governments, agencies, institutions and employers in different countries have increasingly had to reach a contextually agreed definition in relation to antidiscrimination legislation, or to the funding of special training and employment schemes for the under-represented sex. The most widely used cut-off point in the USA,

Sweden and the UK has emerged as between 30 and 33 per cent; that is, if one sex is represented by less than about a third of those involved in an occupation or discipline, the latter was designated as non-traditional for the under-represented sex. Some individual schemes have, however, used a figure of as low as 20 per cent or as high as 40 per cent. It is noted that in Hite's (1985) study of 481 men and women doctoral students in twenty-seven fields at a large state university in the American midwest, she classifies traditional for women as an enrolment of more than 40 per cent women and carrying a 'feminine' orientation; androgynous as 20–40 per cent women enrolments; and non-traditional as less than 20 per cent female and historically 'masculine' in orientation. In Hite's classification, biochemistry, veterinary microbiology and biological sciences are classified as androgynous; while physical sciences, computer sciences, geosciences, statistics, chemistry and physics are non-traditional. Somewhat startlingly, botany, however, is also classified as non-traditional (presumably American women do not enrol beyond the 20 per cent level, which would not be the case in Australia [Hite, 1985, p. 10]).

In the specific context of UQ WISTA's examination of recruitment to higher education and the sex-attribution of disciplines and subdisciplines, the Queensland WISTA team started by taking 30 per cent as the cut-off point below which the enrolment of the under-represented sex was seen as non-traditional. On further investigation of the research literature and the reports of many special projects (both in Australia and overseas), however, we noted some repeated patterns in the reported perceptions of either staff or students in the disciplines in which they worked or studied. In studies of the sex-role attitudes of schoolchildren, of higher education students, of the experiences of minority women in the labour market, there is a consistency in reported evidence. Different kinds of research reports of pupil attitudes to opposite-sex involvement in science and technology disciplines have, in particular, identified further subdivisions within the non-traditional area to show degrees of untypicality through to perceived abnormality. The boys in the British GIST (Girls into Science and Technology) project were, for example, already labelling girls of 11–13 years who did physics in secondary school as not only untypical but 'a bit peculiar' (Smail *et al.*, 1982).

Reviewing the literature against these questions, we arrived at a clearer but subdivided conceptual definition of sex-role perceptions. Where girls and women were in a minority but still formed a relatively significant statistical group (approaching a critical mass), they have tended to be described as untypical and as a minority, but they have not necessarily (indeed, rarely) been described as unfeminine or as acting abnormally for their societally ascribed sex-role. But, by contrast, where girls and women are in a smaller minority they have constantly been perceived as and described as abnormal rather than merely untypical. This is significant because if peer group and staff–student interaction reflects this perception, girls and women have to face not only the practical difficulties of minority status but also an attack on the normality of their sex-role identity. Moreover, it affects both role-model theory and mentorship. Typical adolescent girls will not identify with an abnormal (sex-role abnormal) role model. The character of mentorship is strongly affected by perceptions of normal or abnormal status in protégés.

There is one further subdivision within this second band. When girls and women are a very small minority indeed (one of the 3 per cent female professoriate in Australia; one of only four girls in a tertiary physics or engineering class of fifty or more; one of only eight women plumbers or electricians in a firm's workforce of a hundred), they are described both as sex-role abnormal and as the rubric of exceptions. That is, they are peripheralized and the general transferability of their experience and their achievement is denied. This is a serious policy issue. As long as a group can be written off as so exceptional as to be the constant exception to the rule, it cannot be used as a transferable basis for change.

Finally, we distinguish between sex-normality and sex-neutrality. These are not the same in the labelling of disciplines and occupations. If a discipline is seen as untypical for girls to the point of sex-role abnormality, attitudinal barriers present a major hurdle to all but the very gifted, middle-class and/or confident. If the discipline is seen as non-traditional in numbers but sex-normal, in behavioural and identity terms, there will still be some attitudinal barriers but there is likely to be more encouragement from relevant adults for girls to overcome them. If the discipline is seen, however, as sex-neutral, it will have been presented as normal for both sexes from the start and attitudinal barriers will not have been there, especially in progression (as distinct from access).

For example, physics is regarded as sex-normal for boys but non-traditional (or sex-abnormal) for girls, while the complete reverse applies to biology. Neither can therefore be regarded as sex-neutral. By contrast, the perception of English (or the language of origin) is that it is essential and normal for both sexes, and both enrol in almost equal numbers in the main secondary years. It is possible to see this subject as sex-neutral. But mathematics, which ranks equally as a

Table 1.1 The Byrne Scale of Non-Traditionality

Recruitment of both sexes above 30% of enrolments (e.g. 70:30, 60:40, etc.)	Students and teachers seen as sex-normal for both sexes, therefore the discipline is seen as sex-neutral
Recruitment of either sex at 16–29% of total	Seen as *sex-normal* for the majority sex and *untypical* but sex-normal for the minority sex
Recruitment of either sex at 9–15% of total	Seen as *sex-normal* for the majority sex and *abnormal* for the minority sex
Recruitment of either sex at 8% or less of total	Seen as *sex-normal* for the majority sex and *both abnormal and 'the rubric of exceptions'* for the minority sex, i.e. they do not count as in any way representative or as transferable models

mainstream core foundation subject in secondary education, acquires an early sex-normal label for boys, and thus a 'male' attribution and an untypical label for girls. It is not, therefore, seen as sex-neutral.

For the purpose of analysis in the UQ WISTA research, a scale of non-traditionality has been created. The actual statistical percentages may be negotiable (upwards), but the important issue is the concept of different *thresholds* of untypicality. This should be related to the definition of critical mass, to image (how 'male' is a subject?), to adolescent curricular choice (how does it affect normal sex-role identity [which is critical at that age]?), and to role modelling (is the role model seen as sex-normal, abnormal or so exceptional for that to be irrelevant?). The scale in table 1.1 has been used as a frame of reference throughout the UQ WISTA research. The scale is designed to be conceptual and interpretive and not a tool of precise empirical measurement; it will be used later as a framework against which to interpret our statistical analysis.

Redefining Science and Technology

How we define and see science and technology has begun to emerge as causally related to the issue of gender and science. Writers ranging from Kuhn to modern feminist academics have challenged past received wisdom about the nature, construct and characteristics of science as such. The *image* of science and technology proves both to be inaccurate and to be a critical filter; a filter not only to most girls but also to the androgynous boys of whom fewer enrol in science and technology in each generation. In reviewing the research and philosophical writing about science, several aspects of image have emerged. Science has been traditionally (wrongly) portrayed as:

- objective, factual and non-negotiable
- dealing with phenomena and not people
- culture-free and value-free
- male, masculine and exclusive
- harder than other areas of study

The place of image in ecology theory is discussed further in chapters 3 and 6. Because of its contextual importance as a backcloth, or a tapestry canvas on which our interpretive theory is woven, the resetting of science and technology in different constructual contexts is discussed briefly here in the context of the images of science and technology which influence enrolments in these disciplines.

Science is not Objective or Value-free

Science is itself a concept, not a clearly definable phenomenon as such. At one end of the scale, of course, *scientia* originally simply meant 'knowledge', and as late as 1903 the *Shorter Oxford English Dictionary* (*SOED*) gave one definition as the philosophy and logic included in the Oxford *Literae Humaniores*. But as early as 1725 the concept of scientific rigour as we now understand it meant

> study concerned with a connected body of demonstrated truths or with observed facts systematically classified and more or less colligated by being brought under general laws, and which includes trustworthy methods for the discovery of new truth within its own domain. (*SOED*, 1978)

This is also a still defensible generic definition, which allows a more general interpretation of the scientific approach than the previous century's location of the scientific within the area of demonstrated proof rather than demonstrated truth: 'of a syllogism, a proof; producing knowledge, demonstrative (1667)' (*SOED*, 1978).

The general perception of science has been as an intellectual, principle-based area of curiosity leading to knowledge, but located in an abstract attempt to explain the world by systematic, objective, ordered analysis. The perception of technology emerges as the applied arm, working principally through production and systems. In neither case can the 'objective' label be fully sustained in the sense of so designing experiments that there is no vested interest in the outcome. Researchers do not come to research with a *tabula rasa*; results are often presented to a retrospectively constructed rationality or are the product of prejudged expectation. Albury and Schwartz, for example, cite the 130-year-old research of Paul Broca, a French brain surgeon who measured the weight of the brains of 292 men and 140 women taken from cadavers after autopsies at four Parisian hospitals in the early 1860s. He found that the female brains averaged 14 per cent lighter than the male, and his published results became for fifty years a rallying point for the belief in men's alleged cognitive and intellectual supremacy. Only when the evolutionary biologist Stephen Jay Gould re-examined the implications of the data 120 years later was it discovered that the brain-weight difference was not due to sex as such, but to differences in age and height and to a prevalent degenerative brain disease more common in women than men at the time. Broca had seen no need to crosscheck his results against other factors than the first-level weight difference, since they confirmed the prevailing received wisdom of the time (and his own personal belief) that women were inferior to men and that there was a straight biological reason for this. His work helped to hinder the secondary and higher education of women for fifty years, by bolstering the alleged biological justification for their exclusion from advanced intellectual study. Albury and Schwartz cite other examples from science or technology which were heavily influenced by strong value-based or ideological stances and which masqueraded as 'objective' science (Albury and Schwartz, 1982).

Technology is no more value-free than science. The traditional view that 'technology is essentially amoral, a thing apart from its values, an instrument which can be used for good or ill' (Buchanan, 1965, p. 163) is as characteristic of its period as the equally limited educational view of technology as only applying to systems or products which was then prevalent. Two decades later, Pacey distinguishes those aspects of technology which, like basic science, have a transferable theoretical core, and those which are heavily contextual or culturally based in the country or sector in which they are practised:

So is technology culturally neutral? If we look at the construction of a basic machine and its working principles, the answer seems to be yes. But if we look at the web of human activities surrounding the machine, which includes its practical uses, its role as a status symbol, the supply of fuel and spare parts, and the skills of its owners, the answer is clearly no. Looked at in this second way, technology is seen as part of life, not something that can be kept in a separate compartment. (Pacey, 1983, p. 3)

Why does this matter? Firstly, because of bias where researchers do not concede (or are not aware of) their value bases; and, secondly, because there is considerable research evidence that more girls than boys reject the physical sciences and technological disciplines when they are imaged or marketed as value-free and abstract.

Science as Male or Masculine

This perception emerges as one of the greatest barriers to adolescent girls who, in terms of the Byrne Scale of Non-traditionality (or sex-normality) want to be seen as 'normally feminine' while pursuing tertiary study. There are three aspects highlighted in previous writings:

1 The *perception* of science as a male area by adolescents and young adults making curriculum and discipline choices (which filters young females out from an unconditioned choice).
2 The *actual* male-dominance of science and technology in terms of the participation of teachers, learners and producers (which creates an ecological niche supportive to males and not to females and raises issues of critical mass).
3 The construction and design of science in disciplines on a paradigm seen as male, patriarchal and instrumental (which is described by some as creating an inappropriate teaching: learning environment for females and for many males).

Bowling and Martin identify three overlapping influences of patriarchy on scientific knowledge: 'the choice of topics of study, the content of scientific theories, and the boundary between science and nonscience' Bowling and Martin, 1985, p. 312). One might note at this stage one or two aspects relevant to higher education. For example, a committee set up jointly by the Royal Society and the Institute of Physics in London to look at physics education gave particular emphasis to what it called 'the masculine image of science' which, the report stresses, had two effects. It was likely to lead parents and teachers to see scientific studies as inappropriate for girls, and to make girls themselves likely to see achievement in science as incompatible with femininity (Easlea, 1986, p. 133).

There is more subsumed within the attitudinal question than is immediately apparent, however. It is more complex than the more easily measurable questions of boys' territoriality, sex-appropriate labelling and peer pressure or self-esteem. A deeper problem is what Evelyn Fox Keller calls 'masculinist distortions of the scientific enterprise' which she sees as creating a potential dilemma for scientists who are also women and who have acquired the alternative perspective on the world which feminist analysis produces (Keller, 1982, p. 590). Debates about masculine bias or perspective have centred on very different issues. Some argue that the predominance of men in the sciences has led to a bias in the choice of which problems scientists have chosen to investigate and which they have left totally unresearched; and how the problem is defined. Others argue that the actual design of empirical science is male-biased. Keller is prominent among those who see the actual design of research as male-biased, citing among her examples that almost all animal-learning research on rats has used only male rats: that is, male equals the normal prototype (*ibid.*). One might also note that the English Crowther Report *15–18*, which was so influential in the redesign of upper secondary education in the 1960s, was based on major commissioned research limited to a sample of young male National Servicemen: no young females. Similarly, Bernstein's work on elaborated and basic codes in language was first based on a sample of young males only.

Pacey's reassessment of technology as needing to bridge what Fee calls 'the previous separation of human experience into mutually contradictory realms' (i.e. science and non-science) (Fee, 1981, p. 86) also argues that

> a profound contribution that could be made toward creativity in science and technology would be to encourage the involvement of women in this field at all levels. Not, I must add, as imitation men, copying all the absurdness of men, but to challenge and counteract the male values built in to technology. (Pacey, 1983, p. 107)

Elizabeth Fee suggests that 'the sciences have been seen as masculine, not simply because the vast majority of scientists have historically been men, but also the very characteristics of science are perceived and seen as sex-linked' (Fee, 1981, p. 86). That is, the alleged 'objectivity' we spoke of earlier (rational, authoritative, logical, impersonal, hard and cold) is ascribed by a kind of circularity as characteristic of masculine traits, and then endorsed as scientific. The 'female' antithesis is seen as subjective, irrational, intuitive and deductive, warm and soft, widely ascribed as normally female (Zillborg, 1974; Gelb, 1974). This has been institutionalized structurally within the hierarchy of the sciences — 'the "hard" sciences at the top are seen as more male than the "soft" sciences at the bottom' (Fee, 1981, p. 86). Fee sees science as essentially part of the power structure of social democracy, and no longer as an academically detached intellectual area. She also regards it as part of a male-dominated power structure: 'The production of scientific knowledge is highly organized and closely integrated with the structures of political and economic power' (*ibid.*).

Science as People-oriented

If one view of science lies in the arena of demonstrated truths, of proofs, of knowledge tested by process, an alternative view is as a means of understanding the world by deepening one's knowledge of it. This antithesis is important in relation to female and male motivation for choosing to study science, as is the antithesis of the perception of science as objective and finite and the converse view that it is value-loaded and negotiable. Albury and Schwartz, for example, hold that 'the scientific method, if such a thing exists at all, is not a universal process for arriving at the truth, but a way of deepening the knowledge available within a particular framework for looking at the world' (Albury and Schwartz, 1982, p. 78). Robin Clarke defines science as 'a means of constructing models of reality', and 'alone claiming unique access to an objective understanding of the world' (Clarke, 1985, p. 7). He sees as encouraging the move away from reductionism (viewing reality by examining its constituents in smaller and smaller particles) towards more holistic thinking. Studies of interrelationships thus become an increasingly important part of scientific activity. Clarke also believes that 'if . . . no longer to be trusted as the sole arbiter of truth, [science] remains an immensely powerful — and probably the most powerful — 'means of imaging the world' (*ibid.*, p. 7).

Feminists would argue that a scientific world which is only informed by the knowledge and 'construction of reality' of the male experience of life is incomplete and flawed. Yet we also know from research that both girls and 'androgynous' boys are put off by subjects that are presented as not set in a social context, are not people-oriented or people-friendly. Technology is often (wrongly) presented as user-unfriendly.

To the extent that Robin Clarke argues that historically 'all of the societies which have ever existed on this planet have possessed a technology: very few of them indeed have possessed a science', (*ibid.*, p. 9) he appears to accept the somewhat false or artificial antithesis that science is curiosity-driven knowledge and that technology is the application of invention. He argues that traditional or indigenous technologies are not, in fact, produced only as a result of scientific research. Innovations, from steam engines to zip fasteners, were more often the result of individual ingenuity than of science-based laboratory work. Clarke differentiates between technology arising out of innovation and inventiveness, and 'sciencebased technology' which tends to produce social impacts of greater magnitude: nuclear weapons, electronics, data processing (*ibid.*, p. 9). Arnold Pacey, in turn, recognizes a general public assumption when he discusses the culture-base of technology; technology is seen to be about 'machines, techniques, knowledge and the essential activity of making things work' (Pacey, 1983, p. 6). He goes on to distinguish technology-practice from 'technique' (in Jacques Ellul's sense) or 'technics', as 'the application of scientific and other knowledge to practical tasks by ordered systems that involve people and organisations, living things and machines' (*ibid.*, p. 6).

Pure or Applied? The Applied Filter

For reasons not yet clear, and again discussed further in later chapters, the statistical evidence shows consistently that women enrol more easily, frequently and in greater numbers in science and maths studies that they see as pure, creative and free-floating than in those whose image and content is applied. Chapters 3 and 6 discuss this in the context of new Australian data. Here, we note the extra filter which technology (as distinct from science) represents: women are proportionately filtered out more significantly from subjects and disciplines described as technological or located in Faculties of Applied Science and Technology.

Technology has traditionally been seen as the applied arm of science, the particular rather than the theoretical or conceptual: 'the scientific study of the practical or industrial arts (1859)' (*SOED*, 1978), or latterly 'the practice of any or all of the applied sciences that have practical value and/or industrial use' (*Chambers Twentieth Century Dictionary*). By the mid-1960s in Britain, technology in education was seen as 'the purposeful application of man's [sic] knowledge of materials, sources of energy and natural phenomena' (Schools Council, 1968, p. 29). Nearly twenty years later, the UK Schools Inspectorate identified technological (as distinct from scientific) work as involving the application of scientific ideas to production; improving design and efficiency of devices or systems; using these to tackle a scientific discipline; applying scientific principles to modify a product by problem-solving; using scientific knowledge to make balanced and informed judgments about technological innovation (Department of Education and Science, 1985b). In Australia, a recent definition by the Australian Education Council (AEC) locates technology clearly in the power area of production rather than in the power of ideas circuit of society: 'Technology implies much more than the tools and technical inventions of a society. It involves the whole complex of skills, techniques and processes by which a group maintains production and applies knowledge' (Australian Education Council, 1985). The AEC's view of technology as an instrument of industrial power reflects views characteristic of many writers on the role and status of science today.

While science is related in the ordinary mind with principles, rigour, objective truth and abstract enquiry, technology usually carries a public image of association with machines, systems, or even what Jacques Ellul calls 'la technique'. By this, Ellul means far more than machine technology, or principles of advanced mechanics applied to systems, but rather any complex of standardized means for attaining a desired technocratic result and a predetermined result. Ellul argues that 'in the modern world', the most dangerous form of determination is the technological phenomenon. It is not a question of getting rid of it, but by an act of freedom, transcending it' (Ellul, 1954, passim). Galbraith defines technology as 'the systematic application of scientific or other organised knowledge to practical tasks' and as an activity involving complex organizations (Galbraith, 1972). He also sees technology as in no way value-free, and indeed as heavily value-laden (*ibid.*).

Empirical evidence from a range of countries has confirmed that consistently fewer girls enrol in the applied sciences than the more free-floating ones, fewer in applied than pure maths, fewer in technology-based subjects than curiosity-driven disciplines. The differences are too strong and consistent to be a peripheral matter. We have raised, therefore, issues of the ecology of learning; the need to shift paradigms; and the need to look more qualitatively at different patterns of female and male enrolment between disciplines and subdisciplines which require different policy approaches. We question dyadic approaches (looking at only the effect of factor A on factor B); we argue in the final chapters for a cluster approach in policy formation. If we do not, Jacqueline Nonon's warning to the Seventh International Congress of Women Engineers and Scientists in Rouen in 1978 will become sadly prophetic:

'The transition from one century to the next cannot be made without women; if it is made without women, it will fail: it will be a rendez-vous with history, lost.' (Galbraith, chapter 2)

References

ACOTAFE (1974) *TAFE in Australia: report on needs in technical and further education* (Kangan Report), Canberra, Australian Government Publishing Service.

ALBURY, D. and SCHWARTZ, J. (1982) *Partial Progress: The Politics of Sciences and Technology*, London, Pluto Press.

ALDRICH, M. and HALL, P. (1980) *Programmes in Science, Maths and Engineering for Women in the USA 1966–1978*, Washington, DC, AAAS and Office of Opportunities in Science.

AUSTRALIAN EDUCATION COUNCIL (1985) *Education and Technology*, Melbourne, AEC.

BOWLING, J. and MARTIN, B. (1985) 'Science: a masculine disorder', *Science and Public Policy*, 12 (6), December, pp. 308–16.

BYRNE, E.M. (1978) *Equality of Education and Training for Girls*, Brussels, Commission of the European Communities.

BYRNE, E.M. (1980) *Men's Work, Women's Work? New Perspectives for Change*, Paris, UNESCO, Ed/80/CONF 708/3.

BYRNE, E.M. (1985) *Women and Engineering: A Comparative Overview of New Initiatives*, Canberra, Bureau of Labour Market Research, Australian Government Publishing Service.

BYRNE, E.M. (1989) 'Grounded theory and the Snark Syndrome: the role of the international organisations in research in gender in education', *Evaluation and Research in Education*, 3 (3), pp. 111–123.

CASS, B. *et al.* (1983) *Why so few? Women Academics in Australian Universities*, Sydney, Sydney University Press.

CERCLE DES FEMMES INGENIEURS (1978) *Ingénieur au Feminin*, Paris, Cahiers CEFI.

CLARKE, R. (1985) *Science and Technology in World Development*, Oxford and New York, Oxford University Press/UNESCO.

COMMONWEALTH SCHOOLS COMMISSION (1984) *Girls and Tomorrow: The Challenge for our Schools*, Canberra, Australian Government Publishing Service.

COMMONWEALTH SCHOOLS COMMISSION (1987) *The National Policy for the Education of Girls in Australia*, Canberra, Australian Government Publishing Service.

COUNCIL FOR SCIENTIFIC POLICY (1968) *Enquiry into the Flow of Candidates in Science and Technology in Higher Education* (Dainton Report), London, HMSO.

DEBLÉ, I. (1980) *The School Education of Girls*, Paris, UNESCO.

DEPARTMENT OF EDUCATION AND SCIENCE (1985a) *Science 5–16: A Statement of Policy*, London, HMSO.

DEPARTMENT OF EDUCATION AND SCIENCE (1985b) *Technology and School Science: An HMI Enquiry*, London, HMSO.

EASLEA, B. (1986) 'The masculine image of science with special reference to Physics: how much does gender really matter?', in HARDING, JAN (Ed) *Perspectives on Gender and Science*, London, Falmer Press.

ELLUL, J. (1954) *La Technique ou l'enjeu du siècle*, Paris, Armand Colin, translated as *The Technological Society*, (1964), New York, Vintage Books.

FEE, E. (1981) 'Is feminism a threat to scientific objectivity?', *Journal of College Science Teaching*, 11 (2), pp. 84–92.

GALBRAITH, J.K. (1972) *The New Industrial State*, 2nd edn., London, André Deutsch.

GELB, L. (1974) 'Masculinity and femininity' in MILLER, JEAN BAKER, (Ed) *Psychoanalysis and Women*, Harmondsworth, Penguin.

HESS, B. and FERRÉE, M. (1987) *Analyzing Gender: A Handbook of Social Science Research*, Newbury Park, Calif., Sage Publications.

HITE, L.M. (1985) 'Female doctoral students: their perceptions and concerns', *Journal of College Student Personnel*, 26 (1), pp. 18–23.

KAMINSKI, D.M. (1982) 'Girls and mathematics: an annotated bibliography of British work 1970–81', *Studies in Science Education*, 9, pp. 81–108.

KELLER, E. FOX (1982) 'Feminism and science', *SIGNS*, (7) 3, Spring, pp. 589–602.

LANTZ, A. (1982) 'Women engineers: critical mass, social support and satisfaction', *Engineering Education*, April, pp. 731–7.

LANTZ, A. (1985) 'Strategies to increase mathematics enrolments' in CHIPMAN, S., BRUSH, L. and WILSON, D. (Eds) *Women and Mathematics: Balancing the Equation*, NJ, Lawrence Erlbaum Publishers, pp. 329–54.

MYERS, R. (CHAIRMAN) (1980) *Technological Change in Australia*, Canberra, Australian Government Publishing Service.

OECD (1986) *Girls and Women in Education*, Paris, OECD.

PACEY, A. (1983) *The Culture of Technology*, Oxford, Basil Blackwell.

SCHOOLS COUNCIL (1968) *Technology and the Schools*, Schools Council Working Paper 18, London, HMSO.

SMAIL, B., WHYTE, J. and KELLY, A. (1982) 'Girls into science and technology: the first two years', *Social Science Review*, June, pp. 620–30.

WALLIS, E. (1972) *A Most Rare Vision*, Otago High School Board of Governors.

WILLIAMS, B. (CHAIRMAN) (1979) *Education, Training and Employment*, Report of the Committee of Enquiry into Education and Training, Canberra, Australian Government Publishing Service.

ZILLBORG, G. (1974) 'Masculine and feminine' in MILLER, J. BAKER, (Ed) *Psychoanalysis and Women*, Harmondsworth, Penguin.

Chapter 2

The UQ WISTA Research:
a Holistic and Policy Approach

A change of heart is the essence of all other change and it is brought about by a re-education of the mind. (Emmeline Pethick-Lawrence, *My Part in a Changing World* [1938], ch.7)

We suggested in chapter 1 that just such a re-education of the mind was needed: a shift of emphasis from examining girls and women to examining their learning environment, experience of teaching and peer environment. We wrote of an institutional ecology approach; a concept which we develop further in the next chapter. But we should be clear that the nature of the problems being investigated in the area of women and science are simply not susceptible to 'scientific proof'. However many attempts at replication of empirical research may attract researchers and grants, there will always be a range of projects whose findings appear to contradict each other. We suggest that the following principles can be accepted as bases for reinterpreting what research does and does not tell us, and as bases for future action.

1. Problems governed by interaction of human behaviour are not susceptible to unambiguous 'scientific' truth.

Thus the policymakers, journalists, teachers and parents who ask us for 'the answer', for a neat formula diagnosis of why girls do not enrol in certain sciences, may be disappointed by a lack of blueprint solutions. We can, however, produce a range of sound, research-supported probable causes of female non-access to some sciences, of drop-out or lack of progression in others, or reversion to stereotype, from which institutions and educators must diagnose their particular educational ailments (much as a good doctor knows a range of many accredited possible causes for a small child with a temperature and a rash). And there may be several simultaneous causes of educational symptoms.

2. Two hypotheses can be simultaneously true even if they appear mutually contradictory. They may be true in different circumstances, or in the same context at different times.

Researchers and educators appear to be obsessed with the doctrine of mutual exclusivity. Either, they argue, single-sex schools or classes are better for girls, or they are not. Either girls' differential performance in maths is due to maths anxiety in the girls (blaming-the-victim), or to sex-differentiation of teacher–student interaction in learning. But in practice, single-sex learning is better for some aspects of learning and coeducation better for others, as we discuss in more detail in a later chapter. The maths anxiety may be caused by teacher-differentiation, which in turn may cause a critical filter effect.

3. Insights into causes of human behaviour are unlikely to be achieved by dyadic studies: qualitative research requires a holistic approach.

Not infrequently, widely cited research has been dyadic (that is, it has dealt with the relationship of two factors only with each other) and even where several factors have been identified, some were excluded from research on pragmatic grounds of practicality rather than of logic or conceptual hypotheses. Approaches have too frequently been linear and narrowly focussed on the somewhat specious grounds of feasibility. But much inaccurate and unscholarly received wisdom has been disseminated into the education system and used as a basis for future policies, based on dyadic or on narrow, single-dimensional studies. This does not necessarily rule out the usefulness or scholarship of narrow linear studies, but it requires greater academic responsibility in publication to point either to the limits of the evidence or to its non-transferability in empirical terms. Thus Snark-effect assertions have been made about the influence of issues such as same-sex role models, single-sex schooling and coeducation, and mathematics and gender, on very constrained empirical evidence and without moderating for other related essential and controllable factors. Many research studies (at least as reported) have also imperfectly distinguished between factors which are cause-and-effect related, and factors which are coexistent. The UQ WISTA research has therefore attempted to review 'not a scattered series of analyses, but a systematic ordering of them into an integrated theory' (Glaser and Strauss, 1972, p. 295).

There is a need also not only to review existing research in the specific contexts of its validity, scholarship and relevance to policy, but to look at clusters of related factors. We sought both to distinguish cause-and-effect from coexistent factors, and to distinguish factors which were two-way related (A affects B, but B also affects A in an interactive cyclical effect) from those which were only one-way related (A affects B but B does not influence A; B affects D but not the converse). Some research-based discussion in the area of girls and science has been imprecise, sometimes to the point of being unscholarly, in generally asserting a relationship without identifying clearly its precise nature in these terms.

The main interaction of dimensions and factors which the UQ WISTA project has investigated is set out in figure 2.1. The interaction of one cluster is illustrated in figure 2.2, showing both two-way and one-way relationships. One issue on which there has been widespread agreement in previous research is at least the 'shopping-list' of influential factors in this area of study.

Ten Core Factors: a Central Framework

Very early in our literature research review, two things became evident and were increasingly confirmed in our work. Firstly, there was a particular core of factors (not all seen as of equal importance) which recurred constantly and which both relevant research from a wide range of countries and cultures and investigative work by the major international organizations had held to be influential. In no case could we find decisive evidence of the precise nature and extent of their impact. But whatever the ultimate relevance or influence these might prove to have in our own work, clearly they ought to provide part of our conceptual framework.

The ten core factors can be summarized as:

- same-sex role models for women
- the mentor process
- the image of different branches of science and technology (male, female or sex-neutral; socially responsible or systems- and machine-oriented)
- male attitudes to females in 'non-traditional' disciplines; female attitudes (self-esteem, or towards peers)

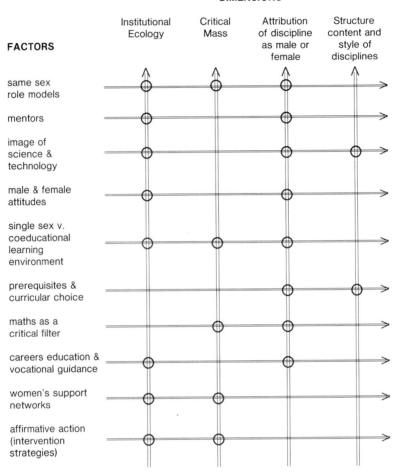

Figure 2.1 UQ WISTA theoretical framework

- single-sex versus coeducation
- prerequisites and school patterns of curricular choices as critical filters
- mathematics as a negative critical filter
- careers education and vocational counselling
- women's support networks
- affirmative action projects in science and technology

Of these, current received wisdom tended to hold that only same-sex role models, women's support networks and affirmative action

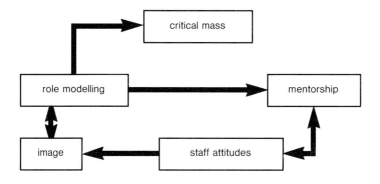

Figure 2.2 Interaction of a cluster of factors

would act as positive influences, and that prerequisites and curricular choices, maths as a critical filter and careers education and vocational counselling acted mainly negatively in relation to women's access to many branches of science and technology which are seen as non-traditional. The four factors of the image of science and technology, male and female attitudes, mentor roles and single-sex versus coeducation have been cited widely as both positive and negative influences.

Balancing the Imaginative and the Critical

It might be argued that if we cannot produce scientific proof of causes of students' biased curricular choices, under-achievement, drop-out or lack or progression without risking further epidemics of the Snark Syndrome (assertions unfounded on sound research), we may lack a policy basis for action. This is to underestimate the policy relevance of qualitative approaches. A rigorous use of a grounded theory approach can help us to form more soundly based hypotheses which would provide an improved basis for systemic and institutional policymaking.

The UQ WISTA research is based on the use and review of what Glaser and Strauss call grounded theory, and on the discovery of substantive theory developed through analysis of both quantitative and qualitative data. 'By the discovery of substantive theory we mean the formulation of concepts and their interrelation into a set of hypotheses for a given substantive area — such as patient care, gang behaviour or education — based on research in the area' (Glaser and Strauss, 1972, p. 288). Glaser and Strauss argue that a specific substantive theory must be formed, in order to see which of the existing formal theories are applicable to the research area on the one hand, and to further refine the substantive (integrated) theory on the other. There is in turn, they argue, a cyclical effect in forming and re-forming formal theory; but based on regular analysis of field data of some kind. 'Thus substantive theory becomes a strategic link in the formulation and development of formal theory based on data. **We have called the latter "grounded" formal theory** to contrast it with formal theory based on logical speculation' (*ibid.*, p. 300).

This interactive approach has a respectable pedigree, and in similar terms, although different words, has been authenticated by one of this century's most distinguished scientists, Sir Peter Medawar, who (writing at much the same time) held that 'scientific reasoning is at all levels an interaction between two episodes of thought — a dialogue between two voices, the one imaginative and the other critical' (Medawar, 1972, p. 22).

His further development of this supports the grounded theory approach. Research and enquiry were he believed, in the nature of

a speculative adventure, an imaginative preconception of what might be true — a preconception which always and necessarily goes a little way (sometimes a long way) beyond anything we have logical authority to believe in . . . *the conjecture is then exposed to criticism to find out whether that imagined world is anything like the real one.* [emphasis added] (*ibid.*, p. 22).

Midrange Theory and Hypotheses

Relationships of clusters of factors are more appropriately analysed specifically in the context of the production of midrange theories which institutions can then use to enlighten their particular situations. Several theories may be simultaneously, but selectively, true, and institutions will need to adopt those which most nearly match their particular ecology in relation to their differing disciplines. We base our conceptualization of midrange theory on Merton's definition,

intermediate to the minor working hypotheses evolved in abundance during the day-to-day routines of research, and the all-inclusive speculations comprising a master conceptual scheme from which it is hoped to derive a very large number of empirically observed uniformities of social behaviour. (Merton, 1958)

The UQ WISTA research was not aimed at what Merton called 'the codification of theoretical perspectives' (*ibid.*), but rather at a systematic approach to the relationship of existing theories to each other, to produce a new model either as a basis for further enquiry or as an immediate policy model.

No researcher starts with a clear mental slate. Medawar's imaginative–critical dialogue produces starting hypotheses which drive a new research initiative or line of investigation. We concur with Borg's view that 'without hypotheses, historical research often becomes little more than an aimless gathering of facts' (Borg, 1963), and with Kerlinger that 'hypotheses are, in essence, about the relationship between variables; and they carry implications for testing these' (Kerlinger, 1970). Kerlinger, however, assumes that subjective belief can be tested against objective reality. Glaser and Strauss regard it as characteristic of fieldwork that multiple hypotheses are pursued simultaneously, and we conform to this. Clearly, in this model earlier hypotheses quickly become integrated to form the basis of a central analytical framework which rapidly crystallizes. One of the processes in moving from these initial deductions to important new concepts, basic classification categories or significant new hypotheses is, however, for the researchers to use replacement (or, alternatively, endorsed) hypotheses to provide a 'central core of theorising which is based on a rigorous review of related hypotheses after non-related ones are pruned away' (Glaser and Strauss, 1972).

In this context, two fundamental hypotheses with which the UQ WISTA project started were that

1 Women's lower representation in the scientific and technological workforce is partly caused by their experiences in higher education institutions, and the causes cannot be wholly blamed on the schooling system or on wider social factors.
2 The institutional ecology of universities and institutes is a major factor in helping or hindering women's access to and progression in science and technology.

It follows that if the grounded theory approach were to explore new theories about the relationships between the ten core factors and the four dimensional issues set out diagrammatically in figure 2.1, we would need to set new substantive theory against new data. The next section describes our methodology for the collection of that relevant data.

Methodology

The UQ WISTA project worked through two dimensions: a scholarly review and policy analysis of existing and earlier research on influential factors in the context of reconceptualization of some current received wisdom; and a partly empirical survey of ten Australian higher education institutions. The project looked at five Universities and five Institutes of Technology, (a) in the context of the ecology of higher educational institutions; (b) as a major sample of Australian institutions from which to investigate the statistical sex-balance and characteristics of different disciplines within science and technology; and (c) as a catchment area for testing current professional opinion on the core ten factors (and possible new factors) which form the central theoretical framework for the WISTA project as a whole.

The work of developing a model of institutional ecology, of statistical analysis of disciplines, and of re-examination of the ten core factors, has been carried out in ten Australian higher education institutions: five Universities and five Institutes of Technology. These were selected to meet a variety of criteria. The sample included both the principal providers of Australia's scientific and technological workforce at tertiary level, and a representative sample from each of the five main states and urban population centres. Selection was moderated by the need to balance the sample between institutions with different provision as between Faculties of Arts, Social Sciences, Humanities, Science and Technology and Engineering, and institutions with different reputations for traditional approaches or for innovation and change. The sample also included institutions at different points of development in relation to the existence of some degree of formal discussion, debate or policy on the status of women, and on affirmative action in science and technology.

This gave us a sample in five of Australia's seven capital cities as shown in table 2.1. Insofar as succeeding chapters refer to UQ WISTA data, it refers to these ten institutions.

Since the start of the Policy Review Project, all of the Institutes have been reorganized as Universities under the Australian post-White Paper general reorganization of higher education of the late 1980s. For the purpose of the discussion of 1985 data we will refer to them as WAIT, NSWIT, QIT, SAIT and RMIT because part of the UQ WISTA ecology case is, in fact, that (at least so far) there are some differences which emerge as between Universities and Institutes as such.

It should be made clear at this stage, however, that the Policy Review survey of ten higher institutions does not involve 'case studies'

Table 2.1 Institutions in the UQ WISTA research project

Name	City	State
University of New South Wales (UNSW)	Sydney	New South Wales
New South Wales Institute of Technology (NSWIT)	Sydney	New South Wales
University of Queensland (UQ)	Brisbane	Queensland
Queensland Institute of Technology (QIT)	Brisbane	Queensland
Monash University	Melbourne	Victoria
Royal Melbourne Institute of Technology (RMIT)	Melbourne	Victoria
University of Adelaide	Adelaide	South Australia
South Australian Institute of Technology (SAIT)	Adelaide	South Australia
University of Western Australia (UWA)	Perth	Western Australia
Western Australian Institute of Technology (WAIT)	Perth	Western Australia

as such. Three levels of data collection from the survey institutions have had three purposes:

1 To produce a compilation of student and staff statistics representing a significant sample of Australian higher education in such a way as to answer detailed, diagnostic questions about female enrolments in different disciplines and subdisciplines and at different levels.
2 To examine the ecology of institutions and of disciplines at a structural, policy-construction level.
3 To explore the prevalent level of knowledge and attitudes, in relation to the issues raised by this research, of some key academic staff in the higher education institutions, as a valuable source of field opinion. The intention was not necessarily to tap a representative sample but to draw on the leading practitioners for firsthand evidence of factors or issues they believed to be relevant.

This will be more fully explained below. It should be noted here that we also wished to see if the practitioners in the survey institutions believed that there was a further factor of influence not already subsumed by our ten core factors, of which we should take note. In other words, the institutions have been used as a catchment area for the development of new theory, or for the amendment or reconstruction of existing theory.

The sample is a significant one. If we express the total number of students in engineering and science in the five Universities, for example as a percentage of all Australian engineering and science students, they are 58.4 per cent and 36.4 per cent respectively of the total (Commonwealth Tertiary Education Commission, 1985a). The five Institutes of Technology in turn account for 50.4 per cent of relevant College of

Advanced Education (CAE) students; that is, they have 59.5 per cent of engineering and 44.3 per cent of applied science students at the relevant level in the CAE sector (Commonwealth Tertiary Education Commission, 1985b).

Because of the complexity of the project, and the work involved for those institutions which agreed to cooperate, some steps were taken at the outset to establish an agreed context and method within which the WISTA Policy Review Project would work. Through the Vice Chancellor of the host University of the three-stranded project as a whole (the University of New South Wales), we obtained the formal approval and support of the Australian Vice Chancellors Committee (AVCC) and the parallel Australian Committee of Directors and Principals in Advanced Education, for the use of the sample Universities and Institutes of Technology as a representative and major sample of higher education institutions. Meetings were then arranged in 1985 at each institution, with the Academic Deputy Vice Chancellors or Directors, with Registrars and with other relevant senior staff. These had two purposes. Firstly, they were essential meetings to set out clearly the tasks which would need to be done each year for three years, their purpose and the degree of cooperation needed. Secondly, they provided the first round of group interviews with staff to discuss the key issues raised by our screening of earlier research, which we discuss later in this chapter.

We defined a range of data which were seen as necessary for the exploration of the concepts (ecology, critical mass, structure of science, etc.) and the ten factors which were central to the enquiry; that is, student and staff statistics, institutional data about the structure and organization of faculties and disciplines and special environmental information such as the state of the institutional debate or policy action programme on the status of women.

A Statistical Database

We wished to set our research review of existing theory against a more diagnostic analysis of Australian data on the patterns of female enrolments and progression. This meant collecting data about staff and students subdivided not only by sex, but also to show

- institutional differences
- differences between disciplines and subdisciplines both between and within institutions, and
- differences between levels of study in each of these.

While several relevant Australian studies have been completed since the inception of the WISTA project in 1984 (on which we comment in a later chapter), there were no objectively researched Australian data which could answer detailed and discipline-based questions other than at a very generalized level. For example, previous research has shown that generalized statistics hide very significant differences between higher education institutions. This provides also a *prima facie* case for supporting our conception that part of the answer to the issues we raise lies in the different institutional ecology of higher education institutions. Connolly and Porter's major American study of female recruitment to engineering, for example, looked at relevant factors across sixty different Schools. At the first level, their data establish that there must be institutional factors of some kind which further influence female recruitment after the generalized effect of such social and educational factors as sex-stereotyping in school curricula, family influence, sex-polarized careers advice and so on. Firstly, although their 1976 data show a USA average female enrolment to engineering of 8.5 per cent of enrolments, four states fell below 5 per cent and eight states exceeded 10 per cent. In looking at sixty schools of engineering (small, under 500; medium, 500–1,500; and large, over 1,500) they found the ten most successful at enrolling women averaged 18.4 per cent female students but the ten least successful had as few as 1.6 per cent. And the interschool (and interdiscipline) differences remained constant over five years or more. Arguably, the reasons are more likely to lie with the Schools, Universities or Institutes than with the women. (Since this reported study, affirmative action in the USA has further increased female enrolments.) The researchers reach, *inter alia*, the fairly obvious premise that 'the strongest predictor of women in engineering at a given campus is the number they have attracted in the past'. They develop this into what they term a '*positive feedback* hypothesis' which suggests that the presence of a 'sizeable number' of women students already ahead, serves to attract new women (Connolly and Porter, 1978a and b). This led the Queensland WISTA research team to look at the need also to link the existing theories on role modelling with theories on the concept of critical mass.

A more recent study of post-secondary education participation in Australia also notes that the female proportion of university education will vary considerably across different higher education institutions, and will be affected by the range of courses offered in any one field and by the alternatives offered by other Faculties in the same University (Anderson and Vervoorn, 1983).

But Australian data have been more limited until recently and have been principally available in relation to overall female participation rates by sector of education (Universities, Schools) or by Faculties (but not disciplines). One valuable Australian research review of women's participation in tertiary education which has been published since the WISTA project started for example, looks both at recent qualitative research in post-schooling and at trends in female enrolments in different tertiary sectors (Universities, Colleges of Advanced Education, Colleges of Technical and Further Education), but to examine contrasting institutional or discipline-based data at a diagnostic level was beyond that study's terms of reference and resources (Powles, 1986).

In Australia, however, as in the USA, institutions vary quite remarkably in the extent to which they succeed (or fail) in recruiting women to, or retaining them in, the same discipline. Published Australian statistical analyses so far have concentrated on figures by Faculty (applied sciences, arts, medicine, etc.), which is unhelpful for qualitative analysis. Firstly, the basis for inclusion or exclusion in Faculties has no commonality. In one University, computing is located in science, in another in arts with mathematics (or both). Faculties of medicine may include physiotherapy or pharmacy. In looking at male-dominated and female-dominated areas in 1984, we found that neither the published analyses from the Commonwealth Tertiary Education Commission nor those from the Australian Bureau of Statistics provided a breakdown which answered simple questions like:

- How many women (and what proportion do they form) are actually studying physics, chemistry, computing or mechanical engineering as distinct from materials or ceramic engineering?
- How many (what proportion of) women are in which level in each discipline?
- How many drop out, go on, etc? Are there different consistent patterns between disciplines?

One first-order question was clearly whether there is a direct relationship (and if so, what) between different clusters of our ten factors of influence on the one hand, and the patterns of female enrolments in different disciplines on the other. To answer this, we clearly needed more detailed statistical analyses of the separate disciplines than could be supplied by the generalized faculty enrolments.

Moreover, our theory of institutional ecology was based on a hypothesis that influences on women's perceptions of sex-normality or traditionality (which strengthen or weaken vocational and aspirational choice) include both the overall institutional sex-balance in the student body and in staffing, and the sex-balance in different disciplines. One essential task was therefore to collect statistics which would show where women students were (or were not) enrolled in terms of discipline, level and programme. What were in fact their rates of access, progression and achievement in each of the disciplines? Were our hypotheses correct, that the same discipline would recruit differently in different institutions for structural, environmental or other reasons? Were progression rates different in the same institution, different for cognate disciplines, and why?

In 1985, institutions were sent a standard proforma setting out the figures we needed. We asked for the breakdown of male and female students at each level, and for the institution as a whole. This proved relatively easy. We then asked for the number of women and men students studying in each of the survey disciplines which we had designated for each institution, and for the study as a whole. It proved, by contrast, much more difficult to achieve a common definition of what was a discipline and a common agreement on how to define (for the purpose of this study), say, a maths student; when did one count chemistry or physics as such and when as a component of, say, engineering?

Since we were hypothesizing that one influence on the cultural environment of the institution was the proportion to which women were a critical mass of the male-dominated whole, it was also necessary to look at staffing profiles. We have obtained staffing figures for the institutions to show the overall sex-balance for each discipline.

The base year for the collection of student and staff statistics was the year 1985, as at 30 April 1985. Because in Australia (unlike Europe and the USA) the academic year runs from February to November, an April date represents a midpoint in the first semester, by which time the preliminary drop-outs or transfers or changes in majors will have taken place but before any significant attrition could be expected. The figures thus represent a realistic annual average.

For student statistics, we asked institutions to supply exactly parallel figures for 1986, which were collated and matched for 1985, discipline by discipline and level by level. In no institution and in no discipline is there a difference in the proportion of female enrolments between the two years of such a significance as to cast doubt on the normality of the 1985 figures. They are remarkably consistent in their patterns, and there is no evidence that 1985 was in any way a 'freak' year.

Our preliminary analysis provided a *prima facie* case for rejecting the current received wisdom that the mere presence of female staff as potential role models will as such increase female enrolments, as unsupported by the data. We therefore asked for staffing figures for 1986 and 1987 to complete our discipline profiles in this respect.

The study is about science and technology, and in our preliminary discussions with Registrars, Deputy Vice Chancellors, Deans and so on in 1985, we made it clear we were concentrating on students who, whatever the balance of individual subjects being studied, were expected to graduate with a degree in science and/or technology. That is, we were not interested in arts or commerce students studying one subject or unit of maths, computing or geology merely for interest.

It had been hoped that we could arrive at a common definition across the ten institutions. We succeeded in reaching a common agreement with all ten that students from medicine, agriculture, veterinary studies and paramedical areas would be excluded from the survey altogether and from the figures for foundation subjects like mathematics, physics and chemistry. Similarly, we asked that the returns for these subjects should exclude engineering students who take these subjects as part of a structured course.

Tables were constructed from raw data supplied specifically for the UQ WISTA Policy Review Project by each institution, providing as universal a presentation as possible. The tables were then sent back to the institution for checking and for appropriate further footnoting, and these amended tables were subsequently returned to the institutions for final vetting. At each stage, amendments to the original figures were made by institutions for one discipline or level or another. This time-consuming process has been essential at every stage both to ensure accuracy and to eliminate any potential ambiguity of presentation. The principal differences of approach and definition have arisen between those institutions whose degrees are more free-floating and composed of the most flexible choice or options systems, and those with more structured degrees with stronger groups of specialisms or routes defined from the first year onward. Registrars were asked to ensure that Deans and Heads of Schools had the chance to comment on the draft tables at the stage at which, in 1986, the full set of statistical summaries for 1985 were available for each discipline or level and for each institution. In 1987, the same process was repeated in respect of the 1986 parallel data which have been checked out by the institutions at the stage of compiling summary and comparative data.

Which Disciplines?

Our early work on tertiary science and technology, however, including such limited statistics as were publicly available, suggested that differences in female and male participation patterns between disciplines in higher education were widespread, complex and subtle. In re-examining the concept of institutional ecology, the University of Queensland WISTA team have worked on the ecology of disciplines, the 'ecological niche' of the institutional 'ecosystem', as well as on the nature of science and technology.

In the original research design, the intention was to focus mainly on those scientific or technological disciplines which had a tradition of poor female recruitment, and our original list centred on a core of very male-dominated areas like physics, chemistry and engineering. It then became evident that other foundation sciences were critical because they were 'service subjects' as well as being sciences in their own right. Moreover, as concepts like territoriality, discipline image, sex-neutrality or the ascribed masculinity or femininity of disciplines emerged more sharply, it also became evident that some disciplines attractive to women would need to be included. Additionally, because the research has been designed from the start as a policy-oriented project set in a context of the importance of technology and science to Australia's economic future, a third criterion, economic relevance, emerged. We discussed our preliminary list of disciplines suggested for inclusion with each institution at the first round of meetings with Deputy and pro Vice Chancellors, Directors, Deans and Heads of Schools and departments in 1985. As a result, some further disciplines were added either because they were of particular interest as acknowledged centres of excellence at the institution, or had unusual profiles, or were seen as of economic or political importance.

On these grounds the following disciplines were finally selected as those which would form the basis for collecting student and staff statistics and for discussion with academic staff, in the ten higher education institutions in the policy review strand:

- *Group A.* Foundation subjects in science and technology which are both a discipline for study in their own right, and a service subject or prerequisite for degrees in science, applied science or technological disciplines like engineering or mining, that is: mathematics, physics, chemistry.
- *Group B.* Disciplines which are clearly non-traditional and which recruit well below the 30 per cent cut-off proportion of female

enrolment (maths, physics and chemistry also qualify under this criterion), that is: geology, geophysics, mining, all branches of engineering, metallurgy, surveying and cartography, building surveying.

- *Group C*. Other disciplines seen as politically important in the economic or political future development of science and technology, that is: computer science, microbiology and biochemistry, biotechnology, genetics, food technology.

It will be evident that we have excluded a number of disciplines which would otherwise qualify under one or more of these three criteria. This is for a variety of reasons. Firstly, some limit had to be set to avoid the data becoming totally unmanageable. Secondly, our prime focus is either on disciplines which, like higher education physics, consistently fail to attract girls (recruiting only one fifth of total enrolments from the equal half of school students who are female), or those which lose disproportionately more women, such as chemistry which recruits two fifths of entrants from women at undergraduate level but tends to revert to the low level of other male-dominated subjects from the second undergraduate year and at postgraduate level.

We were also less inclined to include many disciplines which attract girls and women already because we are not challenging the current received wisdom as to why they do enrol. Female recruitment to medicine or to psychology, for example, is held to be strongly related to societal sex-role stereotyping of the suitability for femininity of disciplines which are 'caring', curative and about human experience rather than the perceived 'objectivity' of thermodynamics or chemical analysis. The exclusion of medicine, agriculture and agronomy, of veterinary studies and of other disciplines which can be seen as scientific or technological, has therefore been based partly on their relatively lower relevance in relation to the criteria of groups A, B and C defined above, and partly on their lesser likelihood to produce new insights which would enlighten policies for change.

These selected disciplines include some which are almost exclusively male, some which achieve intermittent if not constant sex-balance and some which recruit more females than males. This raises, in turn, a new question in terms of 'discipline-labelling', which is a further refinement of mere sex-labelling: the issue of non-traditionality which we discussed in chapter 1. This is important in relation to the four core factors of prerequisites and subject choices, maths, peer attitudes and careers guidance, as well as in relation to critical mass theory.

Dialogue on Research and Theory: a Catchment Area of Attitudes and Issues

It has been a matter of some interest that social science research, even when highly qualitative in nature, has often tended to see a need to authenticate its approval by locating its analyses of earlier theory wherever possible in standardized, quantitative, statistically controlled surveys. Where the required answers can be properly supplied by standardized computerized data ranked on a several-point scale, this is, of course, sound enough. It does not, however, serve the purpose of all qualitative objectives. We used two methods to replace question-naire techniques — group interviews and the circulation of discussion papers to which staff were asked to respond. That is, we have sought to build in a dialogue between two levels of thought which are perhaps a little less polarized than Medawar's (1972) perceived distinction between the imaginative and the critical. We wished to set up a dialogue between the independent researchers creating theory in the area of women's educational under-achievement or stereotypic channelling in science and technology, and the academic staff who actually play a role in constructing the discipline in higher education institutions.

Group Interviews

Accordingly, we asked the survey institutions to cooperate firstly in setting up a series of group interviews in each institution in 1985 and 1986 with senior academic and professional staffs. The groups were to be not fewer than about eight and not more than about fifteen in number, and we aimed to include:

1   as many as possible of the key policymakers from the Faculties or departments in which our survey disciplines were located, viz pro Vice Chancellors, Deans, Professors and Heads of Schools or departments;
2   other academic staff from the survey disciplines interested in attending;
3   professional staff in the areas of careers advice, counselling and student services and (where appropriate) equal opportunity staff.

The 1985 and 1986 meetings arranged with senior academic staff were not only set up in order to explain the complexity of the project and to negotiate agreements on the supply and verification of data.

Also built in to this group interview process and into our written continuing dialogue with the ten institutions was a 'sieving' process using experienced academics as a form of field-monitoring of previous research and of the reality of some of the more relevant research findings, in the normal higher education process. That is, we were applying Cohen and Manion's (1986) principle, that interpretive theory 'must make sense for those to whom it applies', and the pursuit of multiple hypotheses which Glaser and Strauss (1972) regard as central to fieldwork which aims to lead to grounded theory.

Between nine and twelve meetings took place at each institution in both 1985 and 1986, except for the University of Western Australia and Western Australian Institute of Technology which were added to the survey in 1986 and therefore took part only in 1986 interviews. The one-and-a-half-hour meetings were all tape-recorded, and a detailed analysis completed of (a) the issues raised by academic staff in response to our agenda, (b) the comments, reactions, evidence and experience or judgments of academic staff on the ten factors which we raised in each meeting as potential influences, and (c) any new factors or issues raised by staff which were not already covered by our work.

The group discussions were particularly useful in identifying the range of views, or a continuum of opinion, on controversial matters. Discussions sometimes identified polarized central views on some issues. For example, during the tape-recorded meetings with Deans and Heads of Schools in 1985 and 1986, there was a decided ambivalence on the actual role of a Dean or Head of department. At one extreme, the view was taken that it was not in any way the function of a higher education institution or of its lecturing staff to consider where its clientele came from or how representative it was of the sexes (or social classes). 'It's my job to teach the law of thermodynamics, not to indulge in social engineering,' (University physicist). At the other end of the spectrum, some Deans of Engineering had long since accepted that the institution had a role to play in both marketing its courses and in balancing the composition of its student body: 'We visit the girls' schools, go to careers days, we've published brochures with women engineers on the front, and we still don't get them in. Tell us what more to do and we'll try it.' Motivation for seeing a role for higher education institutions varied from an expressed acceptance that Universities are part of the social power structure of society and could legitimately, and indeed should, work consciously towards social as well as educational or economic goals, to a practical concern to increase undergraduate and postgraduate enrolments from the missing half of the age group in order to avoid wasted talent or to prop up a declining discipline.

The group interviews followed a semi-structured format in which an introduction of the project as a whole was followed by a scene-setting description of the main objectives and a sharply focussed introduction to some research findings on the ten factors.

Objectives were described as

1   to attempt to construct a model of institutional ecology as a transferable model for evaluation purposes;
2   to obtain a range of specialist reaction and opinion from practitioners in the disciplines on the perceived or actual relevance of the ten factors to female student achievement in their disciplines;
3   to help in a review of the realism, in applied terms, of the main findings of previous relevant research; and
4   to canvass experienced field opinion on the appropriateness of different policy mechanisms which would help to redress the identified problems, and to test practitioners' views on priorities for action.

There was, however, a fifth general objective which we did not overtly identify. We wished to use the group interviews as an additional source to test the attitudinal climate of each institution as a whole, as identified by its leading academics in the survey disciplines. What appeared to be the overt prevailing attitudes to women's roles in terms of traditionality and non-traditionality as described in the theoretical framework?

As part of this attitudinal climate, we wished to use the group interviews as an additional source from which to identify the apparent state of understanding of or exposure to the now considerable body of knowledge on women and science and technology in the policy-making levels of each institution. It was for this reason that we requested that, where possible, Professors, Deans and Heads should be invited.

We did not have the resources to conduct a full-scale survey on relevant attitudes, even if we had accepted that this was 'scientifically' possible. We did hypothesize that in the same way that questionnaires are answered by the really committed (or responsible, or earnest), those who actually attended the meetings would be likely to represent the potential sharp end of change in the survey institutions. This was because an active voluntary response to an invitation to meet with properly accredited and sponsored academic researchers was perceived as more likely from:

- those already interested in or knowledgeable about gender-related issues in science and technology or involved in intervention strategies;
- those who accepted that female under-recruitment to science and technology was a current policy issue for higher education;
- those policymakers who accepted that tackling the issue was now an unavoidable institutional goal even if they were not personally convinced of a need;
- those who were in any terms normally at the sharp end of generating change in their institutions;
- those who were curiosity-driven or were representing more senior colleagues on request to ensure that their discipline's problems or experience would be aired.

We expected that such an attendance would ensure that a wider range of issues would be canvassed and aired, and this expectation was justified.

How 'representative' was the attendance at group interviews? We saw neither a need nor a realistic possibility of ensuring this (in the same way that one cannot necessarily ensure a representative sample of responses to written questionnaires). Attendance was not necessarily consistent either across institutions or across disciplines or between 1985 and 1986. But we were not expecting to generalize from the responses at interviews in the sense of seeking to argue that because a given number of mathematicians (or physicists, or geneticists) had considered one theory to be more valid, therefore most Australian mathematicians (etc.) would so argue. We were, rather, seeking to ensure firstly that some hypotheses, conclusions and implications of academic researchers previously influential in policy decisions were measured for realism against the reactions of Australian academics actually doing the work of teaching in science and technology; secondly, that any factors not yet researched, but seen as relevant, were aired by the practitioners in institutions: and, thirdly, that each discipline was sufficiently represented to ensure that issues idiosyncratic to that discipline were aired.

Discussion Papers on the Ten Factors

Our second strategy for testing knowledge and attitudes and for seeking informed opinion on needs and priorities was to circulate a series of ten brief discussion papers (one on each of the ten factors) over a period from June 1985 to November 1987, to which academic staff were asked to respond in writing. The papers set out firstly to identify briefly the problem or issue. (What is role modelling and why is it important? Why is single-sex education or coeducation an issue in female achievement? What is the main problem about girls' achievement in mathematics?) We sought, secondly, to report on relevant research in the area which was related both to female involvement in science and technology and to higher education; and, thirdly, to pose questions which would as a result need to be addressed by higher education institutions. The papers were consciously limited in length to between four and seven pages in order to encourage academic staff actually to read them. The responses received in writing from a wide variety of staff (from Deputy Vice Chancellors to lecturers) have been analysed in a policy analysis framework.

Without detracting from the UQ WISTA project's focus on the role of higher education in encouraging female achievement and in remedying or counteracting sex-role stereotypic secondary education, it was seen as essential from the outset to check the male and female patterns of curricular options at Grade 12 in secondary schooling in each of the states where the survey institutions were located. It would be hardly reasonable to expect higher education to produce substantially more science specialists than the schooling system exported, even allowing for mature entrants, overseas enrolments and bridging courses.

We therefore obtained, with the cooperation of the boards of secondary school studies (or equivalents) in each of the states, data on the male and female Grade 12 enrolments in relevant feeder subjects for 1985, the project's base year. Some of these data go further than overall state figures and we look also at the relationship between structure and content of some of the Grade 12 subjects and proportionate female enrolments. The pure–applied antithesis emerges again here in the results, as a relevant sex-differentiated indicator. The secondary data have been used to enlighten our grounded theories in relation to four of the ten core factors, that is male and female attitudes to science, prerequisites, maths as a critical filter and careers guidance. A limited account of this analysis in relation to the secondary tertiary interface appears in chapter 6, but the complexity of this aspect justifies a separate specialist publication, now in preparation.

Scope and Limitations

It should be stressed that the focus throughout the research has been on issues which are seen as either caused by, or are able to be remedied or counteracted by, the educators and by educational institutions in terms of educational policymaking. The causes of women's under-achievement, lack of progression or concentration in areas of educa-tion, training and work socially ascribed as female, are not, of course, solely a result of the influence of the ten factors we have used as our focus. The behaviour of girls and boys in adolescence, for example, has its early roots in primary education. Children also come in to school at four or five years old with sex-stereotypic attitudes already preset, with a strongly developed sense of what is differentially suit-able for boys and for girls — separately and with mutual exclusivity. And indeed, almost the first comment made by Heads and Deans of Schools in our group interviews, in almost all meetings, has been, 'But the problems are made in the schools: they come to us with attitudes already set.'

Similarly, we are familiar with the relevance of the dual work–motherhood and work–wife role, and the problem of childcare. The personal reasons of young women in higher education for dropping out include for example, financial hardship, pregnancy and domestic responsibility (when male students marry they acquire a domestic in-frastructure; when women students marry they acquire domestic re-sponsibility). The possession of an articulate, well-educated working mother who is a successful scientist may well have the possible effect of inspiring a daughter through the role-modelling process.

But these issues are either not remediable within the tertiary edu-cation system, or they are already being quite adequately researched and developed elsewhere. It is not lack of public understanding of the issue which hinders women who have a dual role and no access to childcare facilities, but the lack of public and political commitment to provide such infrastructure. And what hinders progress in schooling is less any lack of understanding of sex-stereotyping in classrooms, given two decades of research in the area, than the lack of will on the part of educational authorities, principals and teachers to admit that it happens at all in their schools, or to allocate resources to deal with the problem.

While therefore the researchers recognize that many social factors external to education and aspects caused by other sectors of education are relevant, they do not explain adequately why, despite lack of childcare provision, or sex-typed careers advice, or inappropriate maths schoolteaching, or male peer hostility to girls choosing science in adolescence, many girls do actually succeed in access to and progres-sion in science and technology in higher education. For these reasons, the research has focussed on higher education institutions and not only on the critical filter effects of a sex-role stereotyped secondary schooling.

The widespread tendency for the Universities and Institutes to argue that there is nothing that they can do further to influence the entry of women to science and technology in higher education, because both research and policy effort should be devoted instead to the schooling system, is an inadequate and facile alibi. We do not accept this over-simple approach.

Firstly, if it were true that all of the influences were unalterably set by the schooling and early social conditioning processes, this would not explain why more girls apply to enter one higher education institution than another; why one University keeps or recruits twice as many women postgraduates in a given discipline than others; or why the female recruitment to the same disciplines in different institutions can vary from double to half the average. Secondly, we hypothesized that higher education institutions, particularly in the first undergraduate year, are at least partially responsible for the non-progression of women after first-year undergraduate studies. Many of the influences which shape the career destination of women interested in science and technology occur in the first year or two in the University or Institute, and this research is premised on the given assumption that changes in the structural and attitudinal environment of tertiary institutions can still remediate very quickly (or reinforce) the sex-role stereotyping of the school and guidance systems. New tertiary policies have been seen to achieve rapid changes in a number of overseas countries. Aldrich and Hall (1980), for example, report on a wide variety of successful intervention programmes which set out to remedy, at the tertiary level, problems relating to competence in or lack of maths, to inadequate science experience, to attitudes or to poor careers advice. Initiatives specifically aimed at opening up engineering to women in higher education are well established in France, the United Kingdom, the USA and Scandinavia to remediate inadequate female scientific and mathematical education in schooling (Byrne, 1985). Broader initiatives to open up non-traditional work in technology and at technician levels in areas like mining and telecommunications have again successfully remedied inadequate and sex-typed schooling in Sweden, the former West Germany and the USA (Byrne, 1980).

Thus, it is argued that the exclusion of socially caused factors from the research does not hinder its usefulness in reconceptualizing and re-examining the educationally caused factors. Whether these are wholly located in schooling, or partly in schooling and partly in tertiary education, it must be stressed that higher education institutions have a proper and responsible role to play both in influencing schooling and in remedying its inadequacies.

Finally it should be noted here that this book does not set out to cover all of the work completed in this research. The scale and complexity of the research completed so far are such that they cannot be encompassed in one book. This publication deals with the fundamental thematic issues of institutional ecology and critical mass, and with some of the ten factors under examination. Other specialist publications will follow, notably unpacking the Snark effect of work on maths as a critical filter, and the merits and demerits of single-sex learning.

John Ruskin wrote that 'not only is there but one way of doing things rightly, but there is only one way of seeing them, and that is seeing the whole of them' (quoted in Sesame and Lilies). While we do not necessarily subscribe to his view that there is only one right way to do things, that the only right way to see things is as a whole is central to the UQ WISTA approach. The next chapter describes how we use a revised concept of institutional ecology to attempt to look at women in science, holistically.

References

ALDRICH, M. and HALL, P. (1980) *Programs in Science, Maths and Engineering in USA 1966–1978*, Washington, DC, AAAS and Office of Opportunities in Science.

ANDERSON, D. and VERVOORN, A. (1983) *Access to Privilege: Patterns of Participation in Australian Post-Secondary Education*, Canberra, Australian National University (ANU) Press.

BORG, W.R. (1963) *Educational Research*, London, Longman.

BYRNE, E.M. (1980) *Women's Work, Men's Work — New Perspectives for Change*, Paris, UNESCO Ed80/CONF 708/3.

BYRNE, E.M. (1985) *Women in Engineering: A Comparative Overview of New Initiatives*, BLMR Monograph 11, Canberra, Australian Government Publishing Service.

COHEN, L. and MANION, L. (1986) *Research Methods in Education*, London, Croom Helm.

COMMONWEALTH TERTIARY EDUCATION COMMISSION (1985a) *Selected University Statistics, 1985*, table 3, Canberra, Australian Government Publishing Service.

COMMONWEALTH TERTIARY EDUCATION COMMISSION (1985b) *Selected Advanced Education Statistics, 1985*, table 6, Canberra, Australian Government Publishing Service.

CONNOLLY, T. and PORTER, A.L. (1978a) *The Recruitment and Retention of Women as Undergraduate Engineers*, Research Report, Atlanta, Ga, Georgia Institute of Technology.

CONNOLLY, T. and PORTER, A.L. (1978b) *Women in Engineering: Policy Recommendations for Recruitment and Retention in Undergraduate Programs*, Research Report, Atlanta, Ga, Georgia Institute of Technology.

GLASER, B.G. and STRAUSS, A.L. (1972) 'Discovery of substantive theory: a basic strategy underlying qualitative research', in FILSTEAD, W. (Ed) *Qualitative Methodology: Firsthand Involvement with the Social World*, 3rd edn, Chicago, Markham Publishing Co, Chapter 28.

KERLINGER, F.N. (1970) *Foundations of Behavioural Research*, New York, Holt, Rinehart and Winston.

MEDAWAR, P.B. (1972) 'Science and Literature', in MEDAWAR, P.B., *The Hope of Progress*, London, Methuen.

MERTON, R. (1958) *Social Theory and Social Structure*, rev. edn, Glencoe, Free Press.

POWLES, M. (1986) *Women's Participation in Tertiary Education: A Review of Recent Australian Research*, Canberra, Commonwealth Tertiary Education Commission.

Chapter 3

Institutional Ecology and Women in Science: Why Women are Where They are and aren't

---

'If you want to slip into a round hole, you must make a ball of yourself — that's where it is.' (George Eliot, *The Mill on the Floss*)

It has been just so since the first introduction of organized secondary and higher education in the nineteenth century, and of systemic education in the twentieth. That is, new kinds of entrants to existing schools, Colleges and Universities have been expected to knock off any corners and to replace any cultures, manners or discourse which do not fit the dominant existing pattern. Any failure to adapt not only to the criteria but also to the behaviour for selection, risked failure of access. Any failure to adapt after entry was highly correlated with drop-out figures. One of the most vivid exposes of this process was documented for working-class children in grammar schools in the 1950s (Jackson and Marsden, 1962). Sociologists, and notably Pierre Bourdieu, have further explored the mismatch between the experience and background of the new cohorts of working-class tertiary students of the 1960s and the different forms of discourse which appear to be generic to the dominant higher education culture.

But it has been most imperfectly realized that this match:mismatch issue is not only a class issue, but also applies to female students entering a male-constructed higher education system inherited in turn from the patriarchal culture of the nineteenth century. The patterns of discourse, of peer group behaviour, of teaching and learning with which most male students are at ease, have proved to be significantly different from those into which most female students have been socialized during the years of schooling and of late adolescence. The male-as-norm process is deeply embedded in higher education culture.

If a plant fails to flourish, to grow or even to survive in our human-constructed garden, we do not blame the plant. We examine the soil (appropriate? needs more lime or phosphate?); the position (needs more sun or shade, shelter or exposure?); the nutrition (too strong? too weak? too wet or dry?) and so on. We accept that it is we who have created an inappropriate ecological environment and that we must adjust that environment if plants, other than the indigenous hardy ones, are to survive and flourish. Yet we refuse to accept a parallel responsibility for the learning environment that we create.

This chapter discusses a new approach to institutional ecology which may help better to explain both why women are where they are in science and technology, and why they are not where they are not. We believe that in using ecology theory as an explanatory framework and as an extended metaphor it is possible to achieve greater insight into why women's access to and progression in different scientific and technological disciplines varies so significantly as between disciplines, between levels and between institutions.

Previous theory has accounted for girls' unequal access or entry to certain scientific disciplines and women's lesser rate of progression to most areas of postgraduate scientific and technological study by a wide range of factors and influences — from one extreme of assumed psychological or biological innate sex-differentiation, to the other extreme of socially constructed conspiracy theories. But factors such as sex-differentiation of teacher–pupil interaction (pedagogic), parental discouragement (social stereotypic), girls' alleged poorer mental equipment for mathematics (alleged biological predestination), single-sex versus coeducation (pedagogic and structural), male discouragement of girls and male territoriality (attitudinal), cannot adequately explain why inter-institutional and interdisciplinary differences are so great. Why do girls from similar schools and social backgrounds, with similar temperaments, enrol consistently more highly in some institutions than others and in some scientific disciplines more than others?

A preliminary statistical analysis of male and female enrolments in higher education in Australia has led to new hypotheses about a cluster of factors which, when related to each other, amount to an ecological explanation which includes some different and new elements in 'institutional' ecology compared with those discussed in former human ecology theory. We look briefly at UQ WISTA statistical evidence for moving to studying institutions and disciplines rather than girls and women themselves, before developing a revised model of institutional ecology as a policy mechanism.

The Statistical Case for Examining an Institutional Ecology Approach

If it were true that the main or exclusive causes of girls' under-recruitment in some scientific disciplines lay completely in schooling or in other pre-tertiary factors (as Universities and Institutes widely allege), one would expect to see minimal differentiation between overall institutional enrolments, or between female recruitment to the same discipline (physics or geology or computing, for instance) in different institutions.

But there is no such consistent pattern. On the contrary, we found considerable variations between the same discipline in different institutions; in different types of institutions; and at different levels in different institutions. Clearly, higher education factors must be at least partly accountable for these differences.

We also found that some disciplines were more susceptible to institutional factors than others; that is, the degree to which female enrolments in a given discipline varied from institution to institution was much more limited in physics and engineering than in maths, computing or geology. We believe that a number of factors influence this: the image of the discipline, its structure and dominant teaching style, its status as 'pure' or 'applied', its location in a given faculty. All are factors controlled more by higher education than by schooling.

The UQ WISTA data analysed are mainly for the survey's base year of 1985, reinforced if necessary by 1986 figures. For this reason, we have frequently looked separately at the five Universities and the five Institutes as such. Since 1985, New South Wales Institute of Technology (NSWIT), Western Australian Institute of Technology (WAIT) and Queensland Institute of Technology (QIT) have been redesignated as the University of Technology, Sydney, the Curtin University of Technology, and Queensland University of Technology respectively. Since we hypothesize, however, that the history, structure and sex-balance of types of institutions usually contribute to their ecology and image, we have continued to record these as Institutes in our analysis, a status they still held at the time of the UQ WISTA survey.

We do not yet know enough about the actual impact on different kinds of minorities of the domination of their ecological niche or their ecosystem in education, teaching and learning by the principal sex,

Table 3.1 Percentage of female enrolments in the five Universities

| Universities | All students | | | | |
| | 1985 | | | 1986 | |
	total	% female		total	% female
University of NSW	17,226	36.3%		18,989	36.0%
University of Qld	17,948	47.5%		18,339	48.4%
Monash University	13,586	47.7%		13,839	48.1%
University of Ad.	9,022	42.1%		8,694	42.8%
University of WA	9,512	44.1%		9,512	45.5%
Total	67,294	43.5%		69,373	43.9%

Table 3.2 Percentage of female enrolments in the five Institutes of Technology

| Institutes of Technology | All students | | | | |
| | 1985 | | | 1986 | |
	total	% female		total	% female
NSWIT	8,673	27.9%		9,435	30.6%
QIT	8,493	27.6%		8,935	29.2%
RMIT	10,875	34.3%		11,163	35.8%
SAIT	6,747	34.7%		6,971	36.5%
WAIT	12,022	42.9%		12,586	44.6%
Total	46,810	34.2%		49,090	36.0%

race or cultural identity. It is, however, reasonable to hypothesize that the better the balance, the more a feeling of normality is achievable. We believe that the actual overall climate of a University and an Institute is bound to be affected by the extent to which women are or are not a critical mass of the whole. Within that concept, their relative actual proportion of a discipline, level of study, or institution as a whole will also affect the image that students have as a whole of the non-traditionality, sex-normality or sex-neutrality of their direct learning environment.

But even overall female enrolments in the five Universities did not reach parity with males in any institution. Within these five, the University of New South Wales had the lowest overall female percentage, although above the probable threshold of critical mass; other Universities ranged from 42 to 48 per cent. That is, two were above and three below the national average in the survey years (see table 3.1).

The Institutes showed a more markedly different pattern in overall enrolments, ranging from a female enrolment of 28 per cent to 44 per cent (see table 3.2). At the most general of levels, the image impact at the Institutes continues to be one of continuing male-domination of

Table 3.3 Percentage of women students in institutions and courses (1985)

All Students		All undergrads		*Masters		PhD		Other P/G	
U of Q	48	U of Q	50	Mon	41	Mon	33	Mon	60
Mon	48	Mon	49	UWA	40	U of A	30	UWA	55
UWA	44	UWA	46	U of A	35	U of Q	27	U of Q	46
WAIT	43	WAIT	45	U of Q	31	UNSW	26	SAIT	44
U of A	42	U of A	43	UNSW	30	UWA	25	UNSW	37

Top five for female enrolments in each category
* Research only.

the overall student body. Even the overall environmental image in terms of critical mass will remain one of non-traditionality for women at NSWIT and at QIT while these proportions persist.

Within all ten survey institutions, however, the pattern changes when the overall student body is further divided by level of study. Three out of four postgraduate students are still male at most institutions. But here the inter-institutional differences become much more sharply marked. If we rank the institutions in an ordinal sequence according to the percentage of women students at each institution, the top five at each level emerge as shown in table 3.3. Institutes, of course, have not offered doctoral programmes and this table omits masters degrees by coursework. But the pattern which emerges suggests that it cannot only be a question of critical mass relationships. We cannot yet draw easy conclusions as to why the two highest female Phd enrolments occur in the institutions with, respectively, one of the highest and the lowest undergraduate female enrolments without looking further at other factors of institutional ecology, and specifically at the mentor role in higher education. It is not an adequate explanation, moreover, to point to Monash University's higher than average overseas enrolment in postgraduate degrees. This alone would not explain why overseas countries not particularly generally or culturally supportive to women's advancement send their women potential engineers or scientists to Monash University more frequently than elsewhere. On the other hand, the University of Adelaide has the lowest female enrolment overall and at undergraduate level, but a higher than average PhD enrolment. It is more likely that factors related to specific disciplines and to institutional and supervisory supportiveness or otherwise affect these patterns.

To summarize so far, one could interpret the undergraduate data to suggest that institutions which have an overall critical mass of female undergraduate students at or near the sex-normal level also tend to have higher than average female undergraduate enrolments in non-traditional science and technology. But there is clearly not a consistent correlation between patterns of female undergraduate and patterns of female postgraduate enrolments, as such, in the same institutions. The postgraduate patterns are skewed by other (tertiary) factors than critical mass alone.

Table 3.4 gives more detail of the overall percentages of women postgraduate students by level for 1985 and 1986. Given a widespread tendency among higher education academics to lay the accountability for girls' under-recruitment to science and technology at the feet of schools, careers advisers, preschools or parents (but to defend higher education as altruistically sex-neutral and gender-unbiased, the patterns illustrated in table 3.4 need much more explanation. It is difficult, for example, to write off these wide inter-institutional variations in female enrolments as due to such generic factors as marital status ('women leave to get married and have babies') or the job market ('women don't go on in geology or surveying because they can't get jobs') or, even more blandly, social attitudes ('it's all a matter of society's perceptions, we can't alter those').

If these were the major influences, there is no reason why they should affect one University or Institute proportionately and consistently more, or less, than another comparable institution. We argue that there are idiosyncratic institutional factors which are more influential. One hypothesis to explain the differential patterns is that the higher level of critical mass of women in the overall student environment in some institutions has created a more gender-neutral or sex-normal environment for progression (as distinct from access). A second (not necessarily mutually exclusive) hypothesis is that proportionately more Deans and Heads of Schools in Monash, UWA and University of Adelaide (the three Universities with the highest 1985 masters research and PhD female percentages of enrolments) may have accepted the mentor role not only as a normal part of their work, but as a particular responsibility towards women students.

This basic analysis would support a theory that once a significant critical mass has been achieved at a gender-neutral level (in the case of undergraduates here, over 40 per cent), other factors then intervene to moderate or to reinforce its effect. The University of Queensland, for example, had the highest female undergraduate enrolment (around 48 per cent) but a relatively low masters research percentage and an average female PhD enrolment. By contrast, the University of Adelaide had a relatively lower (less than 43 per cent) female undergraduate enrolment, but a proportionately higher female PhD enrolment. We

Table 3.4 All postgraduate students by sex and institution

	1985 Masters coursework		1985 Masters res. & thesis		1985 PhD		1985 Other postgrad.		1986 Masters coursework		1986 Masters res. & thesis		1986 PhD		1986 Other postgrad.	
	total	% F	total	% F	total	% F	total	% F	total	% F	total	% F	total	% F	total	% F
U of NSW	1,944	32.4%	501	30.0%	776	25.9%	359	36.5%	2,116	34.0%	534	27.0%	863	26.0%	450	38.0%
NSWIT	317	8.8%	97	25.8%	—	—	524	30.3%	339	13.6%	104	24.0%	—	—	613	28.1%
U of Q	1,010	36.7%	479	30.9%	864	27.4%	1,574	45.5%	1,019	39.6%	472	32.4%	872	27.3%	1,604	46.2%
QIT	61	14.8%	50	8.0%	—	—	635	31.7%	99	20.2%	68	8.8%	—	—	674	32.3%
Monash	1,026	36.8%	610	40.5%	654	33.5%	956	60.4%	1,084	38.7%	620	41.8%	668	34.6%	962	62.3%
RMIT	287	7.3%	110	10.0%	—	—	962	36.3%	350	9.4%	158	15.8%	—	—	1,049	35.6%
U of A	325	29.8%	333	35.1%	504	29.8%	360	41.1%	371	33.7%	341	36.1%	455	30.3%	379	45.9%
SAIT	104	17.3%	84	14.3%	—	—	956	43.7%	98	18.4%	96	13.5%	—	—	1,044	49.6%
U of WA	494	25.0%	399	40.0%	455	25.0%	776	55.0%	507	36.8%	432	40.5%	467	26.3%	497	55.7%
WAIT	—	—	*357	27.0%	—	—	1,705	34.0%	72	32.4%	192	22.9%	—	—	1,870	36.8%
TOTAL	5,568	30.1%	3,020	32.1%	3,253	28.3%	8,807	42.1%	6,055	32.9%	3,017	32.1%	3,325	28.7%	9,142	43.0%

* Masters figures at WAIT not subdivided between coursework and thesis in 1985.

consider that factors moderating the pure or exponential effect of critical mass are likely to lie in discipline-based ecology.

Interdisciplinary and Inter-institutional Differences

The 1985 enrolments for each discipline in each institution have been analysed against the conceptual framework set out in the earlier chapters, in different ways. Given that we have suggested that the general perception of a discipline as non-traditional, or as sex-normal for women, or as sex-neutral, was part of the institutional and discipline-based ecology and was causally related to both access and progression, we have, for example, analysed the disciplines against this theory.

If we look first at tables 3.5a and 3.5b, which illustrate degrees of non-traditionality by discipline, several clear interdisciplinary differences emerge. Firstly, some disciplines are theoretically recruiting at undergraduate level at the sex-normal-for-women level: chemistry in all ten institutions; biochemistry, microbiology, biotechnology and genetics wherever they are offered. When we look at the postgraduate figures for each of these same disciplines we do not, however, find any consistent higher than average progression rate for chemistry in the five Universities, but we do for the other four disciplines. Expressed as percentages, table 3.6 illustrates even more variable patterns between institutions for the same discipline.

It is reasonable, therefore, to hypothesize that progression at a particular level or in a particular discipline reflects such factors as institutional and discipline-based culture, structures, mentorship rather than generic attitudes, and perceptions of job markets. Why, for example, were eleven out of twelve women students in postgraduate biochemistry studying at masters level and only one at PhD level at one University (UNSW), while at another (Adelaide) there were no students in biochemistry of either sex at masters level but all thirty-four biochemistry students were at PhD level, of whom fifteen (44 per cent) were women? Since decisions to carry on to postgraduate level, and on which level, are a matter for significant influence by supervisors, Heads of Schools and Deans, the strong discipline variations require at least partial explanation in terms of the ecology of each discipline. There is a number of possible explanations. Different styles of (or commitment to) mentorship, different departmentally transmitted goals and expectations for students, and different existing levels of critical mass are all relevant factors.

Inter-institutional variations also occur when we look at the average

Table 3.5a Survey disciplines: analysis of 1985 female undergraduate enrolments

Designation of disciplines on Byrne Four-Point Code of Sex-normality and Non-traditionality

Institution	Phys.	Chem.	Maths	Comp. sc.	Biochem.	Microbiol.	Genetics	Biotechnol.
UNSW	2	1	1	1	1	1	0	1
NSWIT	3	1	1	2	0	0	0	1
U of Q	2	1	2	2	1	1	0	0
QIT	2	1	1	3	1	1	0	1
Mon	2	1	1	1	1	1	1	0
RMIT	3	1	1	2	0	0	0	1
U of A	2	1	0	2	1	1	1	0
SAIT	3	1	0	2	1	1	0	0
UWA	2	1	1	2	1	1	0	0
WAIT	3	1	2	0	0	0	0	1

Female enrolment of 30% plus   sex-normal for women   = 1
29–16%   untypical for women   = 2
15–9%   abnormal for women   = 3
8% and below   rubric of exceptions for women   = 4
not offered at undergraduate level in this institution = 0

Table 3.5b Survey disciplines: analysis of 1985 female undergraduate enrolments

Designation of disciplines on Byrne Four-Point Code of Sex-normality and Non-traditionality

Institution	Civil eng.	Chem. eng.	Ceramic eng.	Elect. eng.	Mech. eng.	Minerals	Geology
UNSW	4	2	3	4	4	4	0
NSWIT	4	0	0	4	4	0	3
U of Q	3	3	0	4	4	4	2
QIT	4	0	0	4	4	0	4
Mon	3	2	0	4	3	4	2
RMIT	4	3	0	4	4	4	3
U of A	4	2	0	4	4	0	2
SAIT	4	0	0	4	4	4	3
UWA	4	0	0	4	4	0	2
WAIT	4	4	0	4	4	4	3

Female enrolment of 30% plus	sex-normal for women	= 1
29–16%	untypical for women	= 2
15–9%	abnormal for women	= 3
8% and below	rubric of exceptions for women	= 4
not offered at undergraduate level in this institution		= 0

Table 3.6 Women as percentage of total postgraduates in the five Universities

Institution		Maths %	Chem. %	Microbiol. %	Biochem. %
UNSW	Masters*	0	25.8	33.3	100.0
	PhD	10.0	14.3	40.0	9.1
UQ	Masters*	0	0	57.1	31.6
	PhD	28.6	19.4	32.2	33.3
Monash	Masters*	29.6	44.4	40.0	71.1
	PhD	18.8	23.3	25.0	21.1
Adelaide	Masters*	18.8	20.0	50.0	0
	PhD	7.9	5.9	33.3	44.1
UWA	Masters*	33.3	—	30.8	100.0
	PhD	25.0	20.0	35.7	23.5

* Masters research only

Table 3.7 Female undergraduates as percentage of survey disciplines averaged across the disciplines in each institution (1985)

Institution	%
UNSW	25.8
UQ	24.2
Monash	29.2
U of A	27.9
UWA	23.0
NSWIT	20.2
QIT	14.8
RMIT	21.3
SAIT	12.8
WAIT	15.6

female proportionate enrolment to the survey disciplines (or critical mass) for each institution as a whole. If we express undergraduate female enrolments as a percentage of each survey discipline and average the percentages across these disciplines, we see that women's critical mass of the whole varies markedly (see table 3.7). Despite the levels of recruitment at undergraduate, level, only at Monash University did women science and technology undergraduates as a whole approach the critical mass threshold of 'sex-normality' at almost 30 per cent. In the Universities, about one in four students at this level were women; in the Institutes they varied from one in five (RMIT) to one in eight (SAIT).

Each institution, moreover, shows a different pattern between disciplines. Some disciplines, for example, consistently recruit a proportion of women that is not only higher than the average but also higher

Physics Female Undergraduate Enrolments in 1985

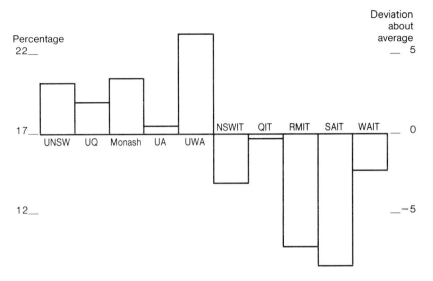

Figure 3.1 Discipline with low inter-institutional variation, showing mean percentage of female enrolments and deviation from average.

than their own institution's average for science and technology. Other disciplines consistently recruit below their institutional average. Still others vary from institution to institution. That is to say that

- Some disciplines (physics, engineering) seem almost impervious to institutional factors and recruit uniformly below the science and technology average both across and within their institutions. Causes for female under-recruitment are therefore likely to lie predominantly with the discipline as such and to require fundamental review of such wider than institutional factors as image, marketing, structure, style and content.
- Other disciplines (chemistry, geology, mathematics, computing) recruit much more variably, and show more evidence of the potential influence of institutional factors. These disciplines need review at both the institutional ecology and the discipline levels.

In figures 3.1 to 3.4, it should be noted that the mean percentage of female enrolments is used as the baseline for comparison between disciplines. This is used because it allows a comparison of enrolment percentages (i.e. proportions in the context of critical mass) independently of actual enrolment numbers. Figure 3.1 illustrates physics as a

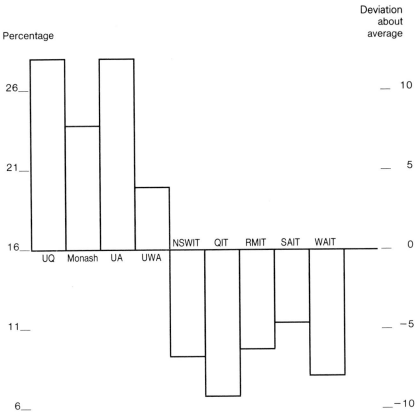

Figure 3.2 University:Institute differentiation showing mean percentage of female enrolments and deviation from average.

discipline with a relatively small inter-institutional variation. It will be seen that the physics average across the ten institutions is only 17 per cent (i.e. females are 17 per cent of all physics undergraduate students), and that the deviation from the average is just over five above and about seven below. It also shows all of the Universities above the inter-institutional average and all of the Institutes below.

In the case of geology (see figure 3.2), with a very similar institutional average (of 16 per cent), the inter-institutional variation is greater. The physics range was from 8.7 to 23.3 per cent, while the geology range is from 6.8 to 28 per cent but with University enrolments all significantly above the average (from five to eleven deviation points) and the Institutes all significantly below the average (from five to nine points).

Chemistry Female Undergraduate Enrolments in 1985

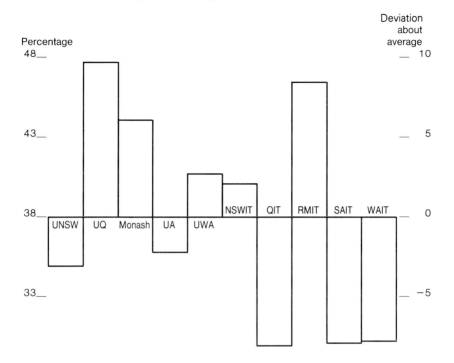

Figure 3.3. Discipline with high institutional variation, showing mean percentage of female enrolments and deviation from average.

By contrast, in figure 3.3 chemistry shows a highly variable inter-institutional variation. There is a much wider deviation from the average, and the mean itself is twice that for physics and is well above the sex-normal (for females) threshold for critical mass. In the case of chemistry, however, the University:Institute differences are less clear — two Universities recruiting below and one Institute above the ten-institutional average. Yet chemistry and physics are usually taken together at Grade 12 in school as a 'package' of correlates. The inter-institutional differences therefore require explanation partly in terms of the tertiary experience. At tertiary level, they begin to diverge, and it should be noted that the chemistry female enrolment deviations from the average are around a mean of 38 per cent while physics is around a mean of only half that figure.

Geology shows a different pattern again. With a mean percentage of 16 per cent across the ten institutions — about the same mean as physics — the deviation from the average is more than ten points above and eight points below the average. But the University female

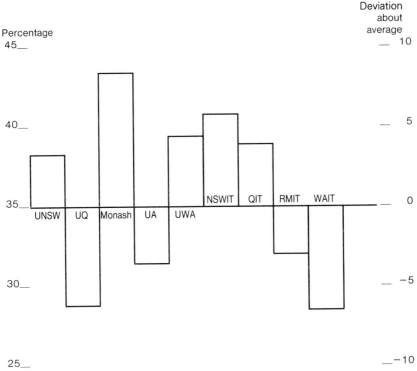

Figure 3.4. Core discipline showing high inter-institutional variation, by mean percentage of female enrolments and deviation from average.

geology enrolments are consistently higher, and the Institute enrolments lower. One hypothesis is that this is because the University geology courses are more free-floating and science-based than the applied structured Institute courses.

Finally, figure 3.4 shows the mathematics enrolments — the most variable of all. Clearly, many more factors are influencing mathematics. These patterns arguably justify a shift to looking at disciplines and institutions, and not solely at girls and women, for explanations.

Physical Environment: Limited Influence

Some earlier researchers have explored institutional ecology as a physical environmental issue, assuming that this impacts significantly on student behaviour. Some feminist theory, for example, has attempted to argue that girls are more put off than boys by an unattractive institutional environment (for example, concrete-massed, unsoftened by landscaping or decor). There is little formal research which records gender differences in this area, and we remain mildly sceptical about its actual importance in terms of UQ WISTA's hypotheses on access and progression. Nevertheless, some of the research is worth a passing glance.

One American model looks at the ecosystem concept in higher education almost entirely in terms of the physical environment. The United States Western Interstate Commission for Higher Education (WICHE) developed an ecosystem model whose basic components are (a) assessing student perceptions of their environment, (b) soliciting recommendations for changing their environment, and (c) redesigning the environment to meet student needs (Schuh and Allen, 1978). The approach is instrumental, based heavily on measurement of student perceptions and actual physical environs. The WICHE Task Force on Epidemiology, Campus Ecology and Program Evaluation saw influences on student performance or adaptability as purely a matter of physical environs, since it addressed the issue in 1973 in terms of campus redesign 'to accommodate a variety of lifestyles' (WICHE, 1973). The five main issues highlighted by students for policy change in Schuh and Allen's (1978) model are an expanded meal service, new policies for room decoration, facilities for quiet study, facilities for 'intense study' and security protection for students on campus at night. Surprisingly, given the state of debate in the mid-1970s on women's relative under-achievement in higher education, neither of these studies looks at sex-differences in attitudes to environment, nor at the impact of peer group pressures or staff attitudes and styles on the learning or cultural environment.

The now massive literature on sex-role stereotyping in the years of schooling tends to suggest in general terms that girls are conditioned to become more susceptible to environments which are civilized, comfortable, clean and softened by decor, and are conditioned to be put off by concrete, dirt, steel, oil, machines and mud. It is, however, difficult to trace any hard, empirical research evidence which validates a cause-and-effect sex-differentiated relationship between harsh or unattractive physical environments and female demotivation in academic learning, in higher or tertiary education institutions. Reports of projects (as distinct from research in particular), often weak in methodology and rigour, report frequent Snark Syndrome assertions that girls' alleged poor motivation to study the manual crafts, engineering, surveying and geology, is influenced by their (perceived) dislike of rough, oily or muddy surroundings. We were prepared to accept some validity in this in relation to image: that is, we were prepared to look at a hypothesis that lower female enrolments might be progressively correlated with disciplines presenting a harsh or unfastidious environment in their image (however incorrectly image describes actual disciplines and their real work). But are girls and their parents really influenced by perceptions of a campus as dominated by laboratories, formaldehyde, rats and machines on the one hand, or of leatherbound books, seminars, comfortable common rooms and philosophy on the other? We were less convinced that the reasons why University A had higher female enrolments in physics, geology or electrical engineering than Institute B would include that University A is softened by green lawns, jacaranda blossom and pleasant student facilities while Institute B is an inner-city concrete jungle round a massive tower block full of grey box-like small rooms with student facilities in a lower basement. While the hypothesis could, we judged, stand some testing in a wider, more integrated model of ecology which we were developing, we saw the main issues as more complex and more cultural.

We therefore discounted this aspect as a factor relevant to access and have not pursued it, although we were less ready to discount it as a factor influencing retention or drop-out, progression in a discipline, or transfer out of it. Since physical environment may contribute to cultural environment, we kept an open mind on its relevance to adaptation theory but ranked it hypothetically low on our list of influential factors, except in regard to male peer behaviour in territorially dominating hands-on facilities in laboratories and computer rooms.

Reviewing Institutional Ecology

We now turn to the resetting of ecology theory in the context of this study. In essence, it is argued that the ecological environment of certain scientific and technological disciplines is the major determinant in both successful recruitment and progression, or failure to recruit, in progression or drop-out. By analogy with natural ecology, in which elements and factors such as warmth, cold, moisture, dryness, soil composition, exposure and shelter are determinants of both survival and growth, we argue that there are clusters of factors common to most disciplines, and specific factors more relevant to some than others, which are determinants for women students. See the illustrations of clusters 1 and 2. Cluster 1 shows that women will see a discipline as sex-normal if critical mass is achieved. Factors influencing the achievement of both critical mass and sex-normality are image, role modelling and mentorship, some of which have two-way as well as one-way

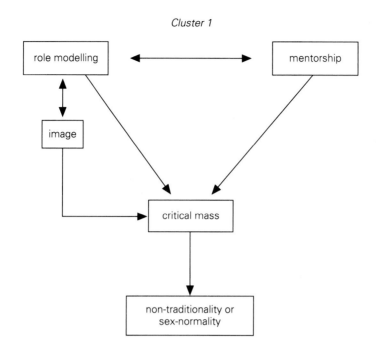

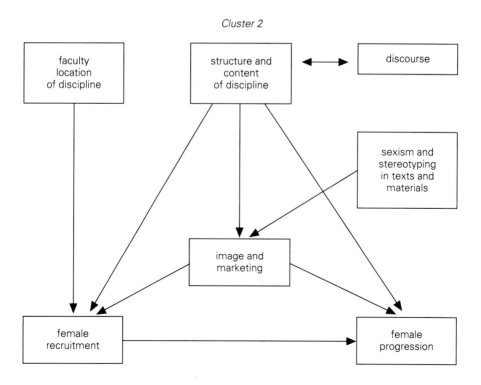

relationships. Cluster 1 can operate at both institutional and discipline levels.

Cluster 2 suggests that a policy which deals only with image without also looking at the structure, content and discourse will be ineffective, particularly in dealing with issues of drop-out or progression. But is there an existing research base for suggesting a higher relevance for these factors?

There is, of course, nothing new about human ecology theory. More than thirty years ago, Duncan (1959) described human ecology as having four principal variables. Population, organization, environment and technology were, he argued, characteristics of an ecosystem. He saw these as reciprocally connected. One of the elder statesmen of human ecology theory, Amos Hawley, argues that it was concerned

> with the elemental problem of how growing, multiplying beings maintain themselves in a constantly changing but ever restricted environment . . . the subject of ecological enquiry then is the community, the form and development of which are studied with particular reference to the limiting and supporting factors of the environment. (Hawley, 1944, p. 403)

In this sense, the study of science and technology in the higher education ecology, or the discipline ecology, is a study of those communities and their limiting and supporting environmental factors. It is a study also of institutional culture, which Hawley describes as 'nothing more than a way of referring to the prevailing techniques by which a population maintains itself in its habitat . . . the morphology of collective life in both its static and its dynamic aspects' (*ibid.*, pp. 403–4).

To reinforce further the paradigm shift of which we spoke in chapter 1, from girls and women (the 'organisms') to the male-constructed environment (the ecosystem or ecological niche), it should be noted that later human ecology theory has developed the concept of collective relationships in the environment: 'organisms, whether plant or animal, establish viable relationships with environment, not independently but collectively, through the mechanism of a system of relationships' (Hawley, 1968, p. 328). We are arguing that it is precisely these collective relationships which are a major influence on female and male achievement and progression in science and technology in higher education: male peer pressures on female peers, sociometric patterns, discourse in collective settings. We also argue that the ecology metaphor explains in considerable measure why the consistent small minority of women who are successful in each generation in carving their way up to the professoriate or top management, do in fact get there. Like Darwin's organisms, those who survive are likely to be those that evolve characteristics which are compatible with the environment: in this case, assertiveness, competitiveness and discourse modelled on 'masculine' styles rather than 'feminine' modes; instrumental values rather than people-oriented values.

Writing in the 1940s, Hawley also reviewed contemporary perceptions of human ecology as dealing with subsocial phenomena. There were, he argued, 'some writers who would have human ecology encompass the whole field of social science, and there are others who prefer to relegate it to the status of a mere sociological research technique' (Hawley, 1944, p. 398). The 1940s debate centred around a typical controversial debate with mutually exclusive standpoints. One group argued that ecology offers an essentially biological approach to the study of the human community and related human to general ecology. The other strongly opposed even a suggestion of association or similarity between the two on the grounds that any assumption of analogy between social and biological phenomena was invalid and impractical.

Hawley rejected both stances, asserting on the one hand that the concept of 'the *sociological* quality of the idea of struggle' does have direct biological analogy: according to Darwin, the struggle for existence relates primarily to the behaviour of organisms towards one another. 'If this be the province of biology, then *ipso facto* all social science resolves itself into biology' (*ibid.*, p. 400). But, on the other hand, he rejected the concepts of competition and spatial analysis as central pivots of human ecology.

In defining the theoretical analogy against which our own policy analysis would take place, the generic definition of ecology has been accepted as 'that branch of biology which deals with the relations of living organisms to their surroundings, their habits and modes of life' (*Shorter Oxford English Dictionary*, 1978). Environments is taken to be 'the conditions or influences under which any person or thing lives or is developed' (*ibid.*, 1827 definition). We discuss both human ecology and institutional ecology at two levels. Firstly, there are valid analogies to be drawn; secondly we will use, in looking at microbial adaptation to new cultures as a transferred metaphor, the concept of an extended metaphor to aid interpretation at a phenomenological level.

We found the distinction between the biological definitions of autoecology and synecology a useful one in terms of an extended metaphor for interpretation. Autoecology is the study of individual living organisms and their environments, while synecology studies the relationship between living groups and their environments. One legitimate criticism of the available pool of previous research in our area could well be that past researchers have been more interested in studying the autoecology of science students and the functioning of individuals (to see why they do or do not succeed or acquire positive attitudes or motivation), rather than the synecology of dominant and subdominant group interactions, in institutional or systemic terms.

In looking at institutional ecology, we have used the basic analogy of an ecosystem (which we are defining as the institution), in which organisms (new women students) adapt to their new cultures and are found in 'ecological niches', which we are defining as the *discipline, School or Department*. In this we differ from Stem (1970) who looked at American college environments in terms of student needs at psychological level but college environment in terms of intellectual or non-intellectual environment. Stem based his analysis on 'the *college* as an ecological niche' (our emphasis) whereas all of our preliminary work convinced us that if role-modelling, mentorship, cultural attitudes etc were *critically* influential, it was at discipline or Departmental level. In this, we ally with Hannan and Freeman who define the ecological niche in terms of human development as the area in which a particular population group (in our case, minority women) 'can survive and reproduce itself (Hannan and Freeman, 1977, p. 947). And we argue that the achievement of critical mass is essential for this ability not only to survive (ie to continue and to complete), but also to reproduce a larger cohort in the next generation through the achievement of a sex-normal image and perception in place of non-traditionality.

There is, of course, nothing new about theories of institutional influence (in terms of environmental impact) on student attitudes and performance. There are several themes which run through the relevant research literature and theoretical studies. One is the *unevenness* of the ecological environment of education, as between regions, districts, institutions. Both the theories of Connolly and Porter (1978) referred to earlier in relation to critical mass, and Eggleston's work on the ecology of schooling, raise issues of the different influences on both access and attainment that different institutional environments exert. Eggleston's study took the concept further. His apparent oversimplification that 'the ecological approach . . . springs from . . . the basic understanding that human beings take on different patterns of behaviour and different life styles and *accept different patterns of achievement* when they find themselves in different locations' (Eggleston, 1977, pp. 15–17) is developed into a clearer definition of the 'ecology of power in a society or community' which in turn requires study not only of the response of individuals to their environment but also of alterations in the creation, maintenance and distribution of the resources (human and material) which constitute the educational environment (*ibid.*) Eggleston reaches a depressing but realistic view that 'there is no evidence that individuals seek through their perceptions, their interpretations or their intentions, to challenge the ecological system of schooling or of the society of which it is part' (*ibid.*).

We have reviewed some earlier models which have been reported as useful in investigating ecology or environment in the context of education or training. We have not, however, found an existing model which would provide a valid way of interpreting holistically the clusters of factors which we have seen as interrelated. Some researchers appear to have replicated the linear approach referred to in our introductory chapter — single dimensional studies, for example, looking at the physical environment, but not simultaneously at behavioural, structural or cultural influences in higher education institutions.

A further analogy can be identified with microbial adaptation to physical cultures. Let it be said at the outset that at no point are we arguing a direct transference of 'behaviour' from microbes or plants to human students! We are simply using a relevant conceptual analogy in the form of an extended metaphor, in order to enlighten and to requestion some received wisdom about the operation of the management of higher education institutions.

When microbes are placed in a new culture, cell growth takes place only under particular conditions. Microbial growth depends not just on physical factors like warmth and humidity, but also on the absence (or presence) of bacteriostatic agents which inhibit growth but on whose removal, growth resumes, or of bactericidal agents which will kill the bacteria off completely. Thus far, we argue that women's retention and progression in non-traditional disciplines is vitally affected by the presence of 'bacteriostatic' or 'bactericidal' agents in the shape of non-supportive or aggressively critical lecturing staff or peer group males, whose role in this regard we discuss in later chapters in discussing attitudes and mentorship.

Also useful as an analogy is the microbial phase of adaptation which includes a 'lag phase'. Jawetz *et al.* (1984) represent the microbial phase of adaptation, growth and decline as shown in figure 3.5. Phase A is the 'lag phase' when, as Jawetz *et al.* put it, 'the cells . . . adapt to their new environment . . . If the cells are taken from an entirely different medium, it often happens that they are . . . incapable of growth in the new medium. In such case a long lag may occur.' (Jawetz *et al.*, 1984, p. 93). When microbes are in the lag phase on their entry to the culture,

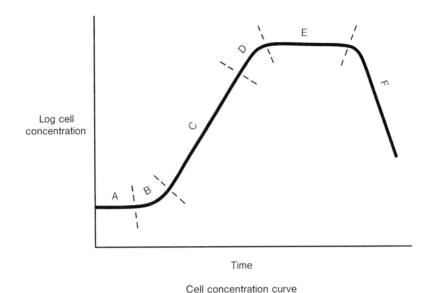

Cell concentration curve

Figure 3.5 Time-lag theory
(Taken from Jawetz et al., 1984, p. 93)

their energy is first spent on adaptation and is therefore not yet available for cell growth. Only when they have adapted will they move on to phase B and multiply. Moreover, the more the culture is identical with or similar to the culture from which the microbe came or to which it is accustomed, the shorter the time-lag phase. Similarly, the more unlike or dissonant the culture, the longer the time-lag phase.

Van Demark and Batzing describe the lag phases as 'a period of rejuvenation or adjustment prior to the onset of cell division . . . in a new physical and chemical environment to which the inoculum must adapt.' If cells are transferred to a fresh medium of the same composition, they 'initiate growth with virtually no lag' (Van Demark and Batzing, 1987, p. 180). By analogy, if the teaching style, teacher attitudes, behaviour patterns and cultural environment are very similar to that from which new students come, the less their time-lag of adaptation, and vice versa. We will argue that girls entering the scientific and technological disciplines come from a more dissonant culture and boys from a similar one.

When, in microbial processes, cells that have been inhibited by a bacteriostatic agent are removed from the harmful cultural environment, washed thoroughly in a centrifuge and replaced in a new growth medium, they begin growth again. So when women students transfer during or after the first year to pursue maths/arts instead of maths/science, or to pursue biological sciences or biochemistry and to drop chemistry and physics, they are removing themselves from a culture which they find alien and negative to their personal and intellectual development to a culture which encourages growth by being more similar to that of their secondary schooling years. We believe this to be cross-related also to the question of the structure and content of disciplines.

The biological metaphor must, for validity, be set against a number of assumptions about the incoming school-leavers and their previous school and adolescent experiences. Firstly, the ethos made up of teaching style, discourse patterns, culture and actual male participation rate of disciplines like physics, engineering, geology and construction is most likely to replicate that of the single-sex boys' non-government schools from which a majority of male school-leavers entering science and technology Universities in Australia come. Secondly, the ethos of the physics and chemistry Grades 11 and 12 classes of the coeducational high schools from which the remaining male students come, also matches the dominant culture of groups in which males outnumber females. We write more of this in our forthcoming more detailed research reports on mathematics, prerequisites and the single-sex versus coeducation controversy. The point here is that males entering science and technology tertiary courses are entering a culture in which they need no time-lag to adjust, because it matches that from which they came.

Girls entering from a single-sex girls' school are held, by current received wisdom, to have an advantage over those coming from co-educational schools. There is, however, no sound empirical base for this assumption yet in Australia. Unless and until longitudinal research following several different cohorts and control groups were to track the intakes through the transition from general first-year to specialized second-year studies (and to check why the choices were made), then from the third year to honours and, where appropriate, to completion of a doctorate, we simply cannot assert that single-sex schools necessarily produce more women physicists or geologists. (And investment in such research would not be justified in policy terms since entry to secondary school is not controllable as a policy issue.) The girls from single-sex schools, moreover, come from a cultural environment where the style of discourse and interpersonal relations has developed throughout adolescence in a very different manner from that of an all-male or mainly male learning environment. Thus they enter a different culture in tertiary science and technology from that from which they came. Girls from coeducational high schools have already been exposed to classes in maths and science which are male-dominated and conducted in styles of discourse and teaching which sit more easily with boys than with girls. Some will have learned to adapt to the male norm (which we describe later in this chapter) and some will be less secure. We hypothesize that one determinant of continuation and progression in the tertiary sector, as against drop-out or transfer, is the extent to which such an adaptation has or has not taken place before entry.

If, of course, higher education institutions accept responsibility for resetting the learning environment, discourse and mentorship roles during first-year teaching into a more sex-neutral mode, the problem becomes realistically remediable. Such actions include understanding the need for a time-lag phase for adaptation — something that would also benefit boys coming from learning environments that are less aggressively male (e.g. small rural high schools with a high proportion of women staff).

Learning Environments

The learning environment is highly relevant to student aspirations. This operates at both institutional and departmental or discipline levels. The premise that 'the environment of a university is shaped by the totality of the university's programs, personnel, policies and procedures which are designed to promote learning' (Gaff *et al.*, 1976, p. 285) is one which we endorse and which underlies the construction of the UQ WISTA model of institutional ecology. In terms of the issues which UQ WISTA investigated, the institutional learning environment was seen as influenced by a number of factors:

1   The attitudinal climate as set by the dominant groups of academics and students. To the extent that there is male dominance, if we accept the prevailing research evidence that there are general differences in teaching styles, manners of discourse, inculcated values and behaviour patterns between mainly male and mainly female groups, then women entering the prevailing attitudinal climate of physics, geology, engineering and so on will experience a mismatch on entry.

2   The construction of disciplines as free-floating or highly structured, as pure or applied, as vocationally oriented or as curiosity-driven.

3 The image and marketing of disciplines as socially responsible or otherwise, or as sex-normal or non-traditional.

4 The academic staff, their representation in terms of sex-balance (in terms of visibility, role modelling and mentorship) and their teaching styles as related to different disciplines.

5 Peer group behaviour, notably by males towards females and by dominant majorities towards minority groups who do not yet form a critical mass and/or whose culture, behaviour and style differs from the inherited norm.

There is some previous research which has investigated the characteristics of the learning environment at departmental as well as institutional level, but with results which provide an ambivalent basis for generalization. In Richard Wakeford's (1984) study of student perceptions of twenty-five British and Irish medical schools across eleven dimensions (from flexibility and friendliness to course content and ethics), the schools showed variations in three dimensions: their extra-curricular emphasis, intensiveness and a 'vocational versus scientific' orientation. (Some schools taught medicine in a vocational ethos, others with a more enquiry-oriented scientific approach.) However, Wakeford does not report his results at all qualitatively. The inter-school differentials on vocational orientation as compared with students' freedom to explore their interests are relevant to this study, although no sex-differential is explored in Wakeford's work.

We spoke in chapter 1 of the perceptual distinctions generally drawn between science and non-science, science and technology. Here, we refer to distinctions between those disciplines which are highly structured and codified and those which are seen and designed as more free-floating and enquiry-driven (in terms of students' capacities to follow their own interests). Previous research does show a marked and relevant sex-differential according to these distinctions. A review of studies on female access, drop-out and progression shows that girls enrol proportionately less than boys in subjects described as applied ('applied' rather than 'pure' maths, 'applied' geology, etc.) and less in subjects marketed as vocational. The UQ WISTA data support this theory. The question of student interest as a motivational factor is also sex-differentiated. Researchers studying adolescent motivation and/or aspiration in school students have reported over some decades that proportionately more girls will choose school subjects or disciplines for intrinsic or interest-based reasons ('I like it,' 'I am good at it,' 'I am interested in this'), while proportionately more boys tend to be guided by extrinsic (usually vocational) reasons of usefulness, relevance to future work, or preparation for higher education studies ('I need it for my job,' 'Maths will be useful,' 'It's a prerequisite').

Thompson *et al.* (1969) argue that the natural sciences have a more highly codified body of knowledge, which is now rooted in clearly defined and accepted methodologies, than the social sciences or humanities do. They hypothesize as a result that this accounts for differences in the extent to which different disciplines are responsive to the needs and interests of students. Our inclusion of structure and style of discipline is supported by Gaff *et al.*'s (1976) study of four departments in a Dutch University, in which chemistry emerges as leaving little time for 'free-floating' critical enquiry or discussion. Chemistry teaching is reported as knowledge-oriented and prescribed and so heavily and tightly timetabled as to leave little time for student-controlled work or for personal academic interests. The departmental style as described by students emerges as instrumental and inflexible (Gaff *et al.*, 1976, p. 285). By contrast, in the same survey, the Psychology Department is described by the researchers as having a 'freewheeling, independent atmosphere (*ibid.*). This contrast was sharpest in the time required of students for set, controlled work, which of the four disciplines surveyed was highest for chemistry and lowest for psychology.

It is not only women who show a will to reject the artificial constraint of knowledge into a straitjacket of what Lowe and Warboys call 'the objective, rational and calculating consciousness' in favour of 'a more subjective, intuitive and feeling type of knowledge' (Lowe and Warboys, 1980, p. 443). Lowe quotes Roszak (1973), among respected scientists, as giving value-based 'feeling type of knowledge' legitimation in his proposition that the normal image of science and the model science should be the value-driven ecological sciences, not the instrumental high-energy physics.

We have therefore investigated, so far as data are readily available, the profile of the survey disciplines in relation to their reported structure and content as published in higher education institutions' calendars and handbooks, and have crossrelated this to the statistical data showing the pattern of female:male enrolments in each discipline. A positive relationship has emerged, that is, the more the discipline is described as applied and not theoretical, vocationally oriented and not curiosity-driven, and is structured into a tight, compulsory non-negotiable degree, the lower the female enrolment. This may well be partly because women are not attracted, but partly also because males are more competitive for these degrees precisely because they are described as job-related.

Teaching style is also relevant. The research literature is ambivalent on how far there is, or is not, a general sex-differential in male and female teaching styles. On balance, the evidence suggests that more males prefer to teach in a directive, information-transmitting style and more females prefer a student-oriented, discursive style. Welch and Lawrenz (1982), for example, have looked at characteristics of male and female science teachers randomly selected from a fourteen-state region of the USA, and report that the female teachers also scored higher on measures of interest in science (intrinsic motivation) and receptivity to change, while more males scored more highly on science knowledge. There are other such studies. (One could hypothesize that only the very interested women survive the barriers to training as a science teacher in a perceptually male domain, of course.)

In higher education, Gaff and Wilson (1971) postulate that natural scientists are, *per se*, less student-centred and less permissive towards students than social scientists are, and more conservative and less will-ing to tolerate nonconformist behaviour (Gaff and Wilson, 1971). This cannot wholly be explained by size of department (e.g. that very large classes may dictate more inflexible methods), since in the Gaff, Crombag and Chang (1976) study, law and medicine were larger than chemistry but were still relatively more personal, and psychology had a more disadvantageous staffing ratio than chemistry (12:1 compared with 7:1) and yet was more student-centred. Their (1971) study of professors in a wide variety of disciplines shows that the least discursive were in mathematics and engineering, who self-rated items like 'discuss points of view other than my own', 'relate the coursework to other fields of study' and 'encourage students to discuss issues which go beyond class reading' the lowest of professors in all disciplines surveyed. This has been held to be because the knowledge-base in maths and the natural sciences is the most highly codified and systematized in analytical and instrumental terms. Thus there is, arguably, a cause-and-effect rela-tionship between the structure of a subject and the teaching style adopted by most academics in that field. In the same study, mathematics and engineering were the disciplines where student-centred teaching ap-proaches were least used. Gaff and Wilson's (1971) data support the theory that the prior imposition of highly codified knowledge is highly correlated with lecturer-domination of teaching and learning styles. Another possible interpretation is, of course, that it is, in the first place, those who prefer an authoritarian and directional style with relat-ively little 'negotiation' involved who are attracted to the neatness and codified nature of certain of the scientific and technological disciplines in the first place.

It should be noted that theories which set out to explain human behaviour patterns will never account for all individuals in the groups studied and will always be subject to exceptions. (Often these exceptions can still be explained in the terms of the theory, however.) Given the reassuring persistence of human individuality in inherited temperament and social variables like class and parental attitudes, there will always be some girls and some boys who do not conform to the sex-stereotyped norms of expected behaviour set by both adults and peer groups in a highly socialized and standardized schooling system. But research evidence in western industrialized countries over several decades, whether from major longitudinal studies like the British Child Development Study (Davie, Butler and Goldstein, 1974) and the Luxembourg Etude Magrip (Institut Pédagogique, 1977), or from a plethora of specific studies focussing on one particular aspect of learning, teaching and socialization, converge to confirm across social, psychological and cognitive dimensions that

- more girls than boys grow up concerned about the social consequences of their own actions, and of the actions of others;
- more girls than boys value the maintenance of interpersonal relations more than the competitive achievement of future success, if these are seen to be in conflict;
- more girls than boys in adolescence appear to prefer a series of dyadic relationships; more boys than girls work through gangs, groups or sets with common peer-identification goals and motivations;
- more girls than boys use language in discourse which contains negotiating skills, relativities, conditions, value judgments and cues to reach consensus;
- more boys than girls use language as a tool to assert dominance or subordination, to establish rankings in gangs, groups or sets, or to establish territoriality.

Gender, Language, Culture and Institutional Ecology

We now look at culture, language and discourse as part of a process in which school students entering higher education may experience a mismatch between their previous learning environment and their current one: an ecological mismatch. Moreover, in some circumstances, this mismatch is sex-differentiated according to not only the different environments of, say, single-sex or coeducational schools, but also the conditioning processes of female and male adolescence. Finally, the

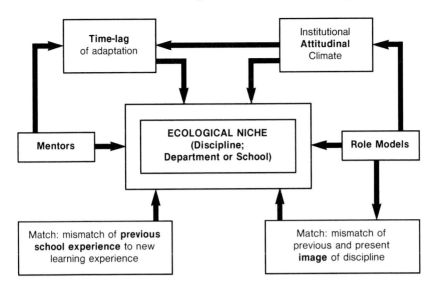

Figure 3.6 Interaction of factors in institutional ecology

culture, language and discourse interaction in these contexts is seen as contributing to a mismatch process in which more female students than male students need to expend initial energy (mental and psychological) in adapting to new and more alien forms of discourse or culture in scientific and technological disciplines instead of being able to use the energy for immediate intellectual growth. That is, by the 'time-lag' analogy, the average (as distinct from gifted pioneer) female student will need longer to adapt and more help in doing so.

Hawley, in his early work on human ecology, implicitly recognizes this when he writes that 'culture is nothing more than a way of referring to the prevailing techniques by which a population maintains itself in its habitat' (Hawley, 1944, p. 404). We argue that these prevailing techniques maintained by the existing (and therefore male-dominated scientific community) involve the language and style of teaching and peer discourse as well as the structure and content of disciplines, and that these differ firstly between arts and sciences, and secondly between predominantly male and predominantly female environments. Indeed, it will be recalled that at much the same time that Hawley was developing his later ecological conceptualization, C.P. Snow was arguing that the scientific disciplines and the literary disciplines in academe were sufficiently different in construction, delivery and ethos as to constitute 'two cultures . . . with little in common in intellectual, moral and psychological climate' (Snow, 1959, p. 2). It is now recognized some decades later that this is not unlinked to the quite different prevailing sex-balance in these two areas of studies.

The Construction and Reproduction of Knowledge-based Culture: a Male Model

Among sociologists prominent in developing theory on the role of systemic education in reproducing itself in each generation, Pierre Bourdieu's work has some immediate relevance to UQ WISTA issues. In essence, we suggest that the mismatch which Bourdieu highlights between the prescribing ethos of French higher education institutions and the new clientele of student entrants of the 1960s has its parallel in the non-adaptability of higher education to a new clientele of women to science and technology in the 1970s. The pioneer women scientists and engineers of earlier decades (forming around 5–10 per cent of all such students) were untypical high achievers. They had to be, to carve their way in. The more widely spread female cohorts seeking entrance in the 1970s and 1980s are arguably not replicas of the pioneer women.

Bourdieu has developed a theory of the role of the education system as an agent for reproducing a culture, a code, a set of transmitted values and expectations of behaviour identical with that of the historically inherited elite who control the education system. This work was primarily developed in the context of the lesser ability of working-class students to adapt quickly and effectively to the elitism and culturally mannered middle-class authoritarianism of French *lycées* and Universities in the 1950s and 1960s. Bourdieu's theory is, however, seen to be highly transferable to the situation of women students entering male-constructed non-traditional disciplines where the women's previous cultural environment, patterns of discourse and peer relationships also differ from that of the disciplines they are now entering in greater numbers.

Pierre Bourdieu sees pedagogy, especially in higher education, as the 'imposition of a cultural arbitrary' (Bourdieu, 1985, passim); arbitrary because the structure and functions of the culture cannot be deduced from any universal principle. It is also inherited unaltered. The cultural arbitrary is in turn endorsed and legitimated by a 'genesis amnesia' which believes that things have always been as they are and therefore should continue so. This in turn leads to a 'cultural unconscious' in the leadership of education who construct what we learn and how we learn it (Bourdieu and Passeron, 1977, pp. 5–9). Bourdieu crystallizes this into a term central to his work, a 'habitus' (which in its original Latin means a condition, appearance and, philosophically, a moral culture), which, he argues, is 'the product of *internalisation* of the principles of a cultural arbitrary' (Bourdieu, 1985).

Applying this to WISTA, many of the male academics who have traditionally constructed the cultural norms of teaching and learning in science and technology are apparently unconscious that these disciplines have in fact been constructed on a male norm. Or so we found in the UQ WISTA group interviews with Professors, Deans and Heads of Schools. This, we argue, constitutes a form of 'genesis amnesia' and a 'cultural unconscious' in Bourdieu's terms. A further example of this comes from Margaret Murray. Born in 1863, she was an early student at University College, London, in 1894 and a lecturer in Egyptology by 1899. Trained by Flinders Petrie, she not only consolidated the training of students of anthropology in the early years of the discipline, but her colonial Indian experience led her to challenge the British Association's Anthropological Section in 1913, urging that it should insist on the government training up women as well as men in anthropology and sending them out to posts in overseas administration. Her challenge was against Hartland's policy at that time that 'anthropology is not a subject for a woman . . . I would not allow a woman to come to my lectures', but Dr Haddon supported her on the grounds that 'it is most important that women should be trained because all we know about the beliefs and customs of the women of these primitive people is what men have told men, and what do *they* know about it' (Murray, 1963). Yet it has taken the work of the wave of feminist anthropologists in the 1970s to follow through the logic of Haddon's academic and cultural stance of 1913 and to question the male cultural bias of the inherited norms of this discipline.

Bourdieu's own language (even in his original French) is usually difficult, jargonistic and at times dense to the point of near-obscurity. When he defines habitus as 'the product of history which produces individual and collective practices' (Bourdieu and Passeron, 1982, p. 82), however, we can recognize the process of institutions reproducing their structures and practices on past models into a definable ecological environment which is then refined into 'ethos'. A more obscure but central dictum that teaching is most effective when 'the habitus it tends to inculcate approximates the habitus accomplished by all prior pedagogical work and family upbringing' (pp. 71–3), can nevertheless be decoded to show that when the teaching content and style and discourse which the inherited cultural base of a University or discipline seeks to transmit, matches more or less the previous teaching and learning experience and family approach to discourse and values of the student entrants, students are most likely to succeed quickly. Among other factors of inherited mismatch to student entrants from different backgrounds from those of previous decades, Bourdieu criticizes the dominant use of *'le langage magistral'* (professorial pedagogical language), which includes style as well as language, as alienating to working-class students (Bourdieu, 1985). We are arguing that sexist language and characteristically male discourse can equally alienate women students.

Sex-differentiation in Language and Discourse

What evidence do we have of generally applicable sex-differences in language and discourse? There is nothing pedagogically new about our knowledge that the socialization process of primary and secondary schooling does produce school students who use mainly different styles and characteristics of language and discourse according to their male or female sex. This is a generalization not universally applicable across the sexes, but it is widely held to be valid at least at the two thirds:one third ratio.

It needs to be stressed at the outset that language is the tool which we use to architect the behaviour around us and to determine our interpersonal relationships. That language is our prime tool for social growth is not a new theory. As long ago as 1848, William Von Humboldt declared that 'man [sic] lives with the world about him principally, indeed . . . exclusively as language presents it'. It was Max Planck, the great scientist, who pointed out that Universities revolve around talk. What has only been recognized more belatedly is that language often presents a different world to girls from that defined for boys. The case is well made in Spender's (1980) research-based analysis of what she describes as 'man-made language'. Here, we will look only at her work on discourse, which she describes in terms of 'the dominant and the muted' (Spender, 1980, chapter 3). Spender bases her theories, *inter alia*, on tape-recordings of mixed-sex conversations over a lengthy period, which have been analysed for a number of factors. She argues that in her research samples women were not in fact able to obtain as much space or time in mixed conversation as men (contrary to popular stereotype). Her conclusion from her research analysis is that 'women are queried, they are interrupted, their opinions are discounted and their contributions devalued' (*ibid.*, p. 87). While Spender tends occasionally in her work to overstate her case with a rather elliptical empirical base, her specific conclusions on discourse are well based on serious research which was scientifically conducted. Like Bernstein (1971), Spender does not argue the complete universality of her argument, but uses its undoubted general transferability to reconceptualize our approach to discourse. Thus far, the work is both sound and useful and has provided an important breakthrough in our understanding. (There is no short cut to understanding this issue, however, without reading the full text.) There is little doubt that Spender's claim that 'women cannot have equal access to discourse undisturbed' (Spender, 1980, p. 89) has been validated not only in her own research, but subsequently in further fieldwork.

At much the same period, Goodwin's (1980) work with American children has also confirmed that the organization of tasks differs considerably when undertaken by groups of all boys and all girls respectively, and that this is reflected in the language and discourse used in order to establish roles in completing the tasks:

> Among the boys the coordinating of such tasks is handled through hierarchical organization. This type of organization is uncommon in girls' games generally, and in accomplishing a task activity . . . all [girls] participate jointly in decision making with minimal negotiation of status. (Goodwin, 1980, p. 165)

This consensual approach by girls remains increasingly more characteristic of female students than of male as they grow through adolescence.

Elliott's (1974) work on sex roles in discussion in classrooms in the early 1970s tends also to confirm that there are, at school level, 'sex role constraints on freedom of discussion in the small [mixed] group . . . such constraints were a major obstacle to any kind of radical innovation in teaching and learning' (Elliott, 1974, p. 147). A wider research literature generally identifies discourse in later adolescence and young adulthood as reflecting power relations for more males than females, and interpersonal relations for more females than males.

This kind of sex-differentiation is confirmed in a different mode by work by Carol Gilligan whose (1982) published research *In a Different Voice* has joined the ranks of seminal books making an immediate and diversified impact on relevant theory. Gilligan writes of men and women as having 'two ways of speaking about moral problems, two modes of describing the relationship between other and self', and traces the differences 'as a contrapuntal theme woven into the cycle of life' (Gilligan, 1982, p. 1). Women, she alleges, speak and discourse 'in a different voice . . . characterized not by gender but theme' (*ibid.*). The 'female' theme is described in Gilligan's analysis of interviews as being more concerned with balancing ethics, moral standpoints and human relationships; the 'male' with balancing a different moral framework with sharper, more polarized decisions (*ibid.*). Her research, set in the USA in the late 1970s, does not, however, assert absolutes. The contrasts between male and female 'voices', or messages, interpretations, themes, rather 'highlight a distinction between two modes of thought and focus a problem of interpretation rather than represent a generalisation about either sex' (*ibid.*, p. 2).

Gilligan's sample of women consistently described their identity as 'defined in a context of relationship and judged by a standard of responsibility and care' (*ibid.*, p. 160). Her male interviewees, by contrast, had a 'clearer, more direct, more distinct and sharp-edged' tone of identity. They defined identity more in terms of separation and independence than in terms of attachment. Gilligan suggests that 'when women construct the adult domain, the world of relationships emerges and becomes the focus of attention and concern' (*ibid.*, p. 167). McClelland, writing on power some years earlier, also concludes that 'women are more concerned than men with both sides of an interdependent relationship . . . are quicker to recognise their own interdependence' (McClelland, 1975, pp. 85–6). These different attitudes to dilemmas involving decisions of social and moral responsibility are not far distant from the sex-differences noted in the research showing general differences in girls' and boys' attitudes to the social implications of science.

Carol Gilligan was primarily concerned with the fact that women's message is allegedly different at the level of generalization (but not universality) as well as the 'voice' showing differences of style and constructed reality. The work of Basil Bernstein, which concurrently with that of Bourdieu unpacks different codes of language used by different groups, adds yet another dimension. We should stress that the criticisms that Bernstein's work has aroused in writers like Labov (1970) and others, relate to controversy about how far his conceptualization of codes is or is not class-linked. They do not in any way invalidate Bernstein's basic identification of different modes and styles of discourse, which he credibly establishes are central factors in the construction of roles and in the transmission of class culture, work culture or subcultures in closely identified groups. It is this central issue of different modes which, when related to gender modes, is relevant to this project.

Bernstein argues firstly that 'forms of socialisation orient the child towards speech codes which control access to relatively context-independent meanings' (Bernstein, 1971, p. 200). He relates the use of language and of role relationships to four interrelated contexts of socialization: the regulative (authority), the instructional (transmission of learning), the imaginative or innovating, and the interpersonal. He concludes that 'the critical orderings of a culture or subculture are made substantive — are made palpable — through the forms of its linguistic realisations of these four contexts' (*ibid.*, p. 206), thus supporting the language stance of researchers from Humboldt through Bourdieu to Spender. Of these four contexts, there is solid research evidence that at least three are sex-differentiated (from the conditioning process in schooling, not by any innate biological determinism), viz language and authority, language of instruction, and the presence or absence of interpersonal (as distinct from group or objective) elements in discourse.

Moreover, Bernstein argues that discourse takes place in two modes, the restricted code and the elaborated code. The former has a style which is functional, ritualistic and fairly standardized, as described. It is also more directional and authoritarian. The conversational exchange 'presupposes a shared cultural heritage . . . [and] . . . closely shared identifications and expectations' (*ibid.*, p. 149). The implication of the research of Spender and Gilligan is that this restricted code style is characteristic of more young males than young females (of any social class). The elaborated code involves more conditionals and subjunctives and (in terms of content) more negotiation, probability and assumption, and is modified in the light of the special attributes and context of the listener (*ibid.*, p. 150). Bernstein points up the difference as inducing 'a sensitivity to the implications of separateness and differences' (*ibid.*), a sensitivity found by many researchers to be more characteristically 'female'.

Relevant to WISTA issues is Bernstein's theory that the elaborated code (which all higher education students must have acquired by definition, by then) itself operates through two modes: elaboration of interpersonal relations and elaboration of relations between objects. Bernstein comments that 'an individual going into the arts is likely to possess an elaborated code oriented *to the person*; whilst an individual going into the sciences, particularly the applied sciences, is likely to possess an elaborated code oriented *to object relations*' (*ibid.*, p. 156). This, of course, can be matched with the female domination of arts and male domination of sciences, reinforcing the socialized antithesis of personal versus objective. Again, we would argue that most of those girls who have so far entered the physical sciences have been those who already conform to the restricted-code style of communication and to the object-relations style of the elaborated code: those nearer the male norm. And in this regard, we note yet another potential element of the match:mismatch issue of the transfer of school female students into higher education male-dominated learning environments. How like the typical male student in discourse and value- or interest-base are the majority of aspiring female science and engineering students? If their discourse style is in fact generally different from that of peer group males (and research in language and gender suggests that it is), the adaptation process and our time-lag phase become areas for policy intervention.

Any readers who doubt, moreover, that the dominant discourse style in higher education in the scientific and technological disciplines is based on a male-as-norm paradigm, may wish to note that Bernstein's (1971) work is important as a frame of reference not in any way because he suggests any sex-differentiation in modes of discourse in young people. He could not, since in common with most sociological researchers in the 1960s he restricted his empirical samples to young males — precisely the 'male-as-norm' syndrome we have criticized. His research is mainly based on empirical work with young male students on day-release at a London College of Further Education. At no stage in his challenging detailed writings do we learn of an attempt to match his early works on males with a parallel study of young females to check their discourse patterns. His control group consisted of elite boys from an English Public School. Similarly, the seminal work of Liam Hudson (1966, 1968 and 1970), looking at arts and science specializations in the context of converger and diverger gifted students, which in turn led to an important further study of creativity and connections in learning, is based exclusively on school*boys* only, and on the perceptions and self-perceptions in language, learning and motivation of male adolescents.

Implications

We discuss further in the last two chapters the interconnectedness of institutional factors, image, environment, discourse and peer attitudes to retention and drop-out in particular. At this stage, it is useful to summarize some immediate implications for policymakers:

1   Statistical data and substantive research from a range of disciplines justify a paradigm shift from blaming girls and women in a deficiency-context for their non-recruitment to certain

scientific and technological disciplines, to re-examining the learning environment of disciplines and institutions to meet the needs of a wider clientele.

2 Some scientific and technological disciplines are more prone to *'genesis amnesia'* and to non-adaptability to new clienteles than others (*vide* sharp inter-institutional and interdisciplinary differences).

3 The concept, characteristics and influence of critical mass need further examination in the context of moving the image and sex-balance of disciplines from non-traditionality to sex-normality for females (in the eyes of males as well as females).

To illustrate the vividness of the real-life application of our construction of the match:mismatch difficulty of minority females becoming integrated into male higher education disciplines, we quote from a study of graduates of the first coeducational class at the USA's West Point Military Academy. The researcher was investigating the mentor role (if any) of the new second-year (sophomore) women towards the new first-year (freshmen) women students, and noting their failure to support those behind them. Yoder *et al.* wrote: 'the major difference between these two groups was the hard-earned, yet marginal and constantly questioned peer acceptance the sophomore women had won from the dominant male group' (Yoder *et al.*, 1982, p. 4).

We return to the issue of peer attitudes in chapter 6. But roles in higher education learning processes are dictated by Professors and lecturers as well as by peer group fellow students. Bourdieu's 'genesis amnesia' is matched by institutional inertia, of which many analysts write. Hannan and Freeman, for example, suggest that organizations eschew adaptation to new demands or to new entrants because 'there are a number of processes that generate structural inertia' (Hannan and Freeman, 1977, p. 930), in which they include internal political constraints ('when organisations alter structure, political equilibria are disturbed' — *ibid.*, p. 931).

This leads us to re-examine two more of our key factors — the influence or otherwise of role models and of mentors, which are discussed in depth in the next two chapters.

References

BERNSTEIN, B. (1971) *Class, Codes and Control*, London, Routledge and Kegan Paul.

BOURDIEU, P. and PASSERON, J.-C. (1977) *Reproduction in Education, Society and Culture*, London, Sage Publications.

BOURDIEU, P. (1985) 'The social space and the genesis of groups', *Theory and Society*, 14 (6).

DAVIE, R., BUTLER, J. and GOLDSTEIN, H. (1974) *From Birth to Seven*, London, Longman.

DUNCAN, O.D. (1959) 'Human ecology and population studies' in HAUSER, P. and DUNCAN, O.D. (Eds), *The Study of Population*, Chicago, University of Chicago Press.

ELLIOT, J. (1974) 'Sex role constraints on freedom of discussion: a neglected reality of the classroom', *New Era*, 55 (6), pp. 147–55.

GAFF, J.G. and WILSON, R.C. (1971) 'Faculty cultures and interdisciplinary study', *Journal of Higher Education*, March, pp. 186–201.

GAFF, J.G., CROMBAG, H.F.M. and CHANG, T.M. (1976) 'Environments for learning in a Dutch university', *Higher Education*, 5, pp. 285–99.

GILLIGAN, C. (1982) *In a Different Voice: Psychological Theory and Women's Development*, Cambridge, Mass., Harvard University Press.

GOODWIN, M.H. (1980) 'Directive-response speech sequences in boys' and girls' task activities' in MCCONNELL, G.S. *et al.* (Eds), *Women in Language and Literature in Society*, New York, Praeger.

HANNAN, T. and FREEMAN, J. (1977) 'The population ecology of organisations', *American Journal of Sociology*, 82 (5), May, pp. 929–64.

HUDSON, L. (Ed) (1970) *The Ecology of Human Intelligence*, Harmondsworth, Penguin.

HUDSON, L. (1966) *Contrary Imaginations: A Psychological Study of the English Schoolboy*, Harmondsworth, Penguin.

HAWLEY, A.H. (1944) 'Ecology and human ecology', *Social Forces*, 22, May, pp. 398–405.

HAWLEY, A.H. (1968) 'Human ecology' in DAVID STILLS (Ed) *International Encyclopaedia of the Social Sciences*, vol. 4, New York, Macmillan and Free Press, pp. 328–37.

INSTITUTE PÉDAGOGIQUE (1977) *L'Etude Magrip*, Luxembourg.

JACKSON, B. and MARSDEN, D. (1962) *Education and the Working Class*, London, Routledge and Kegan Paul.

JAWETZ, E., MELNICK, J. and ADELBERG, E. (1984) *Review of Medical Microbiology*, 16th edn, Los Altos, Calif., Lange Medical Publications.

LABOV, W. (1970) 'The logic of non-standard English' in WILLIAMS, F. (Ed) *Language and Poverty*, Markham Press.

LOWE, P. and WARBOYS, M. (1980) 'Ecology and ideology' in BUTTELL, F.H. and NEWBY, H. (Eds) *The Rural Sociology of the Advanced Societies: Critical Perspectives*, London, Croom Helm, pp. 433–52.

MCCLELLAND, D.C. (1975) *Power: the Inner Experience*, New York, Irvington.

MURRAY, M. (1963) *My First Hundred Years*, London, William Kimber.

SCHUH, J.A. and ALLEN, M.R. (1978) 'Implementing the ecosystem model', *Journal of College Student Personnel*, March, pp. 119–122.

SNOW, C.P. (1959) *The Two Cultures and the Scientific Revolution*, Cambridge, Cambridge University Press.

SPENDER, D., *Man-made Language*, London, Routledge and Kegan Paul.

STERN, G.S. (1970) *People in Context: Measuring Person-Environment Congruence in Education and Industry*, New York, John Wiley and Sons.

THOMPSON, J., HAWKES, R. and AVERY, R. (1969) 'Truth Strategies and University Organization', in *Educational Administration Quarterly*, 5, pp. 4–25.

VAN DEMARK, P. and BATZING, B. (1987) *The Microbes: An Introduction to their Nature and Importance*, Menlo Park, Calif., Benjamin Cummings Publishing.

WAKEFORD, R. (1984) 'The medical school learning milieu: a study of students' perceptions of twenty-five British and Irish medical schools', *Studies in Higher Education*, 9 (2), pp. 139–49.

WELCH, W.W. and LAWRENZ, F. (1982) 'Characteristics of male and female science teacher', in *Journal of Research in Science and Teaching*, 19 (7), pp. 587–594.

WICHE (1973) *The Ecosystem Model: Designing Campus Environments*, Boulder, Colo., Western Interstate Commission for Higher Education.

YODER, J., ADAMS, J., GROVE, S. and PRIEST, R. (1982) 'Mentors: a debt due from present to future generations', paper presented to the Annual Convention of the American Psychological Association, 23–7 August.

Chapter 4

Role Modelling: an Acute Attack of the Snark Effect

Dux femina facti (a woman the head of the enterprise). (Virgil, *Aeneid*, I)

It is difficult to see why the belief that same-sex role modelling is an effective policy mechanism has become so entrenched, given the almost total lack of hard, scholarly evidence that it works. It is even more perplexing to see that mentorship (which everyone who reaches the top in the face of any significant difficulties knows has been a major and critical influence) still has a low profile in terms of research investigation, and an almost non-existent place in policymaking.

We started the UQ WISTA Policy Review Project with a healthy scepticism towards same-sex role modelling as a process. We had noted with concern an extremely loose use of the term not only in lay policy reports, but also in allegedly scholarly research. Much of what has been described as role modelling is no more than the actual, passive presence of a woman. More serious is the constant and widely occurring use of the term role modelling to describe processes which are clearly mentorship. Over half of the written work on role models that we have sieved shows an apparent lack of understanding of the essential characteristics of role modelling, a concurrent unshakeable conviction that it is present as a policy mechanism and that it works. We question this.

In developing this argument, we should make it clear that we are not necessarily challenging all aspects of role-model theory, some of which are still valid and relevant to the understanding of female and male aspiration in adolescence. What is in question is the assumption that aspiration alone (when strengthened by same-sex empathy) will be translated into motivation and then into decision-making, merely by the visible but passive presence of women in non-traditional settings. In this chapter, we seek to clarify more precisely the various stages of each of the two processes, and the extent to which our data so far support the validity of either in terms of policy mechanisms or outcomes.

Role Modelling and Same-Sex Modelling?

At the heart of the role-modelling process is the question of identity. Only when two things happen does role modelling take place at all. Firstly, children, students or trainees identify with an older and very visible person important to them, and secondly they then change their behaviour to imitate that of the adult on whom they feel they should model their actions. Only when both processes are present does role modelling take place.

The original concept of role modelling derives from educational psychology and is a process by which a child models her or his behaviour on that of an adult, receiving praise or negative reactions to different behaviours. It is thus that we acquire, in particular, our sex-role identity in the first place; by praise-reinforced encouragement of same-sex modelling (a girl on mother, aunt or grandmother; a boy on father, uncle or grandfather), or by very negative and overt disapproval of 'cross-sex' behaviour modelled on the opposite sex.

Kagan identifies a sex-role standard and sex-role identity. The former is a 'learned association between selected attributes, behaviours and attitudes, on the one hand, and the concepts of male and female on the other' (Kagan, 1964, p. 145), and works partly through identification with role models in the adult–child interaction process (parent or teacher). He identifies sex-role identity as rather 'the degree to which an individual regards himself or herself as masculine or feminine' (*ibid.*), and in acquiring this sex-role identity the role model needs in Kagan's view to be a caring one, to be seen to have the control of goals and skills the child wishes to acquire. The child also needs to be able to see a realistic similarity between himself or herself and the adult. Kagan is inconclusive on whether the strength of the sex-typing of the role model does or does not affect the child's security of sex identity. The role-model angle of role identity has been debated further since — Mischel (1966 and 1970) for example argues that more of our identity comes from the social learning of behaviour reinforcement or negative influence, while Gelb sees sex identity as having been in fact distorted by 'coercive institutionalisation of sex roles' (Gelb, 1973, p. 366). Overall there would be agreement with the view that when children move from undifferentiated sex-roles (stage I) to polarized sex-roles (stage II) in which societal values and pressures produce a perceivedly 'normal' set of behaviour patterns for each sex, (Robinson and Green, 1970), the role-modelling process as described by Kagan still plays an important part.

Kagan's work can be criticized for its assumption that anyone who rejects sex-role identity is pathologically abnormal. He acknowledges that 'some children either resent or experience anxiety over the behaviours that are assigned to their biological sex' (Kagan, 1964, p. 145), but he endorses the assumption that all children 'have a need to acquire a self-label that *matches* their biological sex' (*ibid.*; emphasis added). He concedes that some adolescents and adults 'strive to avoid adoption of sex-typed responses because of anxiety over the behaviours that are prescribed for their sex role' (*ibid.*, p. 146), but reasserts the predominance of sex-role ascription over actual individuality. 'These individuals are typically in conflict and are likely to manifest a variety of psychopathological symptoms' (*ibid.*). It is true that Kagan concludes by conceding that 'unnecessary conflicts are generated because of anxiety over deviation from sex role standards. Once learned, these standards are not easily altered. But they are modifiable during the early school years' (*ibid.*, p. 163).

We argue in this study that sex-role standards can be altered much later and that staff in tertiary institutions have a direct responsibility for creating a different and more sex-neutral environment for students who precisely do not wish to be labelled, in Kagan's terms, as showing 'psychopathological symptoms' merely because they are choosing to act out of the socially ascribed sex-role standard in the male-dominated higher education milieu. And, indeed, this ascription of psychopathological status to girls who wish to follow a non-traditional curricular or occupational career is precisely our argument in relation to the minority women in the two more extreme minorities in our survey, below 15 per cent and below 8 per cent respectively on the Byrne scale of perceptions of the sex-neutrality/sex-normality/sex-abnormality of minority women in disciplines as set out in our theoretical framework (see chapter 1). It will be recalled that we argued that women who comprise 8 per cent or fewer of the students in a discipline (i.e. had acted very considerably in contradiction to their normally ascribed traditionality) were perceived as both abnormal and so exceptional as to be unable to be used as a 'normal female' model.

The other foundation concept which forms part of role-model theory is that of the reference group. We use other people as reference groups when we begin actually to use them as models for our own behaviour. Kemper defines a reference group as

> any group, collectivity or person which the actor takes into account in some manner in the course of selecting a behaviour from among a set of alternatives . . . A reference group helps to orient the actor in a certain course, whether of action or attitude. (Kemper, 1968, p. 32)

(By actor, of course, Kemper means the person taking active steps to model on another.) Kemper holds that reference groups do influence the achievement of those who use them as a guide. Thus groups set the norms and values to be followed, but until individuals test these on an 'audience group' which will give feedback (either reward:punishment or approval:disapproval feedback, achievement levels and influences on decisions will not, according to Kemper, actually occur.

It is at this stage in Kemper's theory that the individual role model becomes important in that what was a mere desire to adopt a course of action or a set of behaviours is transformed into a real decision:

> using an individual rather than a group . . . the role model demonstrates for the individual how something is done in the technical sense . . . The essential quality of the role model is that he [sic] possesses skills which the actor lacks (or thinks he lacks) and from whom, by observation and comparison with his own performance, the actor can learn. (*ibid.*, p. 33)

Young *et al.* describe the token woman as using the academic world as her reference group by adopting the prevailing academic ideology which, they allege, includes that the token woman 'by virtue of talent and effort in measuring up to the high standards and superior attributes of academic men, is not only exceptional, but an exception to the social category "*women*"' (Young *et al.*, 1980, p. 509). This is interesting in the light of our UQ WISTA theory about the relationship between critical mass and perceived sex-normality or sex-neutrality.

The role-modelling concept has now been widely extended to a belief that in the process of shaping 'normal' or 'deviant' vocational aspirations in adolescence or adult life, or of forming occupational goals, members of each sex are reinforced more securely in decision-making by seeing same-sex role models ahead of them in the power structure (leadership), in the relevant occupational area (science, technical work), or in the sphere of influence they aspire to (politics). In this, relevant theoretical and empirical research tends to support Kagan's perception that the person being influenced by the role model needs to be able to see a 'realistic similarity' between herself or himself and the role model; that is, the rubric of exceptions should not operate.

But if role modelling occurs when we use a person or a group as a reference point to imitate them in our behaviour because we feel identified with them, even if it means altering our behaviour patterns in order to be like them, does the model also need to be of the same sex for us to feel that particular identification? Do we only alter our behaviour (choose different subjects at school, look for a different career or job) as a result of the influence of a model of the same sex? Research suggests that we only identify with a model in a way which leads actually to imitating them if we can see a 'realistic similarity' between us and the adult model. But we still do not know what the real messages are which reach adolescents and young adults when they see a same-sex role model ahead of them. Does a Grade 12 girl only think that 'women can do that' when she sees a woman engineer or a female University Professor, and not that 'I, Jane, can do that'? And what is 'that'? Having a career? Combining a career with marriage? Settling happily for a single life with a rewarding career independence? Or handling machines or management ascribed in her circles as 'male', and therefore being an untypical woman if she follows her model? And at what point does the adolescent see it as normal to follow a role model?

The UQ WISTA research postulates that the adults providing potential same-sex role models (principals, female physics teachers, male preschool teachers, etc.) are only likely to be seen as 'sex-normal' in terms of the particular society's sex-role standards, if they are a critical mass. Minorities, and particularly very small minorities, will, by definition, not be seen as typical or 'normal', since it is the very characteristics of the majority which are, by definition, the norm.

Moreover, role modelling has been discussed in the research literature predominantly in relation to its effect on the same-sex student rather than the opposite-sex student. Its value in the breaking-the-stereotype phase is arguably equally influential where male students see women in non-traditional roles, which can also alter male attitudes and help to liberalize them. That is, until male school students see women in non-traditional roles, presented so far as possible as increasingly normal, they will not alter their repressive, territorial and negative attitudes towards women entering 'male' disciplines and occupations. The debate on female role modelling needs to shift from being seen as a process to influence girls' attitudes, to a strategy for altering boys' attitudes towards girls.

An Inappropriate Policy Approach

In the last decade or so, a particular belief has therefore become widespread in most countries and cultures concerned about sex-role stereotyping and about women's under-achievement in non-traditional areas. Policymakers, inservice trainers and field personnel have acquired an entrenched belief that the existence of more women role models would, automatically and by itself, increase female enrolments in the area represented by the female role models. Thus, it has been argued, the personal visibility of more women school Principals, Vice Chancellors, technical College Principals and Heads of departments, Cabinet Ministers, physics teachers, electrical technicians and plumbers, would result in more girls enrolling in, or seeking leadership in, higher education, technical courses, politics, physics, electrician training and plumbing respectively.

Because of this belief, projects have been increasingly funded which have had as a central or main policy mechanism the conscious use of minority or non-traditional women as visible role models to school and college students. This has typically involved women engineers, plumbers, lawyers, accountants, University science lecturers and other women who form a minority in male-dominated areas in travelling long distances for time-consuming visits to schools or colleges for careers talks or conventions, or to institutions handling apprenticeship recruitment or trade and technical training. It has also involved non-traditional women extensively in inservice training programmes for staff involved in education, training or management.

In particular, the received wisdom has been based on an assumption that the role-modelling process acts in one single, simple step in a direct cause-and-effect relationship between girls seeing or hearing inspiring women and girls and therefore, as a result, altering their curricular choice or vocational aims in one step. This is wrong, and is founded on a serious misinterpretation of the available relevant theory and research.

The present writer reviewed existing published research in this field as part of the UQ WISTA policy review. The UQ WISTA analysis (reported in the next sections of this chapter) identified a number of weaknesses in the conclusions drawn from much of the evidence cited. For example:

1 Some widely cited research articles proved to be based on assertion and conviction without a research base.
2 Some did not follow up their introduction of role models as a

conscious policy, to check whether female enrolments actually did increase at all in relevant disciplines or sectors in subsequent years.

3 Where some increase was recorded in women's enrolments, most projects did not record any research or evaluation methodology which controlled for role modelling to separate it from other coexistent social or educational or psychological factors.

4 Some research was based on questionnaires so loosely compiled that they either did not distinguish same-sex role modelling from cross-sex role modelling, or they did not define what they meant by role modelling at all.

5 No research can be readily traced which follows through oversimplified questionnaire-based student information on female role modelling with interviews to probe the contextual reality of the answers or the relative importance of the process.

6 Some research with graduate students simply reports that more women than men cite same-sex role models in their department and assumes a cause-and-effect relationship, but no methodological steps are reported which check whether the women were already more career-oriented and confident on entering higher education or graduate school.

7 Some research actually concedes that the research design was so imprecise that 'participants' in the study may have had differing views of what constitutes a role model.

8 Most research describes as role modelling activities which are active mentorship and have nothing to do with any of the three stages of role modelling described above.

Alternative Role-Model Theory

As a result of the research review and subsequent UQ WISTA analyses (reported later in this chapter), the present author concludes that there are either three or four distinct phases in the role-modelling process, not one. Insofar as phases two, three and four occur, they are sequential. They each result in order from the previous phase.

1 In phase one, female role-modelling functions as a strategy to break the stereotype of the exclusive masculinity of the image of maths, science or technology.

2 In phase two or three, a personal role-modelling process then takes place in which adolescents or young adults use same-sex

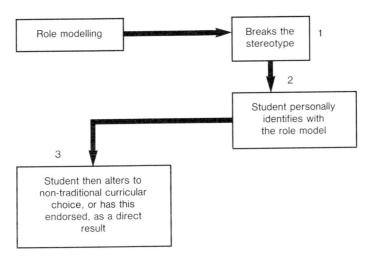

Figure 4.1 Traditional Role Model Theory

identification to strengthen personal decisions to make a vocational or subject choice non-traditional for their sex.

3   In phase three or four, same-sex role modelling acts to 'normalize' an area as either sex-neutral or acceptable or suitable
for either sex in the minority — in this instance generating a
feeling of female normality. This only occurs where the role
models form a critical mass.

These are usually consecutive phases, and most of the effective
achievement in female role modelling so far has remained at phase one,
the breaking-the-stereotype stage. At this first stage, role modelling
can alter or improve female aspiration insofar as it removes the negative barrier of a perception that 'women can't do engineering' or that
'women can't handle management'. The breaking-the-stereotype phase
can also be seen to be related to the image of scientific disciplines and
can remove a negative perceptual access barrier. But unless and until
phases two, three and four are also achieved, there is no evidence that
the mere removal of the perceptual barrier as such will in turn remove
the actual barriers of curricular choice in such a way as directly to
increase female enrolments.

Traditional role-model theory is illustrated diagrammatically in
figure 4.1. It demonstrates the assumption that simply because same-
sex role modelling breaks the stereotype by mere visibility, the student
immediately identifies with the model and therefore alters her or his
curricular choice behaviour — and persists in this. Under no other

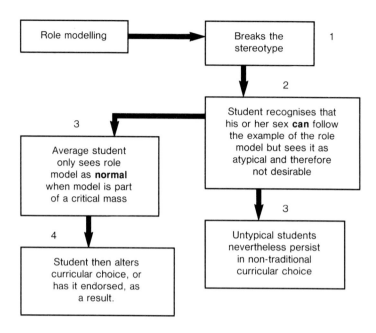

Figure 4.2 UQ WISTA Role Model Theory

assumption could the belief that more women role models, as such, will increase female enrolments have become so widespread.

UQ WISTA role-model theory is set out in figure 4.2. This shows, firstly, that there are in fact clearly two routes. Under that following steps 1 to 3, the student accepts the stereotype and identifies immediately with the role model either because the student is already as untypical as the model (i.e. is middle-class, highly intelligent, independent, has high self-esteem, does not mind or can handle peer pressure) or is quite prepared to become untypical. This accounts for the steady small minority (5–10 per cent) of female entrants to engineering and other male-ascribed areas, whom other research has already recognized as being a highly untypical group (Byrne, 1985).

But students who continue to conform generally to their sex-role identity, and for whom socially accepted concepts of sex-normality remain important, are less likely to identify and less likely to persist in non-traditional choices against negative pressure. These students will follow the second 1-to-4 step route of only identifying with role models when they are normalized by comprising a critical mass within the whole.

We accordingly started our policy review with several working hypotheses in mind:

1 That same-sex role modelling is an important influence in breaking the stereotypes of masculinity or femininity in the vocational setting.
2 That the basis for arguing that the mere acquisition of more females in a given discipline or occupation would result in students/trainees using these as role models, is however, not based on well-grounded theory.
3 That role-model theory is an inappropriate basis for the construction of policy mechanisms in relation to phases (1) and (2) of the role-modelling process as outlined above.

What does the Research say?

Let us now look firstly at what previous research really says, and then at the data and evidence of the UQ WISTA research as a basis for justifying our new grounded theory.

It should be noted that our review has been strictly in the context of the educational process, the role of education and the policymaking process. We recognize the importance of parents in the role-modelling process and in particular of 'working mothers' (or, more accurately, mothers in paid employment, since all mothers work). Tangri's doctoral dissertation and (1972) research report on non-traditional occupational choices in American college women has been widely influential in the acceptance of their assertion of the critical influence of maternal role models. Her classification of these into Role Innovators (fewer than 30 per cent women in an occupation), Moderates (30–50 per cent female representation) and Traditionals (occupations with more than 50 per cent women) has also been used for replication studies (Tangri, 1972, pp. 177–199). While we do not dissent from her findings, we reiterate that our research project has focussed on role modelling and mentorship in the higher education process, on the direct grounds that this can be influenced by the policy process and maternal role-modelling cannot.

We should first note that role modelling should be distinguished from mentorship, which is an active process of positive sponsorship by older 'patrons' (teachers, managers, trainers, counsellors, more senior women staff, etc.) towards younger or less experienced entrants or trainees (chapter 5 deals more fully with this).

The current received wisdom is that, hypothetically, a mentor who is also female and a role model will be doubly influential. But sponsorship, grants and the award of jobs are reflections of the power structure.

In science and technology, women account for less than 2 per cent of the top leadership. Mentors will, therefore, more often still be male.

In summary, we wish to distinguish more clearly, in what has become a considerable conceptual muddle, between same-sex role models who are passive visible 'breaking-the-stereotype' agents, and same-sex mentors or sponsors who actively help those following behind. A further distinction needs to be made between same-sex and opposite-sex modelling or mentorship. Finally, a clearer distinction needs to be made between the identification element in role modelling and the counselling role which more female models/mentors are reported as willing to take on than their male counterparts are.

In looking at the available research, we now divide the issue further into different but related questions. What evidence is there that same-sex role models do increase enrolments of the (same) minority sex? What evidence is there that same-sex role models cause a change of behaviour in younger girls or women sufficient to lead to non-traditional behaviour, or to non-traditional behaviour which is also perceived by the student as normal behaviour?

Do Female Role Models Increase Female Enrolments?

If we were to look at the assumption that more women role models lead to increased numbers of women students in statistical terms, we should expect to find some degree of correlation between higher than average female numbers at both staff and student levels, and we investigated this in our ten institutions. This should, hypothetically, apply either by sector of education or by institution or by type and discipline. The data presented later in this chapter show no correlation whatever. But neither could we trace any previous hard evidence of a correlation in previous research. At the level of sectors of education, for example, a recent international study of the school education of girls did not provide evidence even for a *prima facie* case:

> The most recent UNESCO data on the proportion of women
> in the teaching profession and the proportion of girls at school
> show, whatever the level of education, no statistical relation:
> once again the school system reacts differentially to its environ-
> ment. (Deblé, 1980, p. 104)

Frohreich, in writing of measures to increase female retention rates, simply records as a decisive assertion that 'having women on the engineering faculty can be one of the best ways of providing role models'

(Frohreich, 1975, p. 44). She then jumps straight to the strategy that 'women need to be involved in conducting activities to attract more women students to engineering' and argues that because we have few women academics, women engineering students or other female academics should take this responsibility personally (*ibid.*). Sproule and Mathis (1976) provide a useful summary of a survey of twenty-nine American engineering colleges which have been successful in recruiting and keeping women engineering students, analysing and summarizing their techniques. More wisely than some, they do not claim to have hard evidence that the factors will work: 'Success will be based on a combination of commitment, technique, luck and hard work' (Sproule and Mathis, 1976, p. 745). Nevertheless, they also fall into the trap of writing that 'women faculty members and administrators can serve as role models and counsellors for women students' and then go on to describe a series of *mentor* activities (*ibid.*). They write of women giving careers advice to students undecided on majors and — of course — advice on how to combine career, profession, family and children (advice not offered to male students). This is not role modelling but active counselling which forms part of mentorship.

Clark and Abron-Robinson (1975) make the same decisive assertion that 'the presence of minority female instructors in minority engineering schools helps to attract more such females' without any direct empirical evidence or references. Their only recorded evidence in this article is, again, of mentorship: 'It has been our experience that the minority student seeks out the ear of the minority female professor for advice about scholastic problems, scheduling problems and family or personal problems' (Clark and Abron-Robinson, 1975, p. 35). Dresselhaus, one of America's few women Professors of electrical engineering (at Massachusetts Institute of Technology, or MIT), writes anecdotally that she is convinced that the visibility and availability of (female) role models is a resource for raising the aspirations and self-confidence of women engineering students. But the examples she cites are mainly of mentorship and not of passive role modelling. 'I have helped them come to grips with psychological hangups . . . women students really want to know *how* (in very specific terms) I manage to maintain an active professional life together with a happy marriage and family' (Dresselhaus, 1975, p. 33). Dresselhaus reinforces this in mentorship terms beyond her Professor/student role: 'I am asked almost daily by some woman or other (often not connected with MIT) for professional counselling advice on technical careers' (*ibid.*). None of these researchers records any empirical evidence to support their convictions.

Purdue University in Indiana is one of the most successful American Universities to attract women to engineering, with a long-term multidimensional strategy throughout the 1970s and early 1980s. Purdue University has increased its female recruitment into engineering over ten years from forty-seven in 1967, to 817 in 1976, to over 1,000 women engineering undergraduates in 1979. While the Purdue Model Program for Women entering Engineering (funded partly under the Women's Educational Equity Act) needs to be seen as a whole, one of the core elements is the use of lecture discussions of career engineering and contemporary problems by women lecturers explicitly chosen as role models (happy, married, successful, etc.) to first-year undergraduates (Daniels and Lebold, 1982; Byrne, 1985). What the Purdue reports have not done, however, is to separate out the possible actual influence of the role-model factor from all of the other elements in the overall strategy. In particular, the instances cited of the positive effects of the alleged role models are in fact examples of the mentor process. The visiting women engineers talked and advised about dual-role problems (reconciling career with home responsibilities).

One US review of a wide range of affirmative action programmes in vocational education concludes that there are three overriding qualities which teaching staff need in order for sex equity programmes to be successful, one of which is 'an ability to serve as a role model for female participants'. The report assumes as a given that this means a same-sex role model, without providing any empirical or theoretical basis for this (Wheeler, *et al.*, 1979). A second similar review of special programmes for women to enter science, maths and engineering courses in schools, colleges and higher education also notes the building-in of active female role modelling in many (indeed, most) projects (Aldrich *et al.*, 1980). But a fairly sophisticated literature search has failed to reveal any substantial followthrough evaluation to check whether female enrolments increased, and sustained that increase; or whether, and if so how, same-sex role modelling was at all influential. That is, so far the assertions of a relationship between role modelling and recruitment appear to be based on conviction and repetition and not on evidence: the Snark Syndrome.

Same-sex or Cross-sex Models?

The issue of whether a role model needs to be of the same sex for the process to operate successfully as a policy mechanism, continues to be controversial. The question hinges partly on how far, by the time girls reach adolescence, they are seen to be able to identify strongly enough with an adult of the opposite sex, to see themselves as changing their curricular choices or behaviour patterns to emulate the opposite-sex model, or how far they need a same-sex model.

At the University level, Goldstein (1979) has looked at the effect of same-sex and cross-sex role models on the subsequent academic productivity of scholars. She claims that scholars in the two same-sex conditions (female PhDs with female supervisor, male PhDs with male supervisor) published significantly more research than did scholars in the two cross-sex conditions. The results need to be interpreted cautiously; a causal relationship between supervisor/student, sex and productivity cannot be proven. Nor can we know whether and how a role-modelling process takes place without a study of individual cases. The data raise interesting issues. One is clearly the mentor hypothesis that the female PhD students with female supervisors published more, not because of a warm empathetic identification with the supervisor, but because the female supervisor gave more practical help and mentorship both in the form of Martha White's 'biological library' process and direct help in drafting and placing articles. That is, the same-sex empathy and the similarity in styles of discourse and of ethics and 'message' in terms of Gilligan's (1982) research of which we spoke in chapter 3, led to more positive and practical help in supervision because of cultural consonance. Validating this hypothesis would need careful empirical study in contrasting disciplines, one in which the women supervisors comprise a critical mass and one in which their presence is non-traditional. This is because of the possibility (even likelihood) that in the latter case the women will have moved nearer to the male norms of discourse and behaviour in order to survive in an ecological niche which is dissonant to their previous cultural educational style.

Another much-cited study by Gilbert, Gallessich and Evans is equally imprecise. It identifies role modelling most vaguely as 'an *active* relationship between the modeler and the model in which factors such as perceived similarity in values, personal characteristics and life-style are crucial' (Gilbert *et al.*, 1983, p. 597), but does not clearly define the relationship. The researchers asked students in a psychology department to identify a role model in the academic staff 'in regard to their own professional development and goals' in these terms. Gilbert *et al.* concentrated on whether graduate doctoral University students (N = eighty F and seventy-seven M) who identified same-sex models would differ from those who identified opposite-sex models, in their self-evaluations of competency, stress and satisfaction. The researchers attempted also to measure for work commitment and career aspirations, self-esteem and psychological masculinity and emininity, and asked whether males and females differed in their choice of models; whether students with same-sex models would report a higher competency score, greater satisfaction and less stress and conflict. The authors report that although only 10 per cent of the academic staff were female, 35 per cent of women students identified a female Professor as a role model — but 65 per cent of women cited a male role model. By contrast, of the men, only 15 per cent identified a woman role model and 85 per cent a man. The researchers record that while male and female students with same-sex role models 'showed no differences on the measures of work commitment, career aspirations, self esteem and masculinity', by contrast, 'female graduate students identifying professors as female role models viewed themselves as more career oriented, confident and instrumental than did female students identifying male role models' (*ibid.*). But we do not know whether it was the students who already had higher aspirations and confidence, or already had similarities of lifestyle (professional high-status background), who selected the women to interact with. The anonymity of the questionnaire also prevented a check on the students' actual achievement, and the study does not enlighten as to how or why (or, indeed, whether) role modelling was influential in terms of academic choices and achievement. Nor does it identify the process through which the female students reached the greater degree of instrumentality and career orientation. Was it empathy and self-identification — or greater practical supervisory support (which is, of course, mentorship)?

Gilbert's later study of a small sample of American psychology students (thirty-three female and twenty-four male graduate students) concludes that female students valued lifestyle and values more significantly in a role model than did the male students surveyed. She argues that the same-sex role model therefore needs to show that she or he can 'effectively integrate professional and personal roles' (Gilbert, 1985, p. 121). Her study, however, still is (like many which are frequently cited) limited in sample, scope and discipline, and she concedes what this writer considers a critical flaw: 'participants in the present study may have differing views of what constitutes a role model' (*ibid.*, p. 122), because this was not sharply defined in terms of our three phases, or, indeed, defined clearly at all.

Seater and Ridgeway (1976) have studied 269 college students (112 women and 157 men) in the context of role models and other adult influences on college women's aspirations. This report defines role modelling both by Kemper's reference group process, and as a process in which achievement by the role model must show a successful combination of career, marriage and family (Seater and Ridgeway, 1976, p. 50). Seater and Ridgeway do concede that aspirations are influenced also by other significant adults who may not be role models (same-sex or otherwise). They report that the 44 per cent of women students who identified a role model (but by a process that the researchers do not record fully) 'did have significantly higher degree expectations and were significantly more likely to have plans to enrol in graduate school' (*ibid.*) than the fifty-five women students who identified *no* role model. But the research report is unclear as to whether, and if so how, other variables of influence were controlled or eliminated in favour of role modelling. More important in this study is the reported result that 'perceived encouragement from male faculty members was directly related to higher degree expectations, plans to enrol in graduate school and a more favourable attitude for both male and female students' (*ibid.*, p. 58). The study also records that 'one of the groups perceived as *least* supportive, was male faculty' (*ibid.*, p. 61).

Douvan's (1976) analysis of whether, and if so how, role modelling operates in women's professional development is also mainly theoretical, and locates more in the 'breaking-the-stereotype' phase. The women at Vassar who were both 'committed intellectuals and scholars at the same time that they had husbands and children and led rich full family lives' (Douvan, 1976, p. 8) provided her colleague with the possibility of giving 'serious thought' to acquiring a profession. By contrast, Douvan herself perceiving (as a role model) an unmarried female social scientist of international reputation who had 'great charm . . . unambivalent self assertion and a gentle beautiful personhood' (*ibid.*, p. 9), was able to use her to discredit prevalent social assumptions that single women must be unhappy and unfulfilled, or could not have deliberately *chosen* a career over marriage. What is not clear in either case is how the empathetic self-identification took place (if it did), or how influential it was in the women students' curricular or vocational choice, relative to other factors.

The ambivalence grows when we recognize that a supportive role model (of either sex) has been seen by college students as more important than a same-sex role model as such (Almquist and Angrist, 1971). In a later study, however, Angrist and Almquist (1975) still interpret their available evidence to conclude that female students are more likely to major in a department where there are female lecturing staff. In Tangris's study (1972) a supportive boyfriend was seen by some students as at least as important as a female member of staff for those looking at non-traditional disciplines. The Snark Syndrome is particularly evident in this repeated and also largely unsupported assertion that role modelling and mentorship need to be same-sex to be effective.

A new more recent international study of women who teach in Universities in Britain, France, Finland, and the former West and East Germanies provides further detailed and complex evidence to challenge this (Sutherland, 1985). Most of the women interviewed reported that they had benefited from male mentorship because there were very few women in powerful positions, as well as because they encountered genuinely supportive male academics. Even in Finland 'many of the women owed their academic progress to the support and encouragement given by male professors' (*ibid.*, p. 70). But Sutherland's interviewees tend to confirm our UQ WISTA differentiation between degrees of non-traditionality: what we have described as 'the rubric of exceptions' often applies. In Finland 'women who had been the first female assistants or professors in their subject areas had certainly met with a considerable amount of social comment: *they had been regarded as oddities*' (*ibid.*; emphasis added), a view of unusualness they are recorded as having had to 'live down'. Throughout Sutherland's scholarly international study, two concurrent and recurrent themes are recorded: the debt the successful women owed to mentorship from both sexes, but also widespread consistent male prejudice and attitudinal barriers in the institutional environment. (Her evidence on and analysis of the effect of the dual role, family:work conflicts and the childcare factor are convincing in locating these as continuing barriers, but are outside the scope of this study.)

Role modelling has also been discussed predominantly in relation to its effect on the same-sex student rather than opposite-sex student. Its value in the breaking-the-stereotype phase is arguably equally influential where male students see women in non-traditional roles, which can also alter male attitudes and help to liberalize them. A female senior lecturer in computing at one of the Institutes of Technology we surveyed (where women were less than a third of all students in the Institute and just over a quarter of undergraduate computer science students in 1985), attended one of the UQ WISTA group interviews. (That interview also confirmed the thrust of Spender's [1980] findings — the two minority women found it difficult to obtain 'air time' in the discussion.) She wrote later:

> Apropos of role models. I didn't get a chance to say anything on Wednesday but I had all my children while I was a lecturer at the Institute. The students became quite used to seeing me pregnant, carrying babies in pouches and breastfeeding in

meetings and terminal rooms (they were at the Institute creche). I think actually it had a much greater effect on the males than on the females. Presumably they were used to thinking of mothers as people who stayed at home and one who combined a demanding job was a revelation, judging from the comments I received from many of them.

Again, it proved difficult to trace in our literature search any readily available, major and/or longitudinal studies which (when controlling for other factors) supported the ubiquitous and unshakeable beliefs not only that role modelling is an effective policy mechanism, but that the models need to be the same sex as those they inspire. What evidence was there that where same-sex role modelling was really present, it actually then changed girls' vocational behaviour?

Does Same-sex Role Modelling Induce Vocational Behaviour Change?

We have argued above that to validate a hypothesis that the presence of female role models would persuade girls and young women to make more non-traditional choices, research would need to identify much more closely the processes of self-identification, of acceptance of non-typicality or perception of sex-normality, and of the direct application of these to aspiration, motivation and curricular choice. Is there any evidence to support, unambiguously, such a clear cause-and-effect relationship between the modelling process and actual persistence in non-traditional choices?

Bell (1970a and b) looks at this in occupational terms and suggests, for example, that there are two different processes: interaction, and the personal identification of the younger person with the role model. Bell's sample is, however, of 101 young adult American males in 1961–2 who had been out of school for seven years; another 'male-as-norm' project. Moreover, Bell defines a role model as 'any person to whom a subject felt himself to be similar (or dissimilar) or whom a subject wished to be like (or unlike) or whose values the subject claimed to have adopted (or refused to adopt)', a definition lacking in precision (Bell, 1970b, p. 281). Bell argues as a result of his small study that, after seven years of work, subjects with the most positive occupational and personal role models reached a higher occupational level, with better pay and conditions, and were more 'successful' in career development, than those without (*ibid.*). His reported research, however, does not record whether, and if so how, he controlled for other key variables like ability or social class, type of occupation or qualifications on leaving school; and his sample was all male.

To the extent that most widely reported researchers in this field have raised the issue of interaction as well as identification, we are strengthened in our view that much of what is reported is in fact interactive mentorship and not the modelling process, and that it is this which is the important influence.

Some of the seriously cited studies also represent samples too small from which to generalize. In a rather vaguely reported small study of a medical school, Roeske and Lake (1977) note that women students recorded a perceived lack of women role models in their first two years, but third- and fourth-year female students said they did not need them. Their study is not longitudinal, however, and moreover it is not reported whether the first and second-year women, when they in turn reached their third and fourth years, also ceased to see role modelling as important. Nor do the researchers identify where the women who reported a lack of role models actually were in aspiration, motivation or achievement in their later years (as compared with earlier), or what the perceived difference would have been had they seen female role models ahead. Shapley (1975) sees a need in the USA for every college student in science to have the support of an interested Professor to gain entrance to a graduate department and to facilitate the publication of their work. Strauss (1978) doubts that the sponsor or mentor will in fact be available to female students unless the sponsors (usually male) recognize as legitimate a woman student's commitment to a career rather than to fulltime motherhood. Hence yet again the question of attitudinal factors meshes with modelling and mentorship.

Some reported research is even more distant from empirical evidence of actual behaviour changes. Thus Tidball (1973 and 1974) postulates that women lecturing staff serve as role models for women on the basis of an analysis of *Who's Who in American Women, 1966–71*. Graduates from women's colleges (selective and less selective) are, on her analysis, twice as likely to become achievers than women from coeducational institutions, on the basis that the number of women achievers increases directly in relation to the ratio of women faculty members to women students. This is shaky evidence on which to base a theory that the presence of women staff will increase the number of women students in itself, and is a questionable technique. Entry in a biographical index depends on both nomination and the cooperation of the potential entrant. Biographical dictionaries are selective (in both senses of the word) and incomplete. Oates and Williamson (1978) have reworked Tidball's study and looked at women in *Who's Who in American Women, 1974–75*. They conclude that it is the high selectivity of entry to those women's colleges from which high achievers came which is the more influential factor, and not the presence of women staff as such. That is, high socioeconomic status and higher innate ability are more influential than the single-sex environment and the presence of women staff as such.

Later studies confuse the issue further. O'Donnell and Anderson (1978) find no evidence at all that women students have even been able to identify specific lecturers or teachers who have influenced their choice of major through a role-modelling process. Basow and Howe (1980), by contrast, are certain that their evidence shows that having a female teacher is important for the career decision of female college students — even though they only achieved a positive correlation when they reran their abortive first analysis, by balancing the number of male and female students in each group.

Typically, female role models have also been seen as needing to be superwomen if they are to inspire behaviour changes. Strauss identifies societal attitudes or 'sex-role ideology' which lead to sex-differentiated teaching as a major barrier in American education, and sees one strategy as the importation into the careers programmes of schools and colleges of 'a woman scientist or engineer from the Community who is happy, successful and whose work may be perceived as important enough to be an alternative to traditional female careers' (Strauss, 1978, p. 188). Strauss asserts a preference within the female role model range: *'The ideal role model for any girl is a career oriented mother who is happy and successful in both employment and family endeavours'* (ibid., p. 188, 1978). Bowling and Martin (1985) cite four model strategies as necessary to increase women's participation in existing forms of science and to 'democratise science', among which the use of same-sex role models is seen as part of an overall programme of publicity and networking. They see a need for 'successful women scientists to be widely seen as successful and as desirable models to be followed by other women — and to be accepted and admired by men' (Bowling and Martin, 1985). But they also see the existing role models as likely to be 'honorary males' because only these will be likely to breach the barriers of hierarchy, instrumentalism and elitism (*ibid.*, p. 314).

Almquist and Angrist's research report on role-model influences on the career aspirations of college women is well argued but is based on 'a longitudinal study of one class from the women's college of a small, private, coeducational and technologically oriented university' (Almquist and Angrist, 1971, p. 277). The researchers do not distinguish the professorial or occupational role models by sex. They conclude, *inter alia*, that 'for women, the importance of role models lies in their explication of a life style which incorporates work with family life' (*ibid.*). If this were exclusively true, it would imply that single career women are unlikely or unsuitable or ineffective role models — a view decisively rejected by some key careers and counselling staff in our survey institutions. Almquist and Angrist also identify the 'career-salient' women, or those who had deliberately chosen a long-term occupational lifestyle (and not a broken career or one terminated on marriage), as the ones who 'had future mates who fostered their work plans' (*ibid.*, p. 277). But the processes investigated in this study (as in other replication studies) are not the relationship between female iden-tification with a role model and subsequent non-traditional motivation and choice, but student evaluation of the extent to which role models 'provide a technical explication of how various jobs are performed, . . . how positive extra-work relationships develop between role model and neophyte' . . . and so on (*ibid.*). Once again, these are mentor activities.

Douvan describes the task of minority women in academe as 'to become socialised to the higher status world without losing one's iden-tity and touch with one's own history' (Douvan, 1976). One choice she perceives as available is to become like the dominant group and 'abandon one's past', which as a psychologist she defines clinically as 'identification with the aggressor' (*ibid.*). Alternatively, she lists the strategies of abandonment or de-emphasis of competence, or 'a trench-ant continuing effort to integrate professionalism' and what she calls 'feminine goals' (*ibid.*, p. 278).

One of the more transferable studies is that of Erkut and Mokros (1984), who questioned students in six American liberal arts colleges, five coeducational and one women's only college. The 723 students who identified a Professor they considered important for themselves identified the impact by commitment, skills and personal qualities. The researchers conclude that female students neither gravitate towards nor avoid female role models, but that male students avoid female models and identify with high-status powerful males. The Erkut and Mokros study raises a related issue, however, that of same-sex role models and single-sex institutions. Within the sample, women at the single-sex college were perceived to be more academically successful and more successful in relation to their male and female peers, and more of them planned to go on to postgraduate study. Without know-ing more about the women's college, we cannot tell whether the modification of results when controlled for ability and social class applies also here. For example, in Tidball and Kistia-Kowsky's (1976) study of American women PhDs since 1920, the conclusion is that the seven elite women's colleges produced proportionately more female PhDs than mixed colleges. But the elite colleges had a much tougher selection process, and their students might reasonably be expected to achieve relatively more highly than their male and female peers elsewhere.

Selectivity and social class are not the only variables which skew the research on how far same-sex teachers can act as a positive influence to encourage girls' non-traditional choices. Harding's review of science education for girls suggests that it may in fact be partly that 'teaching style and individual behaviour may be more influential than the sex of the teacher' (Harding, 1983, p. 36). When Welch and Lawrenz (1982) looked at the characteristics of male and female science teachers in a fourteen-state region of the USA, they did identify several significant differences between the two groups (for example, female teachers rate higher on measures of interests in science and receptivity to change, male teachers higher on science knowledge). Eggleston *et al.* (1976) suggest that teaching style is highly correlated with sex, more women science teachers tending to use pupil-centred enquiry methods and more men using problem-solving teaching-centred, teacher-initiated styles. The former style used by more women teachers was seen to be more effective in retaining girls in physics and chemistry, in the British schools surveyed. Stasz *et al.* (1985) have examined another aspect of teaching style — the use of microcomputers to teach maths and science. In a survey across sixty classrooms in forty-nine schools in twenty-five districts in California, they conclude that both female and male teachers provide leadership in the microcomputer movement, have relevant training and experience, and 'present equally viable role models', despite their observations that twice as many boys as girls take computer-programming classes in American high schools, that boys monopolize equipment where classroom control is lax, and that war scenes and physical adventure games dominate in software (Stasz *et al.*, 1985, p. 162). Among the teachers surveyed, although males were more experienced in experimental measures 'there were no differences among interviewees' ratings of male and female teachers'. The researchers note that

> our data could not address one important facet of the role model approach, namely, whether these noted computer teachers were sensitive to sex equity issues in their classrooms. *The sex of a teacher is not a predictor of nonsexist practice.* (*ibid.*; emphasis added)

The present author confirms the need to determine the relationship between gender and non-sexist teaching practice. It cannot be automatically assumed that top women support and encourage other women.

In summary, the research we have reviewed, and the diverse and often contradictory findings and conclusions reported in both research and project literature, did not provide a neat and unambiguous basis for a finite scientific conclusion. Nevertheless, we saw a number of themes, issues and hypotheses as emerging rather more clearly in this overview.

We now record final working hypotheses which we believe could be supported. The previous research we have reviewed provided a reasonably consistent and cross-national basis (but not decisive empirical evidence) for supporting the hypothesis that

- same-sex role modelling is an important influence on breaking the stereotypes of ascribed masculinity and femininity in the vocational setting of curricular choice and of career aspiration.

That is, the research so far supports, on balance, that if female role modelling is visibly used to break the stereotype of the exclusive masculinity of the image of maths, science or technology as higher education disciplines, it is likely to be reasonably effective. How this is done, in terms of policy mechanisms, is another matter, and the last section of this chapter discusses a major shift in policy for future projects receiving public or institutional funding which intend to incorporate conscious same-sex role modelling.

We believe that our critique of earlier relevant research and its weaknesses justifies a second hypothesis. This is that

- the basis for arguing that the mere acquisition of more female staff in a given discipline or occupation would, in itself, result in an increase in female students and trainees because they have been inspired to make non-traditional choices by simply seeing female role models, is not founded in either well-grounded rigorous theory or in sound empirical evidence.

We set out therefore to look at both the patterns of participation of women students and staff in our ten institutions and across the survey disciplines, to see how far our data supported traditional role-model theory, and how far our replacement negative hypothesis was supported. That is, we used Glaser and Strauss's grounded theory approach, outlined in chapter 1 above, to test hypotheses in this area.

The UQ WISTA Data Interpreted

It seemed to us from the start tolerably unrealistic to use role-modelling theory as a policy mechanism in the first place, in view of the limited overall numbers of women staff in most scientific and technological disciplines. Even if we could regard as valid the somewhat doubtful expectation that in theory the presence of women staff would result in students working through all three stages of role modelling, the process could not operate in practice unless

- there were enough women staff in the relevant disciplines to provide choices of role models with whom girls and young women could identify and use to strengthen their non-traditional vocational choices; and
- the women staff formed a sufficient critical mass in each discipline or 'ecological niche' to alter the image of the discipline to one of either sex-normality for women or to sex-neutrality.

We expressed some scepticism that the mere visibility of women academics would be correlated with higher female enrolments. One logical first step was therefore to plot the proportion of women staff in each survey discipline and to match this with the proportion of women students in the same discipline at undergraduate level in all of our survey institutions. If the traditional role-model theory were true, we would expect to find a consistent pattern that higher female enrolments occurred in the disciplines with higher numbers and proportions of women staff: and we did not.

Chapter 3 above sets out the main patterns of female enrolments by discipline, level and institution for the survey year of 1985. We give here the numbers and proportions of female students and staff by discipline, in the context of both access (undergraduate numbers) and progression (postgraduate numbers).

The Statistical Evidence

In physics, female undergraduate enrolments average only 17 per cent across the ten institutions. The institutional range shows considerable inter-institutional differences. It will be seen from table 4.1, however, that the institution with the highest proportion of women staff in physics is also that with the second lowest proportion of female undergraduate enrolments. Five institutions have no women academic staff at all in

Table 4.1 Physics (1985)

Institution	Undergraduate women students		Female staff	
	No.	% Total	No.	% Total
UNSW	21	20.2%	5	8.0%
NSWIT	28	13.9%	—	—
UQ	77	19.0%	—	—
QIT	9	16.7%	1	4.3%
Mon	81	20.5%	1	5.2%
RMIT	12	9.8%	7.1	19.7%
U of A	75	18.8%	—	—
SAIT	4	8.7%	—	—
UWA	187	23.0%	2.5	12.6%
WAIT	5	15.0%	—	—

Table 4.2 Chemistry (1985)

Institution	Undergraduate women students		Female staff	
	No.	% Total	No.	% Total
UNSW	44	35.0%	2	3.0%
NSWIT	85.5	40.1%	—	—
UQ	285	47.7%	—	—
QIT	50	29.9%	—	—
Mon	376	44.1%	0.5	1.5%
RMIT	150	46.3%	3.2	8.8%
U of A	260	35.9%	1	+
SAIT	*41	30.1%	2	10.0%
UWA	335	40.7%	—	—
WAIT	32	30.0%	—	—

* Includes chemical technology and microbiology.
+ Percentage is less than 1%.

physics, but two of these recruit women students at just above the ten-institutional mean.

Chemistry recruits at more than twice the physics average, that is an average undergraduate female enrolment of 38 per cent across our ten institutions, and would therefore rank as sex-normal on the Byrne four-point scale of sex-normality and non-traditionality described in chapter 1 above. If role modelling were an influential factor, we would therefore expect to see a higher proportion of women staff. But there were in fact fewer women lecturers in chemistry than in physics in 1985 (see table 4.2). In 1985, three institutions had a female enrolment of over 40 per cent and no permanent women academic staff of lecturer level or above; Monash University had 44 per cent female students and only 1.5 per cent women staff. The numbers were peripheral. SAIT,

Table 4.3 Mathematics (1985)

Institution	Undergraduate women students		Female staff	
	No.	% Total	No.	% Total
UNSW	80	38.3%	4	6.0%
NSWIT	58	40.8%	—	—
UQ	400	28.8%	4	10.8%
QIT	51	38.9%	3	12.5%
Mon	691	43.4%	3	7.2%
RMIT	108	32.1%	4.3	13.9%
U of A	495	31.4%	5	12.5%
UWA	640	31.0%	6.5	17.6%
WAIT	41	28.0%	—	—

SAIT does not offer mathematics at undergraduate level.

with 10 per cent women staff in chemistry, has the highest proportion of women staff and one of the lowest proportions of women students. Women do not form a critical mass in lecturing staff in this subject; but chemistry recruits a higher percentage of women undergraduates than most other sciences.

Mathematics recruited in 1985 a female enrolment which was highly variable across the ten institutions but averaged 35 per cent, or twice the mean for physics and slightly below that for chemistry. Even allowing for some inflation of the female maths students figures at Monash and Adelaide, the proportion of women staff is certainly generally higher than in either physics or chemistry — but within the discipline of mathematics there is no consistent pattern (see table 4.3). For example, the University of Western Australia has the highest proportion of women staff, but one of the lower proportions of women students. Conversely, Monash University has the highest proportion of women students but almost the lowest proportion of women staff.

When we look at those disciplines where women are in a clear majority, moreover, and the discipline is either sex-neutral or sex-normal for women at the level of female undergraduate enrolments, we find that most have no women academic staff at all. In biotechnology women comprise 63 per cent of undergraduate enrolments at WAIT, 55 per cent at NSWIT and 34 per cent at RMIT, all of which have no women academic staff in this area; while at the University of New South Wales 52 per cent of undergraduate biotechnology students and 22 per cent (two staff) of academic staff in the area are women. In biochemistry and microbiology, undergraduate female enrolments average 55 per cent and 59 per cent respectively, or well into the sex-normal-for-women category. But in biochemistry, four institutions

Table 4.4 Microbiology (1985)

Institution	Undergraduate women students		Female staff	
	No.	% Total	No.	% Total
UNSW	50	65.8%	5	36.0%
UQ	136	59.9%	2	16.7%
Mon	95	59.7%	1	4.3%
U of A	90	61.6%	1.8	21.7%
UWA	99	47.0%	2	19.0%

have no women academic staff at all in this discipline; in a further three, women academic staff are fewer than 15 per cent of the total; and at the University of Western Australia, where women academics represent 25 per cent of the total biochemistry staff (one of the three highest proportions), the female student enrolment is in fact the lowest of the six institutions where this discipline is offered. The position in microbiology is equally uneven (see table 4.4). While the student figures are relatively constant, the staffing profiles are not and show considerable inter-institutional variations.

These relationships or non-relationships have been plotted for all the survey disciplines, and women staff are even fewer in the technological and applied disciplines. Nor is there any coherent or consistent significant relationship between relatively higher female enrolments in subdisciplines (e.g. chemical as distinct from civil engineering) and the presence of women staff, in any technologies.

The UQ WISTA analyses lead us to conclude that in our survey:

1   Scientific and technological disciplines which have relatively higher proportions of undergraduate female enrolments do not generally have a higher proportion of female academic staff.
2   Scientific and technological disciplines which have relatively higher proportions of female academic staff do not generally have a higher proportion of female undergraduate students.
3   In a number of disciplines in several of the survey institutions, the highest female student enrolment in fact coexists with the lowest proportion of women academic staff in that discipline in the same institution, and vice versa.
4   There is no traceable consistent pattern of a first-level statistical relationship between the female proportion of student undergraduate enrolments and the proportion of women staff in the same discipline in the same institution.

We do not, therefore, find any data to support traditional same-sex role-model theory in relation to initial access to non-traditional science and technology, and thus also conclude, significantly, that:

5   The UQ WISTA staff and student data in the disciplines in this survey do not support a hypothesis that increasing the number or proportion of women academics in a given academic discipline will necessarily and by itself increase subsequent female enrolments at the level of first access to higher education in non-traditional science and technology.

This is not to say that same-sex role modelling is an irrelevant factor in the question as a whole. It may well be more relevant to progression than to access. It may also be useful as part of a cluster strategy involving several factors simultaneously. It can still help in the breaking-the-stereotype function. Because of its possible influence in progression, we therefore checked out the possibility of a statistical relationship between the proportion of women staff in each discipline and the proportion of women in the postgraduate masters research and doctoral research student body in the same discipline in the same institution.

The patterns of female postgraduate enrolments are given in chapter 3 above. While, occasionally, one individual institution appears to show data supportive to traditional theory in one particular discipline, in no discipline could we find a majority of relevant institutions (Institutes did not offer doctoral programmes) which could demonstrate consistently higher proportions of female postgraduates and higher proportions of female staff, in the same discipline. There was no traceable consistent pattern or relationship. We concluded that:

6   There was no consistent pattern of evidence from the UQ WISTA staff and student data in this survey which supported a hypothesis that the mere visible presence of women academic staff in a discipline is causally related to the female proportion of postgraduate research students in the same discipline in the same institution.

The Snark Effect: The Views of Academics in UQ WISTA Institutions

Not only did we find neither a basis in previous research or data nor any statistical evidence in the UQ WISTA survey to support traditional role-model theory, we also found that, nevertheless, this was one of the most deeply embedded convictions held by the scientists and technologists who attended our group interviews, and/or who wrote in response to our circulated discussion papers.

The discussion papers on role models were circulated to relevant senior academics in the selected survey disciplines in the period March–May 1986. Professors, Deans, Heads of Schools and careers guidance and counselling staff were asked to come to group interviews (or to send a representative) ready to discuss the issues raised, 'both in relation to your own discipline and your institution as such, and in the light of this written research summary'. They were also asked to write after the meeting to the Director of the University of Queensland WISTA project either with further (or reconsidered) views or on possible future action that could be taken by institutions or government, in relation to these two factors. The discussion papers defined the factors, described the most relevant research and ended with four questions to be addressed. In relation to role modelling, we asked:

1   Can you see a full-time or part-time woman in your discipline who you think is performing one or more of the *positive* functions of a role model? What is her level or grade? Can you assess her likely influence on women students?

2   Can you suggest ways, in your discipline or area, in which you could (or do?) create same-sex role modelling as a process of 'normalizing' the discipline for women, by bringing in external women?

3   Given the agreed principle that only *equally qualified* women be appointed or used, what part could you see the issue of positive role modelling playing in the future policy of this University or Institute? What kinds of options do you think are both feasible and professionally acceptable?

4   How influential do *you* think this factor is?

While we asked primarily that those attending the interviews (when the context of the questions being studied was aired) should also respond in writing, Deans, Heads, etc. were also encouraged to circulate the papers more widely and to invite written responses from any academic interested to provide them. It is clear from the replies that in many disciplines in all ten institutions senior staff failed to explain the context or the issues, or to supply the previously circulated introductory documentation on the UQ WISTA Policy Review Project at the time when they circulated the discussion papers. These had been drafted and used in the expectation that the respondents would have seen the written outline of the aims and purposes of the UQ WISTA project sent to all attending the group interviews, and would have heard the contextual discussions in the interviews. In practice, this did not happen. Many who attended the interviews did not respond in writing; many who wrote in had acquired the discussion papers by varied means and lacked the contextual background. In our field analysis of the main essence of the responses, we have accordingly differentiated between those attending the interviews only, those who both attended and wrote, and those who wrote without the additional context of the interviews. We deliberately did not prescribe access to the material, nor restrict input to a controlled sample, because we wished to test our hypothesis that different departments or disciplines would vary in their approaches, reflecting a different cultural ecology. Nor did we consider that the issues being explored were susceptible to reduction to five-point graded questionnaires. The questions were expressly phrased to elicit qualitative, non-numerical, non-formula answers and clearly asked for opinion and judgement, because these determine the institutional attitudes and climate.

We noted with interest that, generally, the more instrumental the discipline (maths, physics, engineering), the greater the difficulty respondents tended to find in handling questions not reducable to a formula. Conversely, the more flexible or 'free-floating' the discipline in its organization and structure, the more discursive, qualitative and contextual were the respondents' answers or contributions.

Widespread Belief but Confused Understanding of Role Modelling

We found the Snark effect to be widely evident both in the interviews and in the written responses. Both in the group discussions and in most of the letters, most academics who commented on role modelling had accepted as unquestionable an unsupported assertion that the presence of women role models would increase enrolments. They failed either to distinguish between the stages of the role-modelling process or to justify the quantum leap from students seeing visible women to students altering vocational behaviour because of this. In particular, we found frequent evidence of the strength of the belief as a panacea for every kind of problem. There was, for example, an unselective belief in the equal validity of role modelling as an access, and as a retention, influence.

A female University lecturer in civil engineering wrote that of the 5 per cent of their students who were female, and who she saw as under-achieving, 'we have an undesirable female show-cause and dropout rate. In terms of these facts I believe role models are vital' (letter, University). In saying this, she had an unsupported belief in role modelling as an influential retention factor. In the same discipline, a colleague from another institution echoed the assertion, but as an access factor: 'I have been persuaded that it would help young women to decide to enter engineering if there were women academics on the staff of Engineering Departments' (letter, civil engineering Professor). Among the more elliptical responses, some simply assumed that women who were brought in to a department did spark off a role-modelling process by their presence alone, and that same-sex models would automatically also mentor students:

> We have recruited [X] specifically for this, a [female] B.App.Sc. in Geology and Biology . . . as a part-time teacher and as a mentor. Role modelling is very influential. It is most negative when no role model is available [but] when several are available, further additions are of less value. (letter, geology, Institute of Technology)

Most of the positive evidence or opinions did support the usefulness of phase one of the process — the breaking-the-stereotype phase:

> The School of Engineering currently has 3FT and 2PT women staff. They are all performing as role models and are achieving a small but significant break in the stereotype of engineers . . . At the moment we are at the stage that males must perform the mentor role for new female members of staff. (letter, engineering, Institute of Technology)

This respondent did not recognize the mentor role as applying to same-sex students. The 'visibility theory' (simply seeing women in academic posts will encourage girls to make non-traditional choices) was held by many, whom space does not permit us to cite in full.

A maths lecturer, in answer to the first question on the discussion paper, wrote 'Yes; Tutor; they [students] are able to see someone female in a mathematically orientated career which has previously been male-dominated' (letter, applied maths, University) without, however, developing in what regard students would change as a result of seeing a non-traditional female. A (male) Professor of biochemistry questioned whether there would be any influence beyond the first phase:

> There are two full-time women in my discipline who are pro-
> viding role models . . . their primary role is to indicate to both
> male and female students that women can succeed in my
> discipline . . . I think the role model is not as important today
> as it was some years ago. (letter, university)

This respondent also assumed, in his extended answer however, that
the role-modelling process took place merely because his colleagues
were visible: phase one only of the process. Other submissions constantly replicated this assumption.

But even where the belief in this process persisted, it was often
linked with a recognition of its impracticability as a policy. In the
previous section, we questioned the realism of a policy for same-sex
role modelling if the women staff simply were not there or even in the
pipeline. This was graphically echoed for metallurgy:

> This Department acknowledges the importance of positive role
> models . . . the difficulty is to find the equally qualified female
> in Metallurgical Engineering . . . There are no external women
> available . . . This factor is very influential but in order to have
> a chicken you must first have an egg. (letter, Institute)

What is important to note here is that the importance of this factor is
strongly reiterated even though the impossibility of achieving it as a
policy mechanism is simultaneously conceded.

Who is a Good Role Model?

There was, however, marked disagreement on who was or was not a
good role model. On the one hand, many saw a need for successful,
married women to role model. Others saw it as important to have
happy, successful fulfilled single women role models; girls needed to
see that marriage was not Nirvana. But in one group interview, a
careers adviser commented in relation to the discussion papers that

> I could see that the stuff about role models and mentors just
> had to be absolutely right, but what I thought hadn't been said
> was the fact that what role models there are tend to be women
> who don't have families, and so that the extra message is passed
> on that not only is it possible to aspire, but there's a price
> attached to it. But men are not asked to pay that price, and so

there's in fact a sort of hidden agenda about what role models are. (interview, University)

This comment echoes the research evidence we referred to earlier, describing projects in which the current definition of role modelling is based on women's perceived need to show success in the dual role, while men have complete freedom in this respect. The 'superwoman' aspect of role modelling was clearly a further problem. Of those who had clear ideas as to which women would visibly encourage others, the following produces a depressing picture of the level of high expectation of female, but not male, achievement in this respect:

Clearly if one can demonstrate to secondary schoolgirls that a woman can be a successful engineer while at the same time being happily married and able to adjust her married life, in cooperation with her husband, in such a way that children can be properly looked after, then the role model is fully useful. (letter, male, metallurgy, Institute)

A (male) colleague from chemistry commented on the unrealism of such an expectation, and shared our scepticism, but he was in a small minority:

I do not see the presence of a female mentor to be an important factor in aiding progress of women in higher education. I believe role models are important [but] the key according to Strauss is to be 'happy and successful in both employment and family endeavours'. This is difficult for either sex: for female academics in science it is most difficult since success in employment will be dependent on postdoctoral appointments abroad. (letter, Institute of Technology)

In another interview, an engineering academic noting the absence of people of either sex providing role models to encourage interest in engineering, saw no need for them to be of the same sex and also doubted the current feasibility of using scarce women engineers as positive models:

Role models, male and female, in engineering and technology are very few and far between and I would suggest to you that as far as women and engineering is concerned, providing role models to children in schools, you could just as reasonably ask about *men* in engineering providing role models to children in schools. There is an absence on both sides . . . there has been a decline in science and engineering enrolments . . . There might be girls out there in engineering, there are, they are our own graduates, but there's no way you would ever be able to parade them as role models. It's just not the way the media operates or that our society operates . . . the problem is to expose them . . . (interview, Professor of engineering, University).

A female masters student of physics at an Institute of Technology attended one of the group interviews in 1986. She wrote subsequently that 'the Department has very few role models. Apart from this lack, I do not think that female students are actively discouraged', but went on to write strongly in support of role modelling as an example to break the stereotype. Her evidence, however, shows the conceptual confusion characteristic of most responses: on the one hand supporting, on the other rejecting the notion that same-sex role models are needed. A female part-time lecturer at her Institute was seen by her as a role model and 'a leading example of what a woman physicist can achieve', and a previous female physics teacher was seen as a strong influence because of her extreme capability, projecting 'enthusiasm, knowledge and commonsense to all her students'. But she describes role modelling as a generic, not a sex-linked process, in writing that

> Role modelling is very influential in that it is a solid example of an area of interest that one may have. One can evaluate the personal characteristics and to a certain extent what you may be in for, if you make a similar choice . . . but I think a role model of the opposite sex can be just as inspiring. (letter, physics, Institute)

We asked that careers and counselling staff also be invited to attend the interviews and to respond to the discussion papers, and some of the more complex and diagnostic responses came from this group of staff. One such University group again saw positive same-sex role modelling as important because its members believed it showed non-traditionality as attainable. They believed the factor to be constantly and recurrently influential. They saw a direct role for female careers and counselling staff in helping to normalize roles seen as non-traditional, 'in the sense of leadership, assertiveness and awareness rather than in terms of our occupational field' (letter, careers and counselling staff, University). They pressed strongly that cultural factors influencing the situation of aboriginal, overseas and migrant women students be re-examined in the context of the need for same-sex role models to show the 'realistic similarity' which the first section of this chapter highlighted as essential to the identification stage of the modelling process.

In one University, a male recognized that, 'As was pointed out at the meeting, it is difficult for a man to imagine what it is like to have no same-sex role models' (letter, male, civil engineering, University); to this extent, the group interview and discussion paper process usefully aired and clarified a confused policy issue.

Our overall qualitative analysis of the interviews and replies led us to conclude, in summary, that in the ten UQ WISTA survey institutions:

1　There was widespread belief in the value of the role-modelling process in breaking the male stereotype.

2　There was, however, widespread confusion and imprecision about what constituted actual role modelling. Examples given in interviews and in writing ranged from mentorship to extrovert affirmative action, and were based on women staff transmitting unconscious messages but not on how students received these.

3　Of those who responded positively that there were visible women in their discipline, almost all assumed that their mere presence, *per se*, caused a same-sex role-modelling process to take place for the female students.

4　Those who believed role modelling in higher education to be unimportant did so either because they believed parents/ mothers to be more influential, or because they believed educational factors to be more important, or because there were (and would continue to be) too few women academics in the discipline to make role modelling viable.

5　Opinion was sharply divided on the need for same-sex role modelling or the equal value of opposite-sex role models. Both views were frequently described in terms of secure belief without any evidential basis for the belief. The strength of the convictions was inversely correlated with the presence of any factual basis.

6　Most frequently, role modelling was completely confused with mentorship, and both male and female respondents and interviewees consistently expected more women than men to act positively to women students in terms of visible example and encouragement.

Why Does it Matter? The Policy Implications

There are considerable implications for policymakers in redefining and resetting role-model theory in relation to women's access to science and technology. Review after review of affirmative action projects confirm that trying to use same-sex role modelling as an active policy mechanism continues to be built in to projects carrying substantial governmental funding. Why does this matter?

An Alibi for Male Inaction

Firstly, it matters because as long as men can write off the problem as one of a lack of women role models, they can simultaneously write off their own male responsibilities — either as causes of women's encountered barriers, in the first place; or as potential remediers in the power structures, in the second. Certainly the most obvious explanation for the widespread adoption of the concept of female (same-sex) role modelling as a useful policy mechanism by the men who currently control higher education in Australia in the scientific and technological disciplines, is that as long as male academics can say 'If only we had more women staff, we would have more women students,' they can place the onus of responsibility for positive change on women staff and students. It obviates the need for men to re-examine male behaviour as a negative influence.

It is significant that almost all of the proposals put forward both in interviews and in writing also involved women taking on more work, but no traceable expected change on the part of men. For example, in the UQ WISTA survey of institutions, both careers and counselling staff and senior academics (predominantly those in engineering, chemistry, physics and computing) proposed that the existing minority women in University and Institute departments should be asked to supervise more field exercises, visit more schools and colleges, go to more careers exhibitions and to counsel more students, all apparently in the interests of increased visibility and a rather vaguely delineated role-modelling process. There were no parallel proposals for more work by men.

It should also be recognized that most young women will more readily believe that they can achieve highly in disciplines when the men in those disciplines (staff and students alike) transmit the clear message that it is normal for women to do so; and not because women tell them so. The untypical, confident woman student may be sufficiently inspired by a female role model to emulate her, but the typical young woman will need both male as well as female leadership and male peer accreditation. Only when male staff also encourage male students to support and accept female students in disciplines seen so far as territorially masculine are we likely to see substantial change. But one of the disadvantageous aspects of placing female role modelling in a prominent place in policy strategies for change is precisely that it enables dominant males to continue to see no need to change their style in relation to a 'new' clientele: women minority students. The concentration on same-sex role modelling diverts attention from the general institutional ecology of the learning environment.

Active Role Modelling Wastes Women's Scarce Time

A second negative effect of the institutionalization of same-sex role modelling as a policy mechanism is that it imposes a fourth role on already overburdened women in a way which is an uneconomic use of their time. Women are now typically and constantly referred to as having a dual role, that is, combining employment and the work of family domestic responsibility; but men who are also husbands and fathers are not so described despite their self-evident parallel status. Moreover, proportionately more employed women than men are widely reported in labour market research as also taking on the personal counselling and caring roles in relation to staff or students for whom they are responsible, in addition to their normal workload: a third and increasingly demanding role. Minority women are now being asked to take on a fourth role, that of the frequent waste of precious days, evenings and weekends, often travelling long distances to far-flung parts of the country to speak to relatively small numbers of adolescents in schools and colleges, or at exhibitions, to fulfil a policy described as being in the interests of female visibility. This is despite a total lack of empirical evidence as to what effect, if any, this might have.

Academic research in many western countries has, however, established that women carrying out the dual role already have considerable difficulty in freeing an equivalent 'spare' time allocation to that of their male peers to spend in writing, research or attending professional seminars. To expect them also to allocate proportionately more time to uneconomic attendance during evenings and weekends at a range of school and college functions specifically to role model, for example, is further to erode that time. Single women are already disadvantaged as well, since in most western societies far more of the elderly parents or adult disabled who are dependent and living in domestic rather than institutionalized homes live with single women than with male relatives. Similarly, more single women than single men have been shown to be likely to commit themselves to a lifetime's complete domestic responsibility with or without paid employment, while more single males, by contrast, live with a female relative or have a full-time paid domestic infrastructure. It is not argued, of course, that women should not carry an equal responsibility for careers work or attendance at necessary functions. But they should not be asked to carry such an additional burden, merely and solely for achieving female visibility, when the function of breaking stereotypes can be achieved more effectively by other means.

A far more effective way to break stereotypes is through imaging in books, materials and the visual media. Yet this is precisely what the men who have written and who control textbooks and the publishing of educational resources have refused to do. A review of the research literature on sex-role stereotyping in educational materials has also been completed in the UQ WISTA research, and three principal conclusions can be authenticated cross-culturally and cross-nationally. Firstly, in every country and culture which has been investigated by researchers in postwar years in this regard, books and educational materials, and notably science and mathematics textbooks, have been found to be sex-stereotyped in a way which not only represents male and female roles as mutually exclusive, but is years, often decades, out of data in relation to the reality of the spread of actual female and male societal and occupational roles in the society concerned. Secondly, males and females are rarely represented as successful and happy in non-traditional roles. But, thirdly, when children and adolescents have been presented with books, careers materials or texts which include women in non-traditional roles or occupations, in leadership, in scientific or technological disciplines, the use of these materials has, nevertheless, been effective in breaking sex-role stereotypes and in widening adolescent perceptions of achievable vocational choices.

Similarly, there is credible field evidence from careers educators and teachers that the use of videos showing women successfully handling engineering, management, technician training or business enterprises is as effective as, or more effective than, personal appearances of individual minority women in widening the vocational perceptions and aspirations of adolescents. Thus a far more effective way in which to achieve phase one of the role-modelling process (breaking the stereotype) is to commission videos showing both women and men in non-traditional roles as if they were sex-normal, and to use these widely in the school, careers guidance and training systems. It is, however, of limited value to show successful women mining engineers, physicists and chemical analysts unless we show, simultaneously, their husbands or partners supporting them and carrying a full and equal share of domestic responsibility. Grants and project money spent on ferrying untypical women to small functions without the context of an overall strategy to attack sex-role stereotyping in books, careers materials and the visual medial is likely to be a total waste of scarce public money.

Policy Implications for Science Educators and Institutions

But in Australia, and in the UK and USA so far as published project reports in those countries are available, active policies for encouraging girls and women to enter engineering, the technical trades and the applied sciences have been heavily based on traditional role-model theory. The Tradeswomen on the Move Australian project in the Hunter Valley and Women in Engineering projects in particular use minority women to travel far and wide to meet relative handfuls of girls in schools and interact with them. A range of *Registers of Non Traditional Women* has been produced across Australia from special project grants precisely for the purpose of pressing those non-traditional women to allocate extra time to travelling around being 'visible successes', as it were.

The need for women to be equally visible with men in all occupations and roles in which they are represented is accepted, but this is a normal mainstream personnel management policy and should not be seen as an added workload for women in schools and colleges out of working hours. The simple policy of ensuring that women are relatively equitably represented on committees, in decision-making groups and bodies, and at public events and forums, and are used on a par with men as delegates to meetings, negotiations and conferences where they are equally qualified, will ensure their visibility much more effectively than artificially constructed personal role-modelling techniques at a single event. Similarly, senior women academics and principals need to be used in the normal way for graduation speeches, public functions and in school ceremonies, where these form part of the institution's ordinary work and do not constitute an extra workload. But schools and colleges can no longer rely on visible female role modelling as an effective influence on adolescent curricular choice (if it ever was). Adolescent students are influenced by the behaviour of both sexes and, in particular, by the attitudes and behaviour of males to females and females to males in their adult community.

Many well-meant efforts have also been made in inservice training programmes, to involve more women as role models by 'bringing them in from outside'. Where there were previously no women in a particular sector or institution, this may have been seen as unavoidable. However, a more effective strategy is first to re-educate male staff in the light of the now massive bank of accredited research on girls' equal capacity for maths, science and technology, of the role of sexism and sex-role stereotyping in hindering equal achievement and of girls' equal right to scarce places in these disciplines. Both male and female staff need then to work as a team to re-educate school and college male students in this regard.

The rigorous application of Glaser and Strauss's (1967 and 1972) grounded theory approach to the previous scholarship and to available data in relation to same-sex role modelling as a policy mechanism to increase female access to science and technology, results in the rejection of most traditional hypotheses and received wisdom as Snark-based.

One outcome of the UQ WISTA Policy Review research and its different levels of data and replacement grounded theory is a suggested alternative set of principles and theory in this area. In relation to same-sex role modelling, breaking the stereotype, we conclude that:

- There is still a reasonable, consistent and cross-national basis for supporting the hypothesis that same-sex role modelling is an important influence on breaking the stereotypes of ascribed masculinity and femininity in branches of science and technology, in the context of female curricular choice and vocational aspiration.
- However, change will not occur through mere visible imaging of female success, but through new knowledge, new understanding and the re-education of both sexes on women's equal capacity for all branches of scientific and technological study.
- The presentation of successful minority women in any role-modelling context should emphasize their normality in social, family and other roles as well as in occupational terms.
- Any strategy to use female role modelling to break the male stereotypes should provide contrasting models (married, single, young, older experienced, etc.) and not be based on a dual-role superwoman image alone.
- Breaking the stereotype though women's increased visibility is better achieved by improving visible female participation in

contexts seen as normal management and decision-making, and at mainstream ceremonial and public functions.

- Same-sex role modelling is effective as a process of breaking the stereotype through printed and pictorial literature, through educational materials and through careers and guidance literature. Federal and state educational authorities and departments, educational institutions and educational publishers should work to provide visible models of both sexes, in non-traditional as well as in traditional roles, in all educational materials.
- Funds for policies to break stereotypes and to accredit non-traditional sex roles should centre on the strategic mainstream use of key audiovisual and print media and not on project-based used of isolated minority women and men in person.

We have considerably more reservations about personal same-sex role modelling as a policy mechanism. We conclude that:

- There appears to be no valid research basis, grounded either in rigorous theory or in sound empirical evidence, for concluding that the mere acquisition or increase of female staff in a given discipline or occupation would, in itself, result in an increase in female students or trainees in the discipline or occupation of the female role model.
- There appears to be no valid research basis for then concluding that female students or trainees would be inspired to make non-traditional choices merely and solely by seeing female role models in person in a particular discipline or occupation.
- The research basis for concluding that the individual use of same-sex role models is more effective than cross-sex models in influencing the curricular or career choice of students, is ambiguous, inconclusive and unproven, and is a poor basis for strategic policymaking.
- Same-sex female role modelling is accordingly not an appropriate policy mechanism where there is an expectation that already overworked minority women will carry it out in person in circumstances uneconomic in time, resources and energy. Women should not be pressured or expected to role model in person, unless they so wish. Projects should not be funded which centre on drafting minority women in to role model in person, in the mistaken expectation that this would in any way increase female enrolments in non-traditional areas.
- Strategies in schools and colleges need to move from the aim

of changing girls and women to altering male attitudes towards females wishing to make non-traditional choices.

It will be evident that role modelling and mentorship are part of a kind of continuum from passive to active. The phases run thus:

1 Passive role models: merely visibility.
2 Active process by women travelling to role model personally.
3 Self-selected mentorship by individuals based on empathy and mutual choice.
4 Formal institutionalized systems of mentorship.

We now turn to phases 3 and 4 of the continuum: different forms of mentorship which help both general career progression and the advancement of untypical students (or staff) over barriers through active sponsorship and encouragement form senior colleagues.

References

ALDRICH, M. and HALL, P. (1980) Programs in Science, Maths and Engineering for Women in USA 1966–1978, Washington, DC, AAAS and Office of Opportunities in Science.

ALMQUIST, E.M. and ANGRIST, S.S. (1971) 'Role model influences on college women's career aspirations', *Merrill-Palmer Quarterly*, 17, pp. 263–79.

ANGRIST, S.S. and ALMQUIST, E.M. (1975) *Careers and Contingencies: How College Women Juggle with Gender*, New York, Dunellen Publishing Co.

BASOW, S.A. and HOWE, K.G. (1980) 'Role model influence: effects of sex and sex-role attitude in college students', *Psychology of Women Quarterly*, 4 (4), Summer, pp. 558–72.

BELL, A.P. (1970a) 'Role modelship and interaction in adolescence and young adulthood', *Developmental Psychology*, 2 (1), pp. 123–8.

BELL, A.P. (1970b) 'Role models in young adulthood: their relations to occupational behaviours', *Vocational Guidance Quarterly*, June, pp. 280–4.

BOWLING, J. and MARTIN, B. (1985), 'Science: a masculine disorder?', *Science and Public Policy*, December, pp. 308–16.

BYRNE, E.M. (1985) *Women in Engineering: A Comparative Overview*, Bureau of Labour Market Research, Monograph Series, Canberra, Australian Government Publishing Services.

CLARK, Y. and ABRON-ROBINSON, L. (1975) 'Minority women in engineering schools', *IEEE Transactions on Education, E-18* (1), *February*, pp. 34–5.

DANIELS, J. and LEBOLD, K. (1982) 'Women in engineering: a dynamic approach' in HUMPHREYS, S. (Ed) *Women and Minorities in science: Strategies for increasing participation*, AAAS Selected Symposium, Chapter 9. Colo., West View Press.

DEBLÉ, I. (1980) *The School Education of Girls*, Paris, UNESCO.

DOUVAN, E. (1976) 'The role of models in women's professional development', *Psychology of Women Quarterly*, Fall, pp. 5–19.

DRESSELHAUS, M.S. (1975) 'Some personal views on engineering education for women', *IEEE Transactions on Education*, E-18, (1), February, pp. 30–4.

EGGLESTON, J., GALTON, M. and JONES, M. (1976) *Processes and Products of Science Teaching*, Schools Council Research Studies, London, Macmillan Education.

ERKUT, S. and MOKROS, J. (1984) 'Professors as models and mentors for college students', *American Educational Research Journal*, 21 (2), pp. 399–417.

FROHREICH, D.S. (1975) 'How colleges try to attract more women students', *IEEE Transactions on Education*, E-18 (1), February, pp. 41–6.

GELB, L. (1973) 'Masculinity and femininity' in MILLER, J. BAKER (Ed) *Psychoanalysis and Women*, Harmondsworth, Penguin, pp. 364–373.

GILBERT, L.A. (1985) 'Dimensions of same-gender student-faculty role model relationships', *Sex Roles*, 12 (1/2), pp. 111–23.

GILBERT, L. GALLESSICH, J. and EVANS, S. (1983) 'Sex of faculty, role model and students self-perceptions of competence', *Sex Roles*, 9 (5), pp. 597–607.

GILLIGAN, C. (1982) *In a Different Voice: Psychological Theory and Women's Development*, Cambridge, Mass., Harvard University Press.

GLASER, B.G. and STRAUSS, A.L. (1967) *The Discovery of Grounded Theory*, Chicago, Aldine.

GLASER, B. and STRAUSS, A. (1972) 'Discovery of substantive theory: a basic strategy underlying qualitative research', chapter 28 in FILSTEAD, WILLIAM (Ed) (1972) *Qualitative Methodology: Firsthand Involvement with the Social World*, 3rd edn, Chicago, Markham Publishing Co.

GOLDSTEIN, E. (1979) 'Effect of same sex and cross sex role models on the subsequent academic productivity of scholars', *American Psychologist*, 34 (5), May, pp. 407–10.

HARDING, J. (1983) *Switched Off: The Science Education of Girls*, London, Schools Council and Longman.

KAGAN, J. (1964) 'Acquisition and significance of sextyping and sexrole identity' in HOFFMAN, M.L. and L.W. (Eds) *Review of Child Development Research*, vol. 1, New York, Russell Sage Foundation.

KEMPER, T. (1968) 'Reference groups, socialisation and achievement', *American Sociological Review*, 33, pp. 31–45.

MISCHEL, W. (1966) 'A social learning view of sex differences in behaviour' in MACCOBY, E.E. (Ed) *The Development of Sex Differences*, Stanford, California, Stanford University Press.

MISCHEL, W. (1970) 'Sextyping and socialisation' in MUSSEN, P. (Ed), *Carmichael's Manual of Child Psychology*, vol. 2, New York Wiley.

O'DONNELL, J.A. and ANDERSON, D.G. (1978) 'Factors influencing choice of major and career of capable women', *Vocational Guidance Quarterly*, 26, pp. 215–21.

OATES, M.J. and WILLIAMSON, S. (1978) 'Women's colleges and women achievers', *Signs*, 3 (4), Summer, pp. 795–806.

ROBINSON, B.E. and GREEN, M. (1970) 'On the nature of sex role transcendence', *Australian Journal of Sex, Marriage and the Family*, 3 (1), pp. 5–12.

ROESKE, N.A. and LAKE, K. (1977) 'Role models for women medical students', *Journal of Medical Education*, 52 (6), pp. 459–68.

SEATER, B.B. and RIDGEWAY, C.L. (1976) 'Role models, significant others and the importance of male influence on college women', *Sociological Symposium*, 15, Spring, pp. 49–64.

SHAPLEY, D. (1975) 'Obstacles to women in Science', *Impact of Science on Society*, 25 (2), p. 115.

SHOCKLEY, P. and STALEY, C. (1980) 'Women in Management Training Programmes: What they think about key Issues', in *Public Personnel Management Journal*, 9 (3), pp. 214–224.

SPENDER, D. (1980) *Man-Made Language*, London, Routledge and Kegan Paul.

SPROULE, B.A. and MATHIS, H.F. (1976) 'Recruiting and keeping women engineering students: an agenda for action', *Engineering Education, April*, pp. 745–48.

STASZ, C., SHAVELSON, R. and STASZ, C. (1985) 'Teachers as role models: are there gender differences in microcomputer based maths and science instruction?', *Sex Roles*, 13 (3/4), pp. 149–64.

STRAUSS, M.J.B. (1978) 'Wanted: more women in science', *The American Biology Teacher*, March, pp. 181–9.

SUTHERLAND, M. (1985) *Women who Teach in Universities*, European Institute of Education and Social Policy, through Trentham Books. Stoke-on-Trent.

TANGRI, S.S. (1972) 'Determinants of Occupational Role innovation among college women', in *Journal of Social Issues*, 28 (2), pp. 177–199.

TIDBALL, M.E. and KISTIA-KOWSKY, V. (1976) 'Baccalaureat origins of American scientists and scholars', *Science*, 193, pp. 646–52.

WELCH, W.W. and LAWRENZ, F. (1982) 'Characteristics of male and female science teachers', *Journal of Research in Science Teaching*, 19 (7), pp. 58–94.

WHEELER, J. *et al.* (1979) *Case Studies and Promising Approaches: Vocational Education Equity Study*, Final Report, vol. IV, American Institute for Research.

YOUNG, C., MCKENZIE, D.L. and SHERIF, C.W. (1980) 'In search of token women in academia', *Psychology of Women Quarterly*, 4 (4), pp. 508–25.

Chapter 5

The Mentor Process: Selective Choice or Policy Mechanism?

> I would venture to urge with the utmost insistence that it is not
> a 'women's question'. Let me entreat thinking men to dismiss
> from their minds the belief that this is a thing with which they
> have no concern. (Emily Davies [on the higher education of
> women] to the Social Science Association, York, 1864)

Like most other influential issues in the politicosocial area, mentorship
has been discussed and studied principally as a male phenomenon in a
male-as-norm paradigm until very recently. Over the centuries since
Homer wrote of the original Mentor (tutor and adviser to Telemachus,
son of Odysseus), it has been accepted as normal that patronage, pre-
ferment, the Old Boys' network, have been male bastions. Yet, as in
other areas of equity and policy, the current political expectation that
what is available to men in economic, political and social arenas must
now be available to women, has still been seen as a women's issue and
not as a responsibility for management or for institutions. We endorse
Emily Davies' rejection of the peripheralization of problems seen as
women's issues.

In our earlier discussion of institutional ecology, we identified
mentorship as one factor present both at the level of the institution and
in the ecological niche of departments and disciplines. We were also,
however, aware from our review of existing published works of the
likelihood of finding the Snark effect in the strength of the belief in
mentorship as a universal and essential panacea but its highly variable
base in rigorous research or monitoring.

While same-sex role modelling has been most extensively debated
as an access question, mentorship has always been seen more as an

influential factor in terms of progression and of advancement. Moving up the promotions ladder, or into influential policy areas, breaking into postgraduate research — these are all correlated with the active help of those ahead, as well as with the ability and motivation of the trainee or student. We believe that mentorship is both a critical element of institutional ecology and a significant influence in women's retention and progression in non-traditional areas of study and employment. At the outset of the UQ WISTA research, we therefore built in a re-examination of this issue as one of the ten core factors. This was partly because a review of the published accounts of the biographies and work of women scientists had revealed very imperfect and imprecise evidence of the role-model factor, but recurrent and quite unambiguous instances of direct mentorship of women by male scientists and mathematicians.

For when we look at the formative years of education and training, the published profiles, biographies and autobiographies of women seen as having successfully broken into non-traditional areas do contain a common theme of the presence of a mentor, a sponsor, an enabler, a senior or leadership figure who has been more than a role model. And while this has been sometimes written off as anecdotal, it is nonetheless real. The mentor emerges as rather an opener of doors, a sponsor to financial scholarships or awards, a colleague who has created an arena for the protégée to show her gifts. The current received wisdom is that, hypothetically, a mentor who is also female and a role model will be doubly influential in helping women. Yet sponsorship, grants and the award of jobs are reflections of the power structure. In science and technology in higher education, women still are fewer than 2 per cent of the top leadership. Mentors will, therefore, of necessity more often still be male. Nor can we assume that women will, in fact, necessarily be supportive or even ready to take on mentorship when they are in a very small minority at the top. High-profile women are not always supportive to women behind them; and our role-model analysis has already highlighted the danger of burnout and overload for minority women required to take on multiple extra roles.

Mentorship in Science

The role of mentors and sponsors is in particular well documented historically in the biographies of male and female scientists alike. T.H. Huxley, in addition to his many other roles, was a key figure in opening up science education to women in Victorian England. In Rossiter's

(1982) account of women scientists in the USA from the early nineteenth century to the 1940s, the key factor in the accessing of science education for early pioneers was the specific sponsorship of sympathetic male scientists. Amos Eaton in particular not only helped early women scientists such as Emma Hart Willard and Mary Lyon, but trained them to train other women. Maria Mitchell, the astronomer and the first woman member of the American Academy of Arts and Sciences, owed her professorship at Vassar College to the specific keenness of Matthew Vassar to have a prominent woman scientist on his staff. She also became a key role model and promoter of science education for women (*ibid.*). Again, it was Leo Konigsberger who thought so highly of Sofia Kovalevskaia's mathematical ability that he persuaded her (and helped her) to move to Berlin in order to work with Weierstrass, who also helped to overcome the discrimination at Göttingen University sufficiently to enable Kovalevskaia to be granted her degree *summa cum laude* in 1874, at a time when degrees were withheld from women. Weierstrass and Mittag-Leffler together continued to advise and encourage her, and finally it was the support and influence of Mittag-Leffler which obtained her a post at Stockholm University in 1883 (Koblitz 1983 and 1984). Kovalevskaia's achievement as a woman mathematician in a world hostile to the idea of intellect in a female head was achieved only with the direct mentorship of contemporary powerful and supportive male mathematicians.

Florence Sabin's breakthrough research on blood, bone marrow and tuberculosis was, in her view, only possible because of the early help, advice and sponsorship of Dr Franklin Paine Mall of the John Hopkins Medical School in the late 1890s (Haber, 1979). Rosalyn Yalow, the second woman to win a Nobel Prize in Medicine and the sixth Nobel woman scientist, records both early mentorship and early prejudice. Her parents wanted her to be an elementary schoolteacher, but her physics professor at Hunter College (now City University) encouraged her to persist in university physics. But when later, as a teaching assistant at the University of Illinois and studying graduate physics, she achieved As in all sections except the laboratory element in which she achieved A minus, the Chairman of the Physics Department saw her three As and one A minus and merely commented: 'That A minus confirms that women do not do well at laboratory work' (Haber, 1979, p. 131). Only active and constant mentor encouragement can help women to persist against this negative stereotypic climate, which Friedl calls 'the universal cultural devaluation of woman and their activities . . . Why is the belief that women are inferior to men so prevalent a trait of human culture?' (Friedl, 1975, p. 5).

What is Mentorship? The Snark Effect

We first reviewed the most frequently cited research literature and analysed it for methodology and interpretation. We believe that it provides clear evidence of the Snark effect. Although mentorship in business and commerce has been relatively well discussed, the process in academe has been so deeply embedded in Bordieu's 'genesis amnesia' that digging out its presence and its characteristics needs the persistence and intuition of porcine hunters of truffles in the Auvergne. And the mentor process, even when present in higher education, has, indeed, often been denied by those who practise it.

Analyses of the mentor literature as at the outset of our research in 1985 showed a general methodological fluffiness undesirable for an issue so apparently influential. One early critic reviewed the role model, mentor and sponsor concepts at the end of the 1970s and found that the available studies were often methodologically flawed, the numbers too small or unrepresentative for generalization, and the concepts ill-defined (Speizer, 1981, p. 711). This poor or muddled definition at the start of, or in the publication of, empirical research is a phenomenon shared with the role-model issue. Speizer asks most pertinently 'why, with so little research foundation, the concepts of role models, mentors and sponsors have caught the imagination of so many people' (*ibid.*, p. 712). In our terms, why is the Snark effect so evident in this issue?

In another review of research methodologies for assessing mentorship, Wrightsman describes the then current received wisdom as a false consensus on the meaning of mentorship (Wrightsman, 1981, p. 3). This reviewer concludes that 'it is only at a superficial level that "everybody knows" what mentoring is', and particularly criticizes wooly definitions proffered with no indications of their sources or justification (*ibid.*, p. 3).

Mentorship in business and commerce has been most simply defined as an active process of positive sponsorship by older patrons (teachers, managers, trainers, counsellors, senior women staff) towards younger or less experienced staff, students or trainees. In the business world, some of the key writers on mentorship in management, including Kanter (1977), have identified it as having and using the power to help someone through a form of patronage or individual personal sponsorship. It is particularly seen as the use of power to help someone to move upward by bypassing the usual hierarchical process, and it involves providing a generalized sponsorship which enables the person receiving it to achieve progress through a form of reflected power.

It is somewhat disturbing to discover how many of the influential researchers or policymakers in the mentorship area have continued to base their definitions, and hence their work, on that of Daniel Levinson (1978), despite the fact that his published study is based on a very small sample of male Americans aged from 35–45 years some two decades ago. As late as the mid-1970s, he was still using a male-as-norm paradigm. Levinson cites the influence of a mentor as critical in ensuring young men's (sic) professional (and, he says, emotional) development into adulthood and the middle years of professional influence. His much-quoted definition follows:

> A good mentor is an admixture of good father and good friend . . . A 'good enough' mentor is a transitional figure who invites and welcomes a young man into the adult world. He serves as guide, teacher and sponsor. He represents skill, knowledge, virtue, accomplishment — the superior qualities a young man hopes someday to acquire . . . And yet, with all this superiority, he conveys the promise that in time, they will be peers. The protégé has the hope that soon he will be able to join or even surpass his mentor in the work they both value. A mentor can be of great practical help to a young man as he seeks to find his way and gain new skills. But a good mentor is helpful in a more basic, developmental sense. The relationship enables the recipient to identify with a person who exemplifies many of the qualities he seeks . . . He acquires a sense of belonging to the generation of promising young men. He reaps the various benefits to be gained from a serious, mutual non-sexual loving relationship with a somewhat older man or woman. (Levinson, 1978)

We should note that despite Daniel Levinson's assertion of its value, he nevertheless concludes that most adults actually give and receive very little mentoring, and that its practice is the exception rather than the rule.

Roche (1979), also writing on the business world, defines a mentor quite decisively in terms of sponsorship. In his survey of 1,250 men and women business executives in the USA, he asked them: 'at any stage of your career, have you had a relationship with a person who took a personal interest in your career and who guided and sponsored you?' Women executives formed only 1 per cent of the total group studied, and 'tended to have several mentors (averaging three to the men's two — Roche, 1979). While the women executives had female mentors more often than men, seven in ten of the women's mentors were male. Only one in fifty of the men had a female mentor (*ibid.*). In another American analysis located in the business world, mentorship is seen as ensuring that the careers of young people 'get off to a good start' (Collins and Scott, 1978). Out of these relationships, it was hoped that young people learn to take risks, accept a philosophical commitment to sharing and learn to relate to people in an intuitive empathetic way' (Franklin Lunding in *ibid.*, p. 89). In interviews with three chief executives in American jewel companies, three issues emerge which are generally explicit in business and almost wholly implicit in academe. Firstly, the business world holds that executive responsibility involves assisting the people down the line to be successful (a role occasionally accepted but mostly rejected by the Deans and Heads of Schools attending our group interviews). Secondly, the concept is prevalent that mentorship involves actually going out and looking for people and telling them that they are good once their talent is spotted. We found this concept, however, to be embryonic at the articulated level in many academic UQ WISTA group interview discussions, and attitudes to deliberate mentorship were, at the least, ambivalent in our UQ WISTA institutions. Thirdly, mentorship in business involves deliberately creating opportunities for protégés to acquire new skills and to enable them to use them visibly to their advantage (Collins and Scott, 1978).

Henderson has looked at what he describes as 'formal mentorship programs' in American federal, state and municipal government, and found the practice much less ideal than in theory (Henderson, 1985). These mentorship programmes were often resented by mentors (too much extra work), recipients (jealousy from others) and non-recipients (felt excluded) alike. His respondents also showed a strong aversion, in fact, to organized mentoring that imposed mentor–protégé relationships. Henderson concludes that the roles of mentors and protégés are best formed under an organizational umbrella that actually promotes and expects mentoring but does not impose it (*ibid.*, p. 862) — or, in UQ WISTA terms, as part of the positive institutional ecology.

Definitions of mentorship vary considerably according to the sector in which they have germinated: education, general business, top management, elite firms. Collins, in a research-based review of professional women and their mentors, identifies five generic criteria for a true mentor: higher up on the organizational ladder; an authority in the field; really interested in the protégé's development; influential; and willing to invest more extra time and personal commitment than mere interest (Collins, 1983). More recently, Hurley records a view, however, that researchers still could not agree on what mentors were, whether they were important to success, or whether and how formal mentor programmes could be effective (Hurley, 1988). Yet the influence of Levinson, Roche and other 1970s researchers is seen by Hurley to have caused a widespread institutionalization of mentoring. Formal mentor programmes are reported to be in place, for example, at nine major and high-profile American corporations. The concept has been further widened — and therefore considerably blurred — by extending it to teachers, parents and children, a stretching of definition and application which Hurley notes that 'most psychologists consider vague and unwarranted' (*ibid.*, p. 42). Hurley comes down clearly against formal arrangements on the grounds that the reciprocity of mentor–protégé relationships involves mutual choosing, mutual respect and liking, mutual give and take, which cannot be systematized without losing these very characteristics.

How far previously published conclusions from the corporate business world can be soundly generalized to other career settings with different institutional ecologies is debatable. Kram (1983) and Queralt (1982) both question the generalization of received wisdom from evidence in one occupational sector to another in the context of this issue. There are some generic elements which appear to be common across sectors; others are highly contextual to a particular sector.

When we come to look at the higher education sector as such, Levinson concluded more than a decade ago that 'our system of higher education, though officially committed to fostering the intellectual and personal development of students, provides mentoring that is generally limited in quantity and poor in quality' (Levinson, 1978, p.334), a comment which was echoed by many of the Deans and Heads of Schools in our group interviews in the Australian survey institutions. Insofar as it exists, a number of different ways in which the mentor role works in education has been hypothesized. At pre-university stage, science teachers in schools may take particular trouble to seek out access to scholarships for their gifted girls. In higher education mentorship is, however, not only more complex but also more hidden, implicit and undefined. The system is seen to work in relation to such aspects as:

- recommendation for awards
- recommendation for postgraduate scholarships
- recommendation and appointment to part-time tutorships to enable concurrent postgraduate research to be undertaken
- advice and encouragement to students to help them to progress over barriers

- giving students more practical experiences in laboratory experiments with lecturers
- enhancing a student's 'visibility' (seminars, joint papers, conference attendance)
- discussing the latest scientific or technological work with students: brainstorming

The last of these is particularly important and relates to what Martha White (1970) calls 'the biological library', or our mentally stored inherited knowledge and understanding. White discusses in some detail the informal professional training processes which operated at the Radcliffe Institute whose women scholars she interviewed. She recognizes that many professions and occupations have periods analogous to that of the medical internship or residency during which the individual learns to behave in ways which other people in the field regard as 'professional'. Such socialization consists of learning the informal valued and attributed roles and the expectations which are an important part of real professional life. The process results in the gaining of a firmer image of self as a competent and adequate professional. This kind of learning is 'caught' not 'taught', and is a valued byproduct of acceptance by and challenging association with other professionals.

When the older professionals share their special knowledge and understanding outside the lecture halls with some, but not other, students, we are talking of mentorship. In science, in particular, the exclusion from informal channels of communication is important since knowledge in this area is growing so rapidly. At any given time only part of it is in the literature, yet women may have more limited access to the brains of the male fellow scientists who dominate the disciplines than their male peers do. When women are hesitant to put themselves forward or to protest at their exclusion, the pattern of exclusion is confirmed. White's analysis stresses what Egerton describes as 'biological storage' rather than mechanical or library storage; access to the knowledge in the brains of scientists and technologists which, it is held by both White and Bernard (1964), is more often shared in brainstorming discussions and informal interaction between male lecturers and male students or male researchers, than between male lecturers and female students or female researchers. These discussions take place over a beer, in pubs or clubs, and in Australia in 'mateship' sessions from which women are often socially excluded (albeit more by cultural custom than by intent).

Another writer refers to the informal and invisible nature of the process. In an American review of women's place in the scientific community, Cole refers to 'informal social networks . . . detailed patterns of social interaction and sponsorship that are an essential part of successful careers' (Cole, 1981, p. 390). He questions whether women have the same opportunities to establish what he calls apprentice relationships with older, eminent scientists. He describes these as 'an important *mechanism* of transmitting a scientific tradition from one generation to another' (*ibid.*). Cole's list of relevant informal processes in this context includes informal scientific discourse with teachers, being asked to join the laboratories and research teams of senior Professors, and being asked to describe one's work at conferences. Cole recognizes that 'there are no multiple regressions that can describe the impact of these social linkages' (*ibid.*, p. 390), but comes down on the side of judging that women are relatively deprived in this regard. One can legitimately argue that the more informal, unidentified and embedded the process, the less likely that women will be freely admitted to what has been a culturally male process.

Daloz (1986) in a wide-ranging study of effective teaching and mentoring in higher education, describes mentors as guides who lead us along our journey, of notable importance at the beginning of our careers. Daloz accepts the embedded nature of the process:

> unless there is some formalized process for assigning or recognising mentorships, the process remains largely invisible — a German instructor spends extra lab time with a particularly promising student, or a biology Professor and student begin to share problems of child care. (Daloz, 1986, p. 20)

Giles and Endsley (1988) have now attempted to define the generic. They have examined the mentor role in PhD programmes (involving twenty-five males and thirty-nine females) in child and family development at an American state University, in the context of psychosocial relationships as well as of the mentor–protégé dyad. They developed a clearly defined model of career development relationships (CDR) as the classical mentoring relationship, consisting of four generic elements: reciprocity in communication (frequency, variety, understanding); an affective bond (trust, respect, affection); the breadth and depth of influence; and the power differential. These researchers conclude that 'high levels of professor influence and power and, to a lesser extent, high quality communication and strong affective bonds between professor and student all promote a positive graduate school experience both objectively . . . and subjectively' (Giles and Endsley, 1988, p. 474).

This well-constructed research also clarifies not only that mentorship did clearly exist, and was influential, but that students thought of their mentoring professors as more than teachers or sponsors. The research also looked at peer relationships and concludes that student–peer communication is not related as such to career success in graduate school, but that emotional and social peer support does have some importance in the initial stage of graduate school. This may have implications for the peer element of the UQ WISTA ecology theory, and particularly for the time-lag factor.

In summary, the available evidence so far suggests that:

1 Mentoring clearly does exist as a practice but is more clearly defined in executive management than in the education sector.
2 The concept and definition of a mentor varies across sectors and areas of influence and is still very imperfectly and ambiguously described.
3 Mentorship in the business world is generally selective and self-chosen, although increasingly it is becoming formalized, while mentorship in academe is informal and rarely visible.
4 There is as yet no clear, empirical research evidence to suggest the range and extent of the influence of mentorship, nor what proportion of young adults has access to this selective and self-selective process.

A further complication is that some published research commentaries on mentoring see this process as highly sex-differentiated. Daloz (1986) criticizes the male-as-norm basis of much of the published work, finding its value for women questionable. His analysis judges research suggesting that 'women define themselves in relation to others differently than men' as valid, and sees this as central to the mentorship issue (*ibid.*, p. 79).

Mentoring and Women

This brings us to whether the mentor issue is, in fact, different for women and, if one accepts that mentoring is equally prevalent (even if imperfectly researched or recorded), whether it is also either sex-differentiated or sex-biased. The same difficulty about lack of clarity and imperfect definitions applies to research on this aspect, but among a number of immediate questions arising from the review of available published research we address the following:

- Is there any evidence that women are mentored more or less than or equally with men?
- Are women mentored differently from men?
- Given that mentorship started as a process by being male-to-male, that is same-sex relationships, are there factors which are now specific to a cross-sex mentor relationship?

We will review the first two questions in the light of available research and the UQ WISTA evidence, and return in the penultimate section to the problems of cross-sex (mainly male–female, as distinct from female–male) mentorship.

Certainly there is evidence, including considerable biographical evidence, that successful women have had mentors. But the research evidence is uneven and inconclusive on the question of both access to and style of this process. Moore and Sangaria-Danowitz define a mentor in the context of female University administrators as an individual who helps the career advancement of others by 'teaching the ropes', coaching and making important introductions; 47 per cent of their sample identified a mentor by this rather general definition (Moore and Sangaria-Danowitz, 1979, p. 15). Shockley and Staley (1980), however, left the definition of mentors to their female subjects, a rather unsound approach, and their sample was limited to thirty women who participated in campus-run seminars for women and management at the University of Colorado. Nevertheless, they did find that in answer to their overgeneralized question, 'Do you have a mentor in the organisation?', 67 per cent replied that they had (Shockley and Staley, 1980). One of the more thorough and substantial surveys is Riley and Wrench's (1985) study of the mentoring of women lawyers (55 per cent of 2,300 members of a county bar association). Their definitions are clear and precise, although too long to cite here, but follow well-trod paths and include the conferring of status, providing essential information, active help and the sharing of resources. Importantly, the researchers conclude that 'the prevalence of mentoring found in this study is relatively low compared with the prevalence that has been reported in previous studies. One reason for this is the research design' (Riley and Wrench, 1985, p. 384). That is, the study distinguishes between being 'truly mentored' according to a clear and strict definition of this phenomenon (only 43 per cent of all women claiming mentors actually proved to be 'truly mentored'), and receiving loosely defined help. The researchers deduce that mentoring does remain important but this depends on the quality of the mentor–protégé relationship itself (*ibid.*, p. 384).

In Henderson's (1985) study of American executives and managers from larger (over a hundred employees) public organizations and government departments (where the survey total was 822 people), more than seven out of ten of his respondents of both sexes claimed to have had mentors. His definition of a mentor is the rather general one used also by Roche (1979), that is someone with whom respondents had had a relationship at any stage in their career in which the person took a personal interest in the career of the respondent, helped to promote her or him or guided and sponsored her or him (Henderson, 1985, p. 858). Women executives in his sample had more mentors (average 2.72 to the male 2.44) and were three times more likely than men to have a woman as a mentor.

In Missirian's (1982) study of an admittedly select group of a hundred top American women executive managers, she set out to explore wider issues. The study investigated whether Levinson's (1978) male-based mentor–protégé relationship was different for women; whether mentorship has stages and patterns of behaviour; whether mentors and protégés need to have shared values and goals; and whether sexuality is an issue to be addressed in the relationship. Significantly, Missirian concludes that the answer is affirmative in each case. She also concludes that her findings support the general hypothesis that mentoring has, in fact, been a significant influence on the career development of successful female managers, and insofar as one relates this to top women who are the 'rubric of exceptions' in terms of the Byrne Scale of Nontraditionality (see chapter 1), her research findings are credible. One should note, before accepting Missirian's results as necessarily transferable, that the men and women in her sample reached the top by different routes: the men through clearly defined power-based line management, the women more typically through the staff-personnel route which Missirian describes as involving only tenuous advisory power. If we look at the female professoriate in higher education, however, it may also be partly true that the reason why women Professors are more highly represented in the social sciences and therapies is that more of us have entered academe directly at the top after a successful career in a less male-dominated profession and where mentoring is more overtly a part of career-structures: that is, also by a different route.

Vertz (1985) also looks at wider issues in the context of the career advancement of seven groups of women in an American district office of internal revenue. She analyses obstacles to be overcome if mentoring is to be successful. Her analysis of what reads as a thorough and well-constructed study, identifies in particular the need for mentors to be aware of the often different career paths of women — for family reasons, or because they cannot relocate so easily or because they are one phase behind in the qualifications queue. One should, however, note that many more professional women these days do not, in fact, have a very different career path from men, particularly at graduate and professional levels. Sullerot's research almost two decades ago confirmed that in France, 'the higher the woman's education, the less likely she is to interrupt her career' (Sullerot, 1973, p. 85). Ten years later, a survey of women engineers in France showed that French women engineers had an initial economic activity rate of 85 per cent, four fifths of working women engineers in young middle age were mothers and a quarter of women engineers put career before marriage until at least age 30, or double the national average (Cercle des Femmes Ingénieurs, 1982). A similar profile is evident in Sweden; that is, some fifteen years ago, economic activity for women with higher education was 84 per cent compared with 65 per cent for those leaving school after advanced secondary education. Within this, women engineers had an economic activity rate of 95 per cent (Women in Sweden, 1973). In the USA, the work activity rate for women engineers and scientists in the late 1970s was already 89 per cent, and 85 per cent of women engineers expected to combine marriage, motherhood and employment as an engineer (Lebold *et al.*, 1983). Thus, any model for improving the mentorship process by male academics will need to take account of both the possibility that some women will have a different career path than men and that, simultaneously, other women will increasingly have a career path indistinguishable from the male one. To use one assumption to the exclusion of the other is to return to sex-role stereotyping.

It is not possible to conclude from these and other more minor studies whether women are generally mentored equally with men. What does emerge is a generally reported high correlation between top women and past mentoring. But while Missirian (1982) found evidence of sex-differentiation in the mentorship of women, other leading researchers did not, with the one exception of the sexual gossip issue which we deal with later in this chapter. The balance of reported empirical evidence is that top women, when they do break through into mentorship, are more likely to receive a male-as-norm range of practical and psychological support. But they cannot receive the same style of mentorship because theirs will almost always be a cross-sex relationship, and while male students and junior staff will have a same-sex mentor–protégé relationship.

How Many Female Mentors?

Notwithstanding an increased number of women scientists and technologists who pursue long-term careers, there is no evidence yet that the proportion of scientific and technological doctorates which are held by women, or the overall cohort of female scientists and technologists moving through higher education, is yet increasing sufficiently to reach a level of critical mass which is above the untypical level on the Byrne Scale of Non-traditionality. In Australian higher education, women still comprise fewer than 30 per cent of those holding doctorates; moreover, the UQ WISTA figures show that in the survey disciplines, only in biochemistry and microbiology were women more than a minority of postgraduate research students. In almost all other survey disciplines, women postgraduates and staff were below one quarter or one fifth of the total. Thus, as far ahead as we can see, even if an above average proportion of women who graduate in science and technology pursues careers and is successful, these women will not reach numerical parity with males in the foreseeable future. And the greater the sex imbalance at student level in a discipline (physics, metallurgy, civil engineering), the less likely we are to find a critical mass of senior women staff a generation later.

There is little sign of significantly changing trends on the international front, moreover. In UNESCO's recent (1987) study of the representation of women in higher education and research, for example, women averaged only between one fifth and one quarter of all students in the natural sciences in the world's regions. We clearly cannot therefore see a time in the years immediately ahead when the maximum proportion of women staff could in fact exceed this level. The female student enrolments in science vary from 18 per cent in 1984 in a sample of thirty-one countries in Asia and 21 per cent in 1983 in a similar sample of African countries, to 24 per cent in 1984 in Europe (excluding the then USSR) and 23 per cent in 1984 in seven countries in Oceania (Australia's region). In the same survey, women as a proportion of all higher education teachers and researchers varied from 6 per cent in Japan, to 10 per cent in Belgium, 15 per cent in Norway, 14 per cent in New Zealand and 22 per cent in Greece. When we subdivide to look at women in the natural sciences, the figures are even more variable (see table 5.1).

It therefore follows that

- most senior academic staff who are potential mentors will continue to be male;

Table 5.1 Women academics in higher education as percentage of all staff in all fields and in the natural sciences

Country	All fields % women	Natural sciences % women
Canada (1983)	20.2	4.6
Belgium (1985)	23.5	18.4
Finland (1983)	21.3	12.7
France (1985)	23.7	23.2
Norway (1984)	15.7	9.9
Portugal (1985)	31.2	38.1
New Zealand (1985)	22.8	25.3

Source: UNESCO, *Survey on ... Women in Higher Education*, tables 4–7

- most female students, if they have a mentor, will therefore have a cross-sex mentor and a male–female relationship;
- most male students, if they have a mentor, will have a same-sex mentor, and a male–male relationship.

Does this matter?

Cross-sex Mentoring: Male to Female

Given that this is so, three issues which emerge as major factors need review: the expectation that any policies for helping women are a women's affair and not a male responsibility; the likelihood of gossip and jealousy from other colleagues and spouses; and the actual risk of sexual entanglement.

When we analysed both the responses to the UQ WISTA discussion papers and the issues and attitudes prevalent in the group interviews, we found that most of the written comments presupposed that women would work with young women. Relatively few suggested that women should work to overcome prejudice in male students, or that men should take on extra work both with young women (to encourage them) and with young men (to alter their negative attitudes to young women where these were visible). The perceived case for women working with women was typically expressed in one submission which came from the ground upwards, as it were, and which identified mentorship as giving an active message of willingness to help, as much as supported same-sex identification: 'I always found it very much easier as a student to approach a female teacher for assistance than a male one' (letter, female, technical officer, earth sciences, University). This behaviour on the part of women students had been sufficiently widely reported and recognized as a phenomenon to gain reasonable acceptance on the part of our survey academics. But their conclusion from it was therefore to expect the women academics to concentrate on helping women. In almost no interview or written submission did male academics see this as a reason for looking at why it is that female students are put off by male behaviour, attitudes, discourse or other transmitted messages. Nor did male academics consider revising their teaching or supervision style or their transmitted attitudes to women as a result.

Male attitudes to women's professional advancement in higher education still remain ambivalent at best, overtly hostile at worst. Some males fear increased competition for scarce promotion of limited scholarships in a recession. Others still genuinely if anachronistically believe that marriage and motherhood are incompatible with careers for women, but that marriage and fatherhood are irrelevant to careers for men. A recent survey of some 3,000 University staff has confirmed the continuation of these negative attitudes as late as the mid-1980s (Wilson and Byrne, 1987, ch. 4). In a male–male lecturer-to-student relationship, the need for a student's career advancement is an automatic given; in a male–female lecturer-to-student relationship, it is not. Where lecturers and Professors hold generally hostile views to employed or career-oriented wives and mothers, this acts as an access filter in cross-sex mentorship.

More overtly problematic are the issues of gossip and of potentially inappropriate sexual relationships, issues referred to in many of the more substantial research surveys. One needs to distinguish the addition of an affectionate element into a relationship from the development of interaction into love or sexuality. In Levinson's research on which so much later work appears to have been based, he writes of mentorship as involving 'a serious, mutual, *non-sexual* loving [sic] relationship with a somewhat older man or woman' (Levinson, 1978). He also assumes, however, that the relationship has the possibility of becoming sexual where opposite sexes are involved. But Daloz, writing nearly a decade later, uses images and examples in his detailed study of effective teaching and mentoring which merit the word affection rather than love as an ingredient in the relationship (Daloz, 1986). Other researchers have written of an 'affective bond — the degree of respect, trust and/or love each feels towards the other' (Giles and Endsley, 1988, p. 471).

Missirian's study attempts to distinguish 'true mentoring' from sponsorship. Not everyone will agree with her that one element in true mentoring is what she describes as 'the intensity of emotional involvement', which she divides into three phases: respect, affection and love (Missirian, 1982, p. 88). Indeed, much of the evidence is for the reverse — that good, professional mentorship may well involve a friendly affection, but should carefully stop short of and avoid its development into something stronger. Indeed, in another contemporary major study of women and mentoring based on detailed and varied case histories, a successful professional woman is clear that 'You have to be careful of appearances in male/female relationships. In my own case, I would have been reluctant to have so obviously attached myself to a male mentor, for fear it would have been misunderstood' (Collins, 1983, p. 136).

There is greater unanimity on this latter issue: the problem of the perceptions of other colleagues, of the spouses of mentors, and of general, damaging gossip even where there is, in fact, no actual impropriety in a relationship. One American survey of thirty female managers concludes that 'a major risk for both mentor and protégé is the perception of others that a close association will evolve into sexual entanglement. This possibility is a concern of both' (Fitt and Newton; 1981). While most respondents to the survey did not consider that this was a major problem provided that the conduct of both was kept strictly professional, the researchers note that sexual tension did exist in several of the relationships they reviewed (*ibid.*). Examining formal mentorship in American governmental public service, Henderson's study records a frequent problem that 'sexual or intimate improprieties' are likely to be suspected by outsiders when the mentor relationship is between different sexes (Henderson, 1985, p. 858). In Missirian's (1982) survey, there is credible evidence that mixed-sex pairs in the mentor relationship will be at risk of gossip, jealous spouses and sexual tension, whether or not there is actual substance for gossip. The issue can be summarized by this written response by a senior academic following one of the UQ WISTA interviews at which mentorship was discussed:

> The general exposure given to the topic of sexual harassment would make the role of male mentor to a female much more tricky, and the males would now prefer to stay clear of the whole thing. If nothing else, it is a convenient excuse to stay clear of any positive involvement with females. With any luck, discrimination is easier to defend and less embarrassing than sexual harassment charges. (letter, Professor, male, University)

This brings us to the UQ WISTA evidence, and before reviewing the overall policy implications of our review of previous research evidence, we look further at the Australian evidence.

The UQ WISTA Evidence

Because the mentorship issue is not susceptible to statistical review to check hypotheses against grounded theory, in the way in which same-sex role modelling can, to some extent, be statistically monitored, one has to look for other more qualitative research evidence. We believe that the available evidence supports the theory than mentorship does form some part of institutional ecology (visibly or invisibly, consciously or at the embedded level). We believe it is critically influential at the level of the discipline: that is, in the ecological niche.

In the discussion paper on mentors circulated in 1986 to academic staff in scientific and technological disciplines in the UQ WISTA survey institutions, we defined a mentor as

> a sponsor, an enabler, a senior or leadership figure who has been more than a role model — rather an opener of doors, a sponsor to financial scholarships or awards, a colleague who has created an 'arena' for the protégée to show her gifts.

We identified the evidence from research sources such as Rossiter (1982), Strauss (1978), Goldstein (1979) and White (1970) described earlier, and asked in the paper:

(a) Which of the mentor roles listed above do you see as more important or more influential in your discipline?

(b) Do you consider that the ways in which sponsorship or mentoring work in your institution either do, or may, disadvantage women students?

(c) Are you able to identify any observed differences in the way in which these operate for male and female students respectively in helping access to postgraduate work?

(d) Is there any way of moving from the current idiosyncratic approach to a more clearly criterion based model? Is this desirable, or not?

In sharp contrast to the almost universal immediate acceptance of the role-model factor, many of those attending the group interviews in both 1985 and 1986 either did not recognize, or did not accept, the presence of mentorship as a process in higher education institutions, either as a self-chosen, self-selective activity, or as a formalized procedure. Those who attended our group interviews were much less ready to concede the strength of the mentor factor than the importance of role modelling. There was also a quite widespread belief that almost all lecturing staff were 'objective', unbiased, almost altruistic, and that even if mentorship existed, it was sex-neutral.

Some respondents were unfamiliar with the concept as such:

> I was totally unaware of the [mentorship] concept until it began to appear in feminist newspaper articles a few years ago . . . I have never been conscious of a mentor/mentee relationship in any [of my] work situations . . . mentorship is much less common in engineering that it apparently is in business. (letter, civil engineering, University)

Even those who conceded its strength appeared to have a form of 'genesis amnesia' about its actual operation and influence. This comment was characteristic:

> Although there is no evidence in the past of my subject [physics] that a mentor scheme, or patronage if you like, has been very strong, and I think that is true of chemistry, and possibly of mathematics, I think when you take the point of how does a student progress from undergraduate to postgraduate and then into the profession, in my subject it is done strictly by references and they are all confidential. I would be surprised if at that level, the mentorship weighed very much. Certainly, if you know the referee who is writing and you know it is your old friend X, then you would probably believe him a little more than your old enemy Y, but that's not the point. I would be very surprised, and I think this is where I share the view of my engineering colleagues, if this factor was as strong as, for instance, attitudes or prerequisites and mathematics. (interview, physicist, University)

That is, the process is conceded for 'the past' but denied as characteristic of current practices. In the same group interview, a geologist pursued the discussion and recognized the importance of mentorship in progression to doctoral studies:

> I think where a mentor is very important is in going on to a higher degree, say PhD level, and that this is where the influence can be the greatest in getting funding . . . people tend to go into industry because our department has been an industry-oriented department. We have discussed this at length and we have been making an active effort to encourage more people to

go on to PhDs and I think the encouragement by the adviser who is involved in an honours project is extremely important, at least in geology in our department . . . It has been very important in our department. (interview, geologist, University)

Others saw difficulties in finding good mentors in average staff either because of allegedly poor communication skills,

On the subject of mentors, we mathematicians are particularly poor [inept?] at personal relations. I suspect that the abstraction and isolation of the subject attracts a certain aloof and incommunicative personality type. If so, finding compassionate mentors will always be difficult. (letter, mathematician, University)

or because of perceived difficulty in obtaining industrial cooperation in placing female students in the necessary work-experience during University technology courses. In the case of mining, mentorship was seen as external to the department and not, in fact, part of its ecology: 'Mentors are difficult to find for male students . . . much of the industry would look with some suspicion and a possible lack of acceptance at a male without industrial experience. You can imagine the problem for a female.' (letter, mining, University)

In analysing the interviews, we found that there was widespread agreement from Professors and Deans that active mentorship was not a role which the majority of their staff recognized or saw as their function. There was little difficulty in the academics in the group interviews, however, accepting a new concept of mentorship as a process beyond the criterion-based formal selection of students for progression (which they saw staff as readily accepting but which they universally saw as totally sex-neutral). But the consensus was that this form of mentorship was not well done in higher education institutions towards either sex.

Some of the most vehement written responses, however, came from academics objecting to a description of current mentorship as idiosyncratic. In all of these cases, they defined mentorship solely in terms of formal structural arrangements for selecting students for higher degrees, a criterion-based process dependent on such factors as grade point averages and references. These respondents saw references to idiosyncratic processes as charges of discrimination, and in no instance did they refer to or appear to accept the existence of the unconscious or 'subcultural' processes identified in our discussion paper and in previous published accounts. This comment is characteristic of many:

My belief as far as the Chemistry Department is concerned is that the teaching staff [all male] have shown no discrimination in encouraging undergraduates in their study and progress through the degree . . . Over the years, female students at Honours and higher degree level have selected a wide range of staff members as supervisors. (letter, Head of department, University)

Certainly the latter point supports the fact that academics hold a firm belief that advice has departmentally been evenhanded, rather than otherwise. Another academic commented that:

I believe that all staff in this Department encourage all students to achieve to the level defined by their natural ability . . . men and women students are treated in all ways similarly in lectures, tutorials and laboratories . . . The proportion of women students in our courses has always been high and women are well represented in the lists of prizes awarded. (letter, chemist, University)

This academic saw progression to a higher degree as 'several years of very hard work in relative penury' and something of a lottery which women would be inclined to turn down because of marriage and family.

By contrast, among those accepting the existence of positive informal mentorship and supporting it, one academic wrote that

I feel the offering of advice and encouragement is the most influential role that mentors fulfil within the Faculty at present. It indicates a caring attitude and can be carried out inconspicuously and privately. It can have a profound effect on self-esteem. (letter, engineer, University)

The range of controversy about whether mentorship is (or should be) solely a formal procedural process, or whether it is additionally (or alternatively) a subconscious process which has a subcultural aspect, showed a greater polarity than that about role modelling. At one end of the spectrum, mentorship was seen as potentially structural for undergraduates but not for postgraduates:

The encouragement of appropriate students to take postgraduate study and to obtain scholarships is the limit of mentor activity at present. An internal proposal to provide a formal mentor structure for staff support of undergraduates is currently being considered . . . [but] . . . criteria inevitably limit flexibility. I would not support any formalism as applied to postgraduate selection. (letter, computer technology, Institute of Technology)

Yet it was precisely in relation to selection for higher degrees that most respondents argued for a criterion-based process and denied the existence of 'flexible' or subconscious processes. Some academics of both sexes did, however, accept the reality of the existence of a mentorship subculture. One academic commented that:

Mentors are most important in scientific academic life. Most crucial would be getting post-doctoral graduates into prestigious overseas laboratories and [the] finding of part-time or temporary appointments while waiting for an opening. Concealed functions include a variable amount of help given in experimental planning and report writing in both honours and postgraduate degrees. I think visibility is less of a problem than it used to be since some societies favour the giving of papers by younger participants. . . . It will sound facetious but women cannot go out and play squash with the boss. Even male colleagues recognise a certain pattern of squash playing prior to promotions. For squash, substitute various other social activities in which it would be unlikely for a Chairman to be seen with a young female lecturer. (letter, chemistry, female, University)

The male head of medical technology in another institution similarly writes of both socialization and prejudice in the mentor role with an insight and honest accuracy not characteristic of the majority:

The most important and influential mentor role is that which occurs during the ['internship or residency'] apprenticeship time when the new graduate is being educated and trained to comply with the social values, sex roles and professional attitudes of the persons in the work place. The extent of this varies from place to place. Certainly, it can override any previous emphasis, taught or observed in the study course, in which the attitudes of equality are fostered. Naturally, it can be very difficult for the new graduate to overcome these 'built-in' prejudices which must be learnt and obeyed for success in that particular work place. These prejudices could also extend to the withholding of scientific and technical knowledge from any women in that workplace. . . . This question presupposes that the mentor role is to be a consideration in dealing with students at both the undergraduate and postgraduate level. I consider that academics need to be made aware of this research, so that examination of their particular conscious emphases may become apparent. No written or structured policy is necessary. Additional education of those currently in senior positions in laboratories needs to be aimed at showing how the 'apprenticeship' scheme affects the new graduate. (letter, Institute of Technology)

We do not suggest whether this description is widely true or rarely true; merely that it is part of the actuality of higher education practice, often hidden by 'genesis amnesia'.

To summarize the main thrust of the subjective comment on and attitudes towards mentorship in the hundred or so group interviews with academic staff and in the written responses, we saw a much sharper polarity of views on this factor than on others. In the UQ WISTA survey institutions, we found that:

1 Some academics, including many Professors, Heads and Deans, rejected even the concept of mentorship as such, seeing the idea of any special help or encouragement to students as a negation of academic 'objectivity' and an indirect accusation of favouritism or discrimination.

2 Others saw mentorship solely in terms of the standard, procedural selection of students for progression to honours, higher degrees, etc., acknowledged its existence in formal terms, but rejected as outrageous any suggestion that this was in any way subjective.

3 The possibility of particular encouragement or discouragement of individual students within a cohort first objectively selected on academic merit, actually to help them to decide to progress, was also rejected. Objectivity was seen by this group as universal in their department and/or in their institution.

4 A small but significant number of academics, from male Professors to female tutors, accepted the existence of an uneven, necessarily subjective and informal system of mentorship in relation to progression to honours and postgraduate work, to industrial placement and to the informal but important sharing of scientific knowledge. This group saw the process as neither intentionally nor overtly discriminatory, but as one

of instinctive identification and empathy. Its adherents tended to believe that more open discussion of the concept and the processes would improve the mentorship process in their institution.

5 The possibility of unconscious sex-bias because of same-sex empathy or opposite-sex antipathy was generally rejected. Some academics still did not believe informal mentorship, where it existed, to be sex-biased; others clearly did.

6 There was marked conceptual confusion on the meaning and characteristics of mentorship within the academic groups attending the group interviews in each of the ten institutions. The published debate about this process in the worlds of business and management, and in the fields of training and supervision, does not appear to have reached the higher education sector in sufficient measure to make an impact. There was little evidence of any general institutional level of knowledge or awareness of the issue before the UQ WISTA research team introduced the discussion on this topic.

References

BERNARD, J. (1964) *Academic Women*, Pennsylvania State University Press.

CERCLE DES FEMMES INGENIEURS (1982) *Ingénieur au Féminin*, Paris, Cahiers de CEFI.

COLE, J.R. (1981) 'Women in science', *American Scientist*, July/August, pp. 385–91.

COLLINS, E.G.C. and SCOTT, P. (1978) 'Everyone who makes it has a mentor', *Harvard Business Review*, 56 (4), July–August, pp. 89–101.

COLLINS, N. (1983) *Professional Women and their Mentors*, Eaglewood Cliffs, NJ, Prentice Hall.

COOK, M.F. (1979) 'Is the mentor relationship primarily a male experience?', *Personnel Administrator*, 24 (11), pp. 82–6.

DALOZ, L.A. (1986) *Effective Teaching and Mentoring*, San Francisco, Jossey Bass.

ERKUT, S. and MOKROS, J. (1984) 'Professors as models and mentors for college students', *American Educational Research Journal*, 21 (2), pp. 399–417.

FITT, L.W. and NEWTON, D.A. (1981) 'When the mentor is a man and the protégé is a woman', *Harvard Business Review*, 59 (2), pp. 56–60.

FRIEDL, E. (1975) *Women and Men: An Anthropologists' View*, New York, Holt, Rinehart and Winston.

GILES, H.W. and ENDSLEY, R.C. (1988) 'Early career development among child and family development professionals: the role of professor and peer relationships', *Family Relations*, 1988, 37, pp. 470–6.

GOLDSTEIN, E. (1978) 'Effect of Samesex & Crossex Role Models on the Subsequent academic Productivity of Scholars,' in *America Psychologist*. May 34 (5), pp. 407–41.

HABER, L. (1979) *Women Pioneers of Science*, San Diego, Calif., Harcourt Brace Jovanovich.

HENDERSON, D.W. (1985) 'Enlightened mentoring: a characteristic of public management professionalism', *Public Administration Review*, November/ December, pp. 857–63.

HURLEY, DAN (1988) 'The mentor mystique', *Psychology Today*, May, pp. 41–3.

INTERNATIONAL LABOUR OFFICE (1980) *Women's Participation in the Economic Activity of the World*, Geneva, ILO.

KANTER, R.M. (1977) *Men and Women of the Corporation*, New York, Basic Books.

KOBLITZ, A.H. (1984) 'Sofia Kovalevskaia and the mathematical community', *The Mathematical Intelligencer*, 6 (1), pp. 20–9.

KOBLITZ, A.H. (1983) *A Convergence of Lives: Sofia Kovalevskaia*, Birkhauser.

KRAM, K. (1983) 'Phases of the mentor relationship', *Academy of Management Journal*, 26, pp. 608–25.

KRAM, K. and ISABELLA, L. (1985) 'Mentoring alternatives: the role of peer relationships in career development', *Academy of Management Journal*, 28, pp. 110–32.

LEBOLD, W., JAGACINSKI, C. and SHELL, K. (1983) *National Engineering Career Development Study*, Indiana, Purdue University.

LEVINSON, D. (1978) *The Seasons of a Man's Life*, New York, Alfred A. Knopf.

MISSIRIAN, A. (1982) *The Corporate Connection: Why Executive Women need Mentors to Reach the Top*, Eaglewood Cliffs, NJ, Prentice-Hall.

RILEY, S. and WRENCH, D. (1985) 'Mentoring among women lawyers', *Journal of Applied Social Psychology*, 15 (4), pp. 374–86.

ROCHE, G. (1979) 'Much ado about mentors', *Harvard Business Review*, 57, January–February, pp. 14–28.

ROSSITER, M.W. (1984) *Women Scientists in America: Struggles and Strategies to 1940*, Baltimore, John Hopkins University Press.

SHAPIRO, E.C., HASELTINE, E.P. and ROWE, M.P. (1978) 'Moving up: role models, mentors and the patron system', *Sloan Management Review*, 19 (3), pp. 51–8.

SHOCKLEY, P. and STALEY, C. (1980) 'Women in Management Training Programmes: what they think about Key Issues, in *Public Personnel Management Journal*, 9 (3), pp. 214–224.

SPEIZER, J.J. (1981) 'Role models, mentors and sponsors: the elusive concept', *Signs*, Summer, pp. 692–712.

STRAUSS, M.J.B. (1978) 'Wanted: More Women in Science', in *The American Biology Teacher*, March, pp. 181–189.

SULLEROT, E. (1973) *Les Françaises au Travail*, Paris, Hachette.

UNESCO (1987) *Survey on the Representation of Women in Higher Education Research*, Paris.

VERTZ, L. (1985) 'Women, occupational advancement and mentoring: an analysis of one public organisation', *Public Administration Review*, May/June, pp. 415–23.

WHITE, M. (1970) 'Psychological and social barriers to women in science', *Science*, 170, pp. 413–16.

WILSON, B. and BYRNE, E. (1987) *Women in the University: A Policy Report*, St. Lucia, The University of Queensland, Press.

WRIGHTSMAN, L.S. (1981) 'Research methodologies for assessing mentoring', paper presented to American Psychological Association (ERIC: 209 339).

YODER, J., ADAMS, J., GROVE, S. and PRIEST, R. (1982) 'Mentors: a debt due from present to future generations', paper presented to the *Annual Convention of the American Psychological Convention*, Washington, DC, 23–7 August.

Chapter 6

The Critical Filters:
Further Cluster Factors

'I was very much interested in the message you sent me about the use of mathematics . . . I have hitherto generally looked upon it as a delightful study, but one which very few people cared about. Now I begin to see that it is rather a source of true pleasure.' (Student to Emily Davies, founder of Girton College, Cambridge, 4 March 1870 [Stephen, 1927, p. 231])

Attitudes and mentorship have been influential from the start, and this quotation could have been taken from one of today's students. Heads and Deans of higher education Schools of scientific and technological disciplines have tended to wash their hands of the attitudinal issues and of factors in higher education, on the grounds that it is all the fault of the schools (or parents, or employers, or . . .). While our earlier argument is that this is specious, it is undoubtedly true that there are factors (clusters of factors) which operate at the schooling level and in the transition years.

The Institutional Ecology of Schools

In chapter 3, we postulated that the institutional ecology of education consisted of a number of generic elements — discourse, role modelling and mentorship, image and structure and content of discipline. Before we return to this in the final chapter, we now look at the cluster of factors at school level which create an institutional ecology (and within school physics, chemistry and maths, an ecological niche). Our 'time-lag' theory in chapter 3 is based on an assessment that boys and girls respectively still live through a different, gender-based experience in the school years, and therefore come to higher education disciplines which are non-traditional for their sex as into a different ecological niche. And we hypothesize that a girl coming from an all-girls' schools to a male-dominated science or technological subject has a greater ecological mismatch and therefore needs a longer time-lag and support in her first year, than a boy from an all-boys' or mixed school coming to a male-dominated higher education discipline. This chapter therefore looks at clusters of factors which are influential in upper secondary education and in the transition from school to higher education.

From a Dyadic Approach to Cluster-factor Policy

Moving to a more holistic approach — dealing with a problem as a whole and not with one or two factors only — is important if policy initiatives are to give a good return for investment. Most of the 1970s' research which looked at girls and science has been dyadic: looking at the interaction of two factors only on each other (the effect of role modelling on careers guidance; the effect of vocational motivation on curricular choice). And some of this research does not even distinguish between one-way related factors on the one hand (innate intellect affects mathematical performance but improved mathematical achievement does not affect innate intellect), and two-way factors on the other (teacher expectations of girls in maths affects their motivation and achievement, positively or negatively, which further influences teacher expectations, which further affects girls' motivation and achievement). In turn, policymakers have tended to centre specific affirmative action policies on one or two factors only: the use of role models, or improved marketing at careers exhibitions.

If we wish to move towards achieving a critical mass of female enrolments in the economically important scientific and technological disciplines and trades, in such a way as to normalize women's participation in them, we need to attack the problem through a cluster approach. Cluster 3 illustrates one group of factors which need to be tackled together if we are to achieve critical mass. That is to say, merely using more female role models will not work unless we also provide both gender-neutral and interchangeable role models in educational books and texts. Similarly, we need actively to remove sex-labels from disciplines and subjects if they are to be seen as 'role model normal' (see cluster 3).

Thus, both girls and boys need to see school subjects and training areas as gender-neutral, which is unlikely to be achieved until we stop

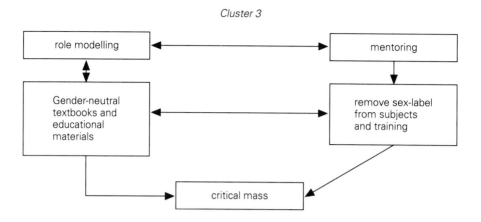

Cluster 3

transmitting sexist and stereotypic messages about the 'maleness' of medicine, mining, management, maths, etc. in educational materials. Same-sex role modelling is most effective through the print and visual media. But, at the same time, positive mentoring of able girls to help them to achieve equally in maths, science and technical crafts cannot be a same-sex process because we do not yet have a critical mass of women teachers in these areas. Male teachers and lecturers need, therefore, to take responsibility not only actively to help women students to see achievement as normal for their sex, but also actively to teach men students that women are equally capable and have an equal right to scarce places in science and technology.

There will, meanwhile, continue to be girls who come out of a gender-biased schooling with the 'wrong' maths; without technical hands-on experience; or lacking adequate spatial development because they have been excluded from practical technical crafts. We therefore need policies from second-chance re-education and 'topping-up' courses in applied maths and technical skills to be available in order to help girls and women to reach the same levels of prerequisite knowledge: bridging courses. Cluster 4 suggests a group of related factors which, again, need to be tackled together.

In the event, the total grant and staffing resources for the UQ WISTA project enabled us to look in depth at some, but not all, clusters of the factors listed on one axis of our theoretical framework. In this work and in monographs planned to follow, we deal with role modelling, mentorship, attitudes, image, mathematics as a critical filter and single-sex schooling versus coeducation. A follow-up three-year grant (1991–3) has been obtained from the Australian Research Council to look at the interaction of prerequisites, curricular choices and career education and career guidance.

Cluster 4

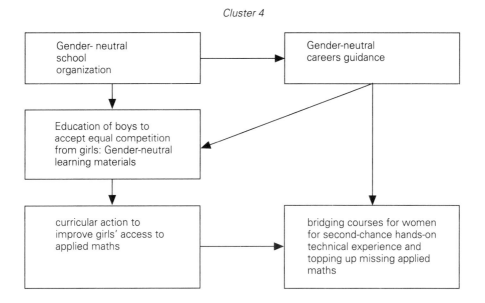

Maths as a Critical Filter

We circulated a discussion paper on maths as a critical filter to the Deans, Professors and Heads of (higher education) Schools who took part in the ten-institution survey. We recorded in an earlier study of women and engineering (Byrne, 1985) that Heads of departments in tertiary institutions who responded to the enquiry cited inadequate preparation in maths as one of the major critical filters which prevented girls from entering physics and engineering courses, or which caused their early drop-out. Returns from Monash, Newcastle and Sydney Universities and the University of New South Wales, in particular, all spoke of either inadequate school preparation, or of the difficulty which women students experienced with first-year physics and maths.

We therefore raised the filter effect of maths in the 1985 and 1986 rounds of group interviews with Deans, Professors and Heads of Schools in the ten WISTA survey institutions as well as circulating a discussion paper. However, academic leaders of disciplines such as physics, engineering, mining and metallurgy commented in almost all institutions that the problem was less that girls do not do maths, than that girls did a more limited maths or 'the wrong maths' and were noticeably lacking in the kind of applied maths needed for physics, engineering and some technology. There was, however, considerable variation between staff in different institutions in their estimate of the scale of this problem.

This diagnosis is not, of course, new. Benbow and Stanley (1982) have reported on their late 1970s follow-up of the American Study of Mathematically Precocious Youth (SMPY) conducted from 1971 to 1974, with a final sample of 2,188 students as college 'freshmen' of whom 57 per cent were male. They found, *inter alia*, that not only did SMPY males take significantly more semesters of high-school maths than SMPY females, and in a significantly earlier grade than their female peers, but that sex differences emerged in which elements of maths were taken at the upper levels. The sex difference was apparently minimal up to trigonometry,

> But then approximately 10 per cent more boys than girls took college algebra and analytic geometry . . . with respect to calculus, approximately two thirds of SMPY boys took at least one calculus course, compared to 40 per cent of the girls . . . We conclude that the gender difference in taking calculus in high school was important. (Benbow and Stanley, 1982, p. 604)

The researchers point out that 'because SMPY girls took their maths later than SMPY boys, they had less time to do calculus and other advanced maths courses in high school (*ibid.*, p. 608). 'Among the SMPY group, almost twice as many boys as girls took calculus in high school.' (*ibid.*, p. 618).

In Fennema and Carpenter's (1981) review of the American National Assessment of Educational Progress (based on 70,000 schoolchildren aged 9, 13 and 17 years), they found that 'only about two-thirds as many females as males reported they had taken either trigonometry or precalculus/calculus', although relatively few of either sex reported taking these courses (Fennema and Carpenter, 1981, p. 554). That is, there is a critical filter process within mathematics, as well as a filtering of girls out of access to Grade 12 maths. Why?

Early theorists attempted to argue that the sex differences in maths performance (which are irrefutable) were due to universal (innate) female incapacity, and if one held this view there would, of course, be no case for attempting a remedy. Among significant studies which reject this genetic theory, the reports commissioned by the American National Institute of Education (NIE) to study maths avoidance in female students and to advise on policy changes challenge the 'female incapacity' theory. (See Sherman and Fennema, 1977; Fox, 1977).

Others have written of 'maths anxiety' (notably Tobias, 1978); Tobias and Weissbrod (1980) review maths-anxiety intervention programmes with some concern that 'practice is moving ahead of theory and experimental research. Viewed negatively, this could produce careless and irresponsible "maths cures" ' (Tobias and Weissbrod, 1980, p. 68). In either event, this blaming-the-victim approach implies a policy of intervention programmes to remove the negative attitudes, unless we regard Frank Besag's latest work at Wisconsin as transferable and delete maths anxiety as a female cause altogether: Besag and Wahl found no sex differences on maths anxiety or self-esteem in a sample of some 7,500 students (Holden, 1987).

Still others blame not the students, but schoolteacher attitudes and practices. That teachers do, in fact (whether consciously or not), treat boys and girls differently in classroom interaction is well documented. In Becker's (1981) study of geometry teachers, teacher-initiated processes were weighted in favour of boys, who received more time, encouragement, attention and reinforcement. Brophy and Bood's earlier (1970) study confirms that boys receive more feedback and evaluative comment 'both absolutely and relatively' and sees the teachers' different expectations of boys and girls as self-fulfilling prophecies. (Brophy and Bood, 1970).

The image of maths is cited by some as the reason for the sex difference in maths results, either in terms of its perceived usefulness vocationally (Armstrong and Price, 1982) or its perceived sex-appropriateness (Leder, 1976; Armstrong and Price, 1982). Yet others argue that the whole issue centres not on female incapacity or inferiority, but on a different female approach to spatial development.

The Queensland UQ WISTA research team accordingly obtained from the boards of secondary school studies (or equivalent) in each Australian state, (a) detailed statistics for secondary enrolments (not achievements) in Grade 12 subjects, including maths, for 1985; (b) a detailed breakdown of the content of the different mathematics courses in each state; and (c) the status of each maths course in the light of its content, for tertiary entrance. The data support the contention that the filter effect is not seen only in overall female maths enrolments, but also in relation to precisely those units or courses which contain the calculus, matrices, and geometric or algebra work, etc. which the UQ WISTA Deans and Heads of Schools identified as missing in the preparation of more women students than men.

In Queensland, in the survey years of 1985 and 1986, girls comprised 43 per cent of maths I candidates, but only 27 per cent of those taking maths II. It should be noted that maths I includes two calculus units, probability and statistics. Maths II includes matrices, vectors, mechanics and a third advanced calculus unit. Queensland ASAT records show maths II students (both sexes) to be consistently more able than maths I students. In New South Wales, the parallel figures were 54 per cent female enrolment in two-unit maths, 40 per cent in three-unit maths and 29 per cent in four-unit maths. Two-unit maths is designed as a general course and is only suitable for tertiary maths being taken as a minor discipline; three-unit maths is needed for tertiary maths being taken as a major, or for tertiary physics or engineering; four-unit maths is of a higher level than three and tests for a 'high degree of understanding of algebra and calculus'.

In Victoria, the differentiation is less sharp. Girls formed 53 per cent of general maths candidates, 33 per cent of pure maths A and 29 per cent of applied maths B. Maths A (pure) covers mensuration, probability, functions and calculus; maths B (applied) involves functions, calculus, linear algebra, vectors, complex number and analytic geometry. In South Australia, interestingly, 52 per cent of general maths, 33 per cent of maths I and 33 per cent of maths II candidates were girls. Maths IS (equals one maths subject only) is an alternative to maths I and II and is not recommended as a pre-tertiary subject. Maths I and II are both seen as necessary for tertiary physics, engineering or tertiary maths. They work as a double major at Grade 12 and are complementary. Unlike the New South Wales three-unit and four-unit maths, which are different in level and standard, the South Australian maths I and II are complementary and of the same standard.

In Western Australia, the pattern is similar to South Australia: female enrolment of 59 per cent in maths IV, 52 per cent in maths I and 32 per cent in maths II and III. Maths IV is not designed for tertiary entrance. Maths I is meant to provide for general tertiary entrance and includes algebra, trigonometry and statistics but excludes calculus. It is less advanced than II and III. Maths II and III are a double major, are complementary and include algebra, trigonometry, analytical geometry, statistics and calculus.

As part of the follow-up research project into curricular choice, prerequisites and career education (the SHEP-APIST Project), we have updated the figures for Grade 12 to 1990. The differential patterns are replicated.

The Australian secondary maths data support the concern of Deans and Heads of Schools, and the findings of earlier research (including major studies not cited here for reasons of space), that the filter effect operates as much within mathematics in secondary education as between maths and other subjects. While this filter effect continues, the answer to it lies not in blaming the schools for Pontius Pilate hand-washing, but in tertiary-based remediation or topping-up programmes.

Special intervention programmes designed to top up missing maths, physics and technical skills in the USA, the UK, Sweden, Denmark and the former West Germany, and which have targeted special groups at the post-schooling stage, have proved to have extremely effective and relatively swift returns for investment. In one American review of over 300 projects to increase the number and status of women in science, maths and engineering, a significant number were located in tertiary and higher education institutions — funded jointly by federal aid and from the institutions' own funds (Aldrich and Hall, 1980). The (West) German schemes, which operate across all Länder and which have increased women's recruitment to scientific and technical training by very significant proportions, are also targeted at the late adolescent and young adult years and carry substantial federal (systematic) funding.

It is not of course argued here that we should not work at long-term programmes of improved mathematics education in schools, but that this — if achievable — will not affect tertiary recruitment for many years and that we cannot wait to produce our missing tertiary mathematicians, physicists and engineers. Concurrently with a long-term programme to attack the schooling issues, we need a mathematics remediation programme which will target, in particular, the female school-leavers and young women who the UQ WISTA data show as having missed out on those particular elements of maths needed for physics, engineering and technological disciplines. This would also apply, of course, to any male school-leavers who have suffered the critical-filter effect through poor curricular or vocational guidance.

In our discussion paper on maths as a critical filter, academic staff were asked, where relevant, how they saw the role of higher education institutions in providing for bridging courses, for topping-up courses, or for late entry to allow for the study of missing elements in maths in a bridging year in the higher education institution. Some considered that prerequisites were too strict and that for some sciences in particular there was a historic inheritance of expectation in advanced maths which the content of courses did not always justify. The filter process referred to above was seen by some as continuing at the tertiary level. This was characteristic of the comments we received:

Another barrier at the University level is the presence in many Universities of two strands of first year mathematics, an ordinary and a higher one. Typically, entry to the higher demands 4 unit maths for entry. Girls (and others) who fail to meet this requirement are *forever* excluded from honours and higher degrees. (lecturer, maths, University)

We raised specific issues on whether higher education had a responsibility to deal with the perceived 'inadequate maths' problem, and if so, how?

Opinions were divided and academic staff adopted three main positions:

1   Some (a significant minority) felt the problem was a schooling one; that it was not the task of Universities and Institutes to take on any remediation of lower-level work; and that the policy issue involved was not one in which higher education had a role.

2   Others (rather more) considered the matter urgent and critical if the problems of female under-recruitment to certain areas of science and technology were to be solved. They regarded the urgent systemic provision of bridging or topping-up courses or of special maths remediation programmes as a priority policy issue. But they tended to see this as the task of tertiary colleges and did not wish to see higher education resources devoted to this.

3   A third view was expressed equally frequently. These staff adopted the main stance outlined in the second opinion above, but considered it essential that those programmes aimed at topping up the kind of work needed for higher education physics, engineering, applied maths, etc. should be taught by higher education staffs in their own institutions. They either did not have (rightly or wrongly) confidence in the technical college system as a whole to teach the 'right' elements at the appropriate level, or they considered the students would benefit from the more integrated approach of remediation programmes specifically designed as pre-physics, pre-engineering, etc.

Within the third group, representatives of several disciplines other than maths were confident that catching up was not impossible:

The aim of maths remediation should not be primarily to provide missing elements but to improve attitudes and motivation towards the subject and to improve general mathematical manipulative skills through practice . . . The missing elements can readily be picked up as required along the way. Such remediation should be carried out within our institutions, and should be funded and credited. It would be a cost-effective investment. (Head of chemistry, Institute)

All who supported the higher education role in remediation or topping up or strengthening applied maths were adamant that this would only be possible with specific additional federal funding for it.

The British Cockcroft Committee on mathematics teaching in schools also saw it as essential that higher education institutions played a more major role in the inservice education of schoolteachers. The Committee, however, recognized that time spent on this was seen by academic staff as being 'to the detriment of their academic careers, because those responsible for making appointments do not value experience gained during inservice work as highly as evidence of published work. If this is the case, we regret it' (Committee of Inquiry into Teaching of Mathematics, para. 742). The Committee recognized this as a sharper dilemma in relation to promotions, but recommended an extension of consultancy work in inservice education not only because of its benefit to schools; it 'also enables those who work in training institutions to gain up-to-date and first hand knowledge of the work that is going on in primary and secondary classrooms' (*ibid.*, para. 743). Such a policy would also have implications for higher education staffing policy in general.

One of the reasons why mathematics is not taken equally by girls is its image and the male peer attitudes towards this. Again, it must be stressed that dealing with maths alone without dealing with related factors, is ineffective. Maths, image, positive mentorship and content of courses are all interrelated in a two-way influential impact.

Image, Attitudes and Curricular Choice

We also circulated a discussion paper on the image of science to the Deans, Professors and Heads of Schools in our survey institutions. In the paper we identified three main aspects of the image of disciplines which have emerged as critical:

1   Ascribed masculinity or femininity of disciplines. Within this, boys subdivide their attitudes; some disciplines are seen by males as beyond girls' capacity (girls 'can't' do maths or physics) and others carry a label of unsuitability (girls 'shouldn't' do geology, surveying or engineering).
2   Image of social irresponsibility or social unresponsiveness of disciplines. Disciplines seen as objective, detached or destructive switch off girls and 'androgynous' boys.

3   Thirdly, different sciences and technologies carry labels of difficulty or ease, and of vocational usefulness (the latter are therefore worth pursuing even if difficult), or of free-floating non-vocational interest.

Different researchers have related each of these aspects to sex-differentiated patterns of enrolment, retention and progression, and in practice it is not possible easily to separate them out because of their interreactions.

In response to the image discussion paper, the 'social' image of maths was seen as possibly more detrimental than its masculine attribution by boys. Characteristic of this angle is the following comment from one leading University mathematician who saw maths as having a major image problem; it was seen as male, lacking a social responsibility image, and anachronistic:

As to its social responsibility image, almost all applications of maths offered in both schools and Universities are 'male' (e.g. the speed of projectiles and the like). Yet precisely the same maths that underlies these [the calculus] is equally applicable in more curative and therapeutic applications that might appeal more to girls. For example, in the modelling of the spread of epidemics, or population growth of interacting species, or the dissipation time of drugs in the body. Something could be done immediately here. (lecturer, male, maths, University)

Engineering, physics and chemistry emerged as the disciplines most seen as having an image problem:

Chemistry has a major image problem. It is related to its social responsibility, which is perceived to be more important by girls than boys. Chemistry compared with biology is seen to be difficult, unimportant and uninteresting, though less so than physics. At this stage, still 'male' on a three point scale. (Head of chemistry, Institute)

Yes, physics has an image problem. No doubt the connection between physics and nuclear bombs and war technology has some effect . . . The image has male attribution since males are naturally more aggressive and in general do not mind the war technology image . . . The media [reinforces], in some way it is the *correct* image. Physics has enormous potential for good or evil and we would be foolish to ignore that the evil part creates many jobs for physicists . . . Physics has to play the earlier role of classics. Without some physics knowledge and understanding, a person in the modern world is uneducated . . . [physics] will have a dramatic effect on our standard of living ten or fifty years hence. Physics with its precise use of language disciplines the mind. This is the positive image (Professor and Head of physics, University)

Yes, mechanical engineering has a major image problem . . . It is confused with mechanical *trades* which are seen as often involving dirty work in unpleasant circumstances and conditions . . . The image is most strongly transmitted through the media (principal lecturer, male, Institute)

A female lecturer from a different Institute echoed this:

There is a problem in building a clear and positive image of engineering; the term *engineer* is used to describe positions ranging from domestic engineer to sound engineer, from locomotive engineer to professional engineer . . . from unskilled labour to high level research . . . the male domination is not perceived in a positive way by the general public. It seems to have acquired all the negative elements of football, motor racing and Big Brother. (lecturer, engineering, female, Institute)

The Maleness of Science

Many researchers have written of the perceived maleness of science; some of a patriarchal structure and bias in content, others of a male attribution. Arnold Pacey, for example, regards technology ('the application of scientific and other knowledge to practical tasks by ordered systems that involve people and organisations, living things and machines' [Pacey, 1983, p. 61]) as not only value-loaded but as focussing on ranges of activities traditionally interesting to men but excluding the work of women, and sees a need to 'challenge and counteract the male values built into technology' (*ibid.*, p. 107). Albury and Schwartz also view science as reflecting 'the prevailing world view of the male researchers of woman's inequality' (Albury and Schwartz, 1982, p. 89). Broca's nineteenth-century work on brain-weights 'proving' that womens' brains were lighter, now proves be highly suspect but his view prevailed for fifty years. Albury and Schwart see the labelling of physics as a boys' subject as an 'effective device for keeping girls confined to the humanities and the arts' (*ibid.*, pp. 87–90). Bowling and Martin (1985) see the masculinity of science as based on its dominant assumptions of competition and hierarchy as well as in the choice of (and exclusion of) topics for study. The scientific disciplines, they argue, are constructed as more process- and system-oriented than flexible and shifting like human behaviour. But they do not define science precisely, and the argument is weakened when one contrasts different sciences whose construction varies between disciplines.

Others see the maleness of science as a transmitted media process which does not do justice to the actual social orientation and human variance of many aspects of scientific research. Rosslyn Ives (1984) also attributes the perceived maleness of science in Australia to the transmission of ideas about the world and conveyed to students by two media: science textbooks and science educators (who in turn learned from books and other educators). In an examination of secondary science textbooks in general science, biology, chemistry and physics in 1984, males were represented in general science and chemistry books in a ratio (to females) of 5:1; in physics books by 8.6:1; and even in biology by 3:1. Authors also used predominantly male language (he, men, his, boys . . .) in examples in the texts (Ives, 1984). There are many other such studies from overseas research.

We are concerned less here, however, with the intrinsic masculinity (or otherwise) of different sciences than with the ascription of maleness in different degrees to different disciplines. For example, Weinreich-Haste's studies with English schoolchildren found that both sexes rate physics, maths and chemistry as more masculine (four and five on a six-point scale), although boys rated all three as proportionately more male than did girls. Subjects rated as scientific were also perceived as 'masculine, hard, complex, based on thinking rather than feeling'. Girls saw science as difficult, 'and they also saw complicated and difficult things as masculine' (Weinreich-Haste, 1981, p. 221).

Ebbutt moves the issue nearer the classroom. His follow-up research examined the perceptions of both boys and girls as to whether there was 'boys' science' and 'girls' science' and if so, what they were. Both sexes, for example, saw elements like metals, batteries and circuits as being for boys, and girls saw chemicals, crystals and tie dye for girls (Ebbutt, 1981). While the origins of this male:female imaging may well lie in the prevailing social stereotypes, researchers argue that science teachers reinforce the image rather than counteracting it.

In the British Girls in Science and Technology Project, the male 'territoriality' of some disciplines rather than others placed a stronger male label on physics than on other school sciences; curriculum materials were seen to be heavily sex-biased, and boys held strongly sex-stereotyped views against girls' active interest in aspects of science which the boys saw as masculine (Whyte, 1986; Kelly *et al.*, 1983).

Peer attitudes are crucial in adolescence and in young adulthood. In our survey, we circulated a discussion paper on male and female attitudes as a barrier, relating attitudes and image. We know that our acquired attitudes are built up from our experiences and from the way in which we interpret these. They derive from 'evidence' presented to us from which we construct what we see as 'reality'. Head describes an attitude in the context of science as an 'underlying generalised construct' (Head, 1984). Certainly, recent research in the areas of the psychology of sex differences, in vocational motivation and aspiration, and in the achievement of adolescents, confirms this. That is, the influence of our attitudes and of other people's attitudes to us does underlie most of our decision-making. From this underlying influence, we generalize to see certain behaviour or goals as 'normal' for our sex, or our ability, or our social background. Adolescents are particularly unwilling to indulge in behaviour not seen as appropriate for their sex or for their age or within their peer group. Hence the labelling of disciplines as sex-normal or gender-neutral or sex-abnormal becomes a major barrier to 'cross-sex' choices. Researchers have attributed up to 25 per cent of variance in science achievement to how students feel towards what they are studying, the learning environment and their self-concept (Bloom, 1976). Earlier research attributes a further 25 per cent to the quality and type of instruction a student receives in terms of cues, reinforcement and encouragement to participate (Dollard and Miller, 1950).

Hostile male attitudes have been found by researchers at primary, secondary and tertiary levels. A Sydney study of 1,119 girls and 1,158 boys in the 1970s looked at the attitudes of 9–13 year-olds. Among the assertions drawn from the children's own sayings, and then empirically tested, were that:

- boys are better at maths and science than girls
- boys are cleverer than girls
- girls would not make good engineers
- boys make better leaders

In fact, 54 per cent of boys but only 5 per cent of girls thought boys were cleverer. Three quarters of the boys from independent schools and half of the boys from state schools thought that girls would not make engineers, and were weak and silly. Overall, 77 per cent of boys (but only 14 per cent of girls) thought boys make better leaders (Phillips, 1975). This clearly has implications for the learning environment of the ecological niche of classrooms and lecture halls.

Attitudes can operate adversely at tertiary level also. A Danish review of special efforts to increase women's enrolment in engineering courses resulted in higher female drop-out rates even after a significant initial increase. One reason given is that women students 'are not taken seriously although they, to start with, have better marks [grades] than the male student on average. In spite of that they are often not regarded as sufficiently skilled technically to study at the place [technical University]', (Due-Billing and Bruvik-Hansen, 1983). The limited Australian evidence is conflicting on this, male academic staff recording an allegedly supportive attitude to women students, and women students reporting, as might be expected, no problems in some disciplines, but male mockery and harassment in others. In an American study, Clark and Abron-Robinson (1975) report a variety of perceptions by peers and lecturing staff of female students' capacity in engineering, including hostility by male Professors towards women undergraduates. Later American studies, however, appear to reflect some changes in the social climate since the mid-1970s, recording that minority women students tend to be more highly qualified and motivated, and therefore (implicitly) supported. Pressure from male peer students is still seen as more influential than adverse attitudes by male staff in Europe and in Australia.

A University lecturer in the UQ WISTA survey commented that:

> When I asked my student daughter to contact a woman lecturer at the Engineering Faculty of [X] Institute of Technology, she refused point blank because of the reaction of the male students during a previous visit. I would describe her as having more than average self confidence and ability to respond to such behaviour. I think only a minority of students actually live up to the coarse, beerswilling image, but it may be a significant factor in discouraging women. (lecturer, engineering, University)

It would be possible, of course, to write off widespread reporting of adverse male attitudes as subjective and anecdotal, despite a growing body of serious research, or to see it as only a problem in schooling. Reports from students in tertiary institutions, however, from counselling staff and from lecturing staff concerned about female underachievement or 'channelling' into limited options, suggest that there is significant replication at the tertiary level of an early ingrained male hostility to females competing in areas seen as territorially male. Males are also widely reported in research and in Australian studies of the status of women in tertiary institutions as having more traditional attitudes to women's long-term role outside the home than females have.

The Social Image of Science

There is a growing literature on the extent to which the way that children and school students may see science as a social process, and its role in society, may influence their decisions to pursue or to reject and drop (a) science in general and (b) certain disciplines of science in particular. By the mid-1970s, a wide range of research had discussed the influence of students' attitudes to science (Ormerod and Duckworth, 1975) and, in particular, sex differences in attitudes. And within the latter, the social implications of science have come to emerge as more influential than they were considered a decade ago.

Ormerod tested the Brunel Attitude Scale to science in 1969–70 on 261 boys and 264 girls drawn from a wider sample taken from seventeen British schools matched for type of school and for single-sex/coeducational classes. The attitude scale distinguished subject preference, and social attitudes to science and the perceived social responsibility of science. He concludes that his data showed a strong significance between high social scores (i.e. seeing science as socially responsible) and later choice of science in the case of girls, but, in his sample, a low correlation in the case of boys. This 'social factor' had emerged strongly by the third year of secondary education, which Ormerod rightly considers has implications for curriculum design (Ormerod, 1971). The research, though useful in accrediting the issue as an issue, has some weaknesses. Ormerod only uses the term 'science' in this early research, not distinguishing between physics, chemistry and biology. The Brunel Science Attitude Scale uses 'science' simultaneously to describe a school subject ('Science is the most boring subject on the timetable', not distinguishing physics from biology, for instance) and a whole area of life ('With the aid of science, I look forward to a brighter future', 'Science is destroying the beauties of nature').

Later research has subdivided the scientific disciplines more thoroughly. By the mid and late 1970s, Ormerod had worked with a number of researchers to test different angles of the attitudinal question. Ormerod developed the Brunel Subject Preference Grid (Ormerod, 1975) which he tested in both mixed and single-sex schools on 1,200 pupils aged 14 plus in the top 25 per cent of the ability range. He found not only that the social implications factor was much less evident with biology than with physics and chemistry, but that those with favourable attitudes to the social implications of science (i.e. regarding science as socially useful, relevant, helpful, exciting, etc.) were significantly more likely to choose physics and chemistry at 14 plus than those with unfavourable or indifferent attitudes (Ormerod *et al.*, 1979). Moreover, work by Bottomley and Ormerod using the Brunel SOCATT Grid found that the social implications factor would also override even dislike of teachers for girls, but the reverse was true for boys. That is, girls with a favourable attitude to the social aspects of science would still choose science even if they scored highly on dislike of the teacher. (The research did not, unfortunately, distinguish the sex of the teacher, and it is therefore difficult to relate this to the same-sex role-model issue [Ormerod, 1979].)

Further study of the social image of science leads back to sex-differentiated perceptions of different elements of science. (For example, boys are more often reported as seeing lasers as useful in war and defence, a negative view; girls more often in relation to their curative and therapeutic uses a positive view.)

A Danish study takes this issue of elements of science further in the context of a major longitudinal study of physics teaching in Danish upper secondary schools. Among other concerns, the researchers investigated students' attitudes towards syllabus topics in physics. One central question was 'What would you like to learn more about in physics?' While the sex differences are not as great as previous research would lead one to expect, boys are overall more interested in everyday technology and in rockets and space technology than girls are; girls are more interested in natural phenomena (wind and solar energy, lightning and thunder) than boys (Nielsen and Thomsen, 1985). This and other research into the elements of different sciences suggest a correlation between perceived traditionally male/female activities and levels of interest — which poses a dilemma for the construction of new curricula, for interest is, in turn, seen by other researchers as highly correlated with a discipline's perceived social responsibility.

Interest is also reinforced (or otherwise) by the media and by textbooks. Pratt (1981), in a review of American elementary school science books, found that four of those most frequently used in 1977 did not cover social problems at all. National Science Foundations materials had only slight social coverage. In a major world review of sexism and sex-role stereotyping in school texts and children's books, UNESCO found that even in countries like Norway with a long established anti-sexist and anti-stereotypic policy in education, 'Discrimination against girls in Norwegian textbooks is particularly noticeable in science textbook illustrations . . . pictures of girls/women are used when electric hairdryers and bathroom scales are to be shown' (Michel, 1986, p. 27).

In this study, it was found that in physics texts references were almost exclusively oriented to interests known to attract boys: electric trains, male sports, factories, industry, astronomy. Even books in the natural sciences were found to have a 'marked mechanistic dehumanization' (*ibid.*, p. 27). In middle-school science texts 'boys solve all problems and are good at do-it-yourself while girls are [shown as] incompetent' (*ibid.*, p. 28). The media replicate this image, but also tend to portray scientists and engineers with negative images. Albury and Schwartz see the coverage of science and technology in the national media in Britain as remarkably consistent — 'the work of scientists and technologists is a vaguely sinister, mysterious activity that ordinary people cannot understand' (Albury and Schwartz, 1982, p. 107).

American research does not wholly support the British data on attitudes of school students, however. An American study of the decline in science achievement in 9-, 13- and 17-year-olds since 1979 led to the National Assessment of Science in 1981–2. The study looked at the image of science defined as 'impressions or perceptions which are held by members of a group and are symbolic of basic attitudes and orientations', or, in Jungian terms, 'deposits of accumulated experience'. The main focus was to identify the current images of science in the USA and to check for variations by sex, race and geographic location (Hueftle *et al.*, 1983). Fewer than half of the 9-year-olds in 1982 recognized that people write stories better than computers. More school students responded positively in 1982 than in 1979 on 'persistent societal problems' (pollution, world hunger, etc.), but there was no overall statistically significant sex difference between males and females. And while boys consistently reported more positive attitudes towards science in general than girls did, the differences were again only of the order of 3 per cent. Boys showed a 'statistically significant decline of 3.0 per cent of socio-scientific responsibility items' (*ibid.*, p. 25); girls were 13 per cent less certain than boys that they could have an impact on the problem of running out of resources.

In the feedback from the discussion paper and in the 1985 and 1986 rounds of UQ WISTA group interviews, engineers most of all tended to see their disciplines as having a major problem of public and educational image — that is, both students and teachers underestimated the social responsibility and human orientation of different forms of engineering, and overestimated its 'oily-machine oriented anachronistic image'. Despite the contrary evidence from research into schooling, few physicists, however, saw problems of image in their discipline. Geologists reported variously on conflicting images: attractive to women if presented as a tidy science, negative to women if presented as a rough outback discipline. In the written replies, image emerged on the whole as an underestimated and oversimplified issue, except for engineering.

In terms of remediation policies, our survey participants were much more inclined to blame the written and electronic media, and schools or parents, for their unfavourable image. The idea of altering content, bias, focus and marketing in higher education as part of its ecological environment, occurred only to the occasional isolated physicist, chemist or mining engineer.

Single-Sex or Coeducation?

There is no issue in which the Snark Syndrome is more evident and the Snark effect more influential than on the single-sex versus coeducation issue. We raised this in the group interviews in 1985 and 1986, and sent out a discussion paper (no. 6) on the question.

The debate about the relative advantages and disadvantages to girls and to boys respectively of being educated in single-sex or mixed schools, dates only from the 1970s, from mainly British evidence. In the popularization of the debate, assertions have become current which are not supported by much of the later, more scholarly and rigorous, research. The matter is considerably more complex than the current received wisdom suggests. There are three main ranges of issues which have been raised. The first relates to girls' relative choices of and achievement in maths, science and technical subjects in relation to girls in mixed schools and to boys in both kinds of schools. The second relates to the role of single-sex (post-school) colleges in helping women's achievement and progression in higher education. The third deals with the environment of single-sex and coeducation in terms of girls' confidence, self-esteem and vocational motivation, and with the apparently different ways in which teachers use language and discourse with girls and with boys respectively in mixed and in single-sex environments.

In the subsequent educational debate, a number of assertions have moved to the status of strengthened hypotheses; some, but not all, of these are significantly supported by subsequent research:

Hypothesis one: more girls choose or succeed in maths, physics and chemistry in 16 plus exams and at Advanced Level (Grade 12) in single-sex than in mixed schools.

Hypothesis two: more girls will go on to higher or advanced tertiary education in maths, science and technology from single-sex than from mixed schools.

Hypothesis three: girls are more likely to acquire confidence and higher self-esteem in a girls' school than in a mixed school.

Hypothesis four: more girls will choose non-traditional vocationally oriented courses (engineering, mining, metallurgy, surveying) from single-sex schools or colleges; fewer will generally drop out once enrolled in a single-sex college from whichever type of school.

Hypothesis five: boys' domination of language and of teacher attention in the secondary years disadvantages girls in coeducational classrooms, discourages them to pursue 'male' subjects like physics, maths and the technical crafts, and reinforces traditional sex-role course choices.

There are several issues which have been raised in the decade since 1975, when Her Majesty's Inspectorate (HMI) in England and Wales published the first review of sex differences in mixed and single-sex schools since the Board of Education's 1923 report (Department of Education and Science [DES], 1975; Board of Education, 1923). The HMI report suggests that in its survey of 10 per cent of all state-maintained schools in England and Wales, 'girls are more likely to choose a science and boys a language in a single-sex school than they are in a mixed school' (DES, 1975, p. 12), but that for pre-vocational and practical courses, 'girls in single-sex schools do not enjoy as wide a variety of these courses as do their contemporaries of either sex in any other types of school' (*ibid.*, p. 14).

The first general point which must be made is that in England and Wales, in Australia, and in most European countries, the majority of single-sex schools are fee-paying, academically selective, private or independent, and middle-class, while most mixed schools are comprehensive (all-ability), state-maintained, and are weighted overall with more lower-middle-class and working-class children. Straight comparisons are thus invalid unless those data have been specifically controlled or adjusted to allow for

- a generally higher ability intake in the majority of single-sex schools which are academically selective, and
- different social class intakes between types of schools.

Wood and Ferguson (1974) have checked out the data for 100,000 pupils entering for the Ordinary Level (Grade 10 equivalent) examinations in Britain. They looked at single-sex and mixed schools across thirteen subjects and conclude that girls in girls' schools appear to have a slight advantage in most subjects; that girls' only schools produce higher rates of female passes in physics and chemistry than mixed schools do; and that when schools change from single-sex grammar to mixed comprehensive, the success rate of girls is reduced and that of boys is improved. It is not, however, clear whether they controlled for relative differences of intake.

Ormerod (1975) applied the Brunel Subject Preference Grid to 1,204 pupils (518 boys and 686 girls) in ten single-sex grammar, five mixed grammar and four comprehensive schools drawn from four contrasting regions of England. Overall, he found that single-sex educated girls 'have their preferences met by less satisfactory choices than do the boys . . . the main weakness (however) is with coeducated girls' (Ormerod, 1975, p. 265). His results on the Preference Grid lead him to conclude also that attitudes towards teachers are likely to play an important mediating role in subject preferences, and should be included as a factor when interpreting sex differences between types of school.

Steedman (1983) questions some of the earlier conclusions about achievement in British single-sex and mixed schools. With a research grant from the Equal Opportunities Commission in the UK, she reviewed the findings of the National Child Development Study (NCDS — a longitudinal study of over 14,000 people born in one week in March 1958). The data were re-examined to check out single-sex and mixed secondary schooling and, in summary, Steedman finds that 'most differences between the examination results in mixed and in single-sex schools are markedly reduced once differences in initial attainment and in home background have been allowed for' (Steedman, 1983, p. 1). In relation to science, the NCDS reworked data show that while girls perform less well than boys in chemistry overall, there is very little advantage in girls' schools over mixed schools in girl's chemistry achievements. Similarly, despite a 'very extreme' sex difference in physics enrolment and performance overall, girls' performance in relation to boys' is only marginally improved by being in a girls' school (*ibid.*, p. 34).

In this study, Steedman was able to adjust the raw data for differential ability intake between the types of schools, and (where appropriate) for social class. Sex differences in previously unadjusted scores showing slight advantages to single-sex schools in achieving four or more 'good' passes (per pupil), then diminished to minimal after this adjustment. Mostly, where girls in girls' schools retained a performance advantage this was in relation to 'high examination performance' (the high fliers). Steedman concludes that the small differences were 'not enough to suggest that single-sex schools (or classes) would remove the sex differences in science performance (nor that mixed classes caused them)' (*ibid.*).

A review of the available evidence over the 1970s (Bone, 1983), while including an overview of the examination success rate literature, raises wider issues. Bone's overall conclusion is that the research she reviewed found that the subject mixes taken by girls, their academic results and the 'responses of schools to their more personal needs' (Bone, 1983) have been more conditioned by the type of school (grammar selective, comprehensive all-ability, independent private) and its style (traditional or not) than by its single-sex or mixed status. However, girls do appear to be a little more likely to look favourably at 'male' curricular areas when educated with other girls than in mixed environments in adolescence, although Bone's review suggests that girls' schools are still not 'notably active' in encouraging departures from sex stereotypes (*ibid.*). Also, girls of very high ability in academically oriented schools were less likely everywhere to be as sex-stereotyped (*ibid.*). On the whole, Bone concludes girls in girls' schools do not generally do better in maths and physics than girls in mixed schools, but girls in girls' grammar schools do in fact do better. The single-sex environment does not of itself have a significant effect on academic performance; only when single-sex schools are also grammar schools is this so. Even then the advantage is statistically quite minor. At the more qualitative level, a first issue is that while girls' interests are closer to those of boys when in single-sex girls' schools, their choices are not necessarily so (*ibid.*, II 3.1 and 3.2).

Work at Chelsea College (now King's College), London, under Jan Harding's direction, has looked at entry and pass rates in both Nuffield and traditional externally examined science courses in the early 1970s. The project investigated sex differences, controlling both for single-sex and mixed schools and for type of school (grammar, comprehensive and independent). The results are interesting in that while the pattern of passes for some science subjects for some examining boards show an apparent advantage for girls in girls' schools, the sex differences in pass rates vary within a subject (e.g. chemistry), either with different boards or with different types of school (e.g. grammar, direct grant, comprehensive), apart from the sex of the school (Harding, 1979 and 1981). That is, there is not in fact a consistent difference between subjects (e.g. chemistry across all boards as distinct from physics across all boards), nor a constant finding when the sex status of a school is matched with the type of school. Harding later questions whether it is not teaching style and organizational style of the school, rather than its single-sex or mixed status, that is crucial (Harding, 1983). Ormerod and Duckworth's review of a range of research dealing with attitudes to science concludes that boys and girls do appear to have generally different learning styles and to respond differently to various teaching strategies and teacher behaviours (Ormerod and Duckworth, 1975).

A second area of controversy is about the learning environment. Research into the area of gender and language (what language is used, how adults talk to boys and to girls, how much attention they give to each sex, etc.) has suggested that (whether consciously or unconsciously), teachers of both sexes appear to treat boys and girls differently from each other in language, conversation and attention, and to treat girls differently when in mixed or girls' only classrooms. Spender's (1980) work on gender and language leads her to conclude that in single-sex groups females are more likely to use a cooperative form of dialogue and males a competitive one; when the two sexes are together, the male competitive mode wins. Spender cites research to support the view that women prefer a balance of talking and listening and are more reluctant to interrupt, and that girls in mixed classrooms are socialized into ceding to male dominance in answering teachers' questions. Hence girls do not acquire confidence in debate (Spender, 1980, p. 2). Spender's work spells out convincingly the importance of language in 'shaping our world' and in 'classifying and ordering the world: our means of manipulating reality', (*ibid.*, p. 2). If her arguments have substance, the different performance of girls in teacher–pupil interaction in single-sex and mixed classrooms is potentially significant in maths and science lessons.

However, the experiments in single-sex classes in mixed schools have, perhaps predictably, produced mixed results. While some single-sex experiments have produced temporary gains in girls' confidence and participation, both staff and girls are more often reported as accepting the need to change the much-reported male domination, aggression or mockery in mixed classes to a teaching and learning process which gives equal opportunity for both sexes to develop (Kelly, 1981; Smith, 1980; Rhydderch, 1984). One survey reported girls as preferring single-sex classes (DES/HMI, 1980). But of the girls who were asked how much they had enjoyed their time at school in the Fifteen Thousand Hours survey of London schools in the 1970s, significantly more in mixed than in girls' schools recorded 'quite a lot' or 'very much' (Bone, 1983, p. 111).

Single Sex: Snark Syndrome or Valid Findings

Among the respondants to our discussion paper on the single-sex issue, the majority (as in the group interviews) were deeply convinced of the positive role of single-sex girls' schools. Otherwise hardheaded scientists and engineers anecdoted from a sample of one ('my wife . . . my daughter . . .'), and those who consulted their colleagues found the same:

> Many of the lecturers believe that girls in single-sex schools do better. However, when quizzed, it transpires that this belief is based on what you describe as the current 'received wisdom' rather than on serious examination of the question. None can quote studies. (Head of maths, University)

So far, we have summarized the main influential findings. However, when one takes these apart for such scholarly elements as size or viability of sample, control of variables, transferability of sample, validity of interpretation from data, a different and more complex picture emerges. This can be summarized as follows. Firstly, when single-sex/coeducational studies are controlled for social class and ability, the sex differences between the sectors almost disappear. A larger majority of single-sex schools are private, socially selective or academically selective and fee-paying than state schools are. It must be stressed that it is the nature of the school, and not its sex base, that is the variable. Secondly, one cannot assume that same-sex role modelling 'works better' in single-sex schools or colleges. In the first place, not all women are actually desirable role models; some female teachers distil highly traditional sex-role views of the world. Nor can we assume that maths and science teachers (particularly departmental Heads) in girls' schools are, in fact, women: a male scientist in a girls' school can often serve to reinforce the perceived masculinity of science. Nor do girls' schools necessarily have a female principal. Governing bodies will readily appoint male principals in girls' schools (notably in Catholic and Anglican schools), where they would not dream of appointing a female principal to a boys' school; this practice is increasing, not decreasing. Thirdly, much of the evidence is unscholarly, or anecdotal, or based on small samples, or inconclusive.

Gill's (1987) review and annotated bibliography of Australian and overseas research on the overall single sex/coeducation issue introduces a healthy note of critical scepticism. When one analyses the range of research which she cites, we can confirm that there is no conclusive evidence on either side of the argument, and we can place strong question marks over the transferability of some of the most widely cited research.

Similar questions must be placed over the research on classroom domination by boys as a factor discouraging on its own (for example) girls from pursuing maths or physics. That it forms part of a cluster of factors may be less debatable. Among the major arguments put forward by protagonists of the 'single-sex schools advantage girls' theory are the apparent findings that, in coeducation, boys dominate discourse; teachers give boys more time, attention, cueing and coaching; boys discourage girls from discussion by interruption and mockery; girls have lower self-esteem, and so on. Doenan (1987) has reviewed several hundred studies of research on these and related issues in relation to coeducation versus single-sex education. His scholarly and rigorous re-examination of the 'evidence' shows up the same Snark Syndrome phenomenon as the role-model 'research' reviewed in chapter 4. He finds the following flaws in the most widely cited research:

- Many widely cited studies are based, on closer examination, on infinitesimal samples (one teacher, ten lessons; one teacher, one lesson), which would make their basis for generalization and their transferability questionable.
- Some studies do not report the number of students involved; many do not report the location and type of school (rural, inner-city, etc.).
- A majority of the studies do not define adequately what they mean by 'praise' or 'interaction', and their observation is often methodologically unsystematic.

As a result of Doenan's review, we can legitimately conclude only the following:

1   No study shows females to have had generally more interactions with or help from teachers than male peers; a substantial body of research shows males to be favoured in interactions and receipt of positive help; but a significant number of studies show no sex differences. We cannot conclude that all coeducational settings are lethal to girls.

2   There is consistently strong evidence that males are cued, prompted or questioned more than females in coeducational classrooms.

3   Twenty-nine studies show no sex differences in positive teacher–student interactions, twenty-six demonstrate that males receive more positive interactions, and seven show that females are favoured.

4   More studies show that males receive both more praise and more criticism than females, but many studies show no sex differences. But the more soundly constructed and reported research shows that it is frequently a small minority of boys in a classroom who dominate, are disruptive and receive more attention — not all, or most, boys.

One implication of this is that the issue is less a question of sex-domination of the environment than it is of discipline and classroom management. A second is that the evidence on this issue does not provide a policy basis for returning to single-sex schooling.

Similarly, some preliminary evidence from the USA is frequently cited to show that attendance at single-sex colleges (post-schooling) is influential. How far this influence is the product of the single-sex environment, however, and how far the maturer age of the women concerned and the nature of their early programmes in colleges are responsible, is hard to identify from the published records. For example, St Mary's College, Indiana, has developed a dual-degree programme which enables women attending a single-sex liberal arts programme to pursue an engineering degree in addition to their two-year degree in humanities (or sciences). It is believed that the women 'have an opportunity to develop intellectually and socially without competing with men for leadership' and they are seen to enter the male-dominated third year with increased self-assurance and confidence (Aldrich and Hall, 1980). Smith College and the University of Massachusetts have a similar dual-degree programme in liberal arts and engineering, and for three years (second to fourth year) students take a balance of both, with a fifth year only in engineering (Ivey, 1982). In both cases, women's participation in engineering in the host University appears to have increased. The reason for this is arguably as much a question of greater maturity on entering the 'male' programme, however, as the fact that they studied with women previously.

Nevertheless, even assuming the continuing protection from negative male attitudes to be the relevant factor, is this the right policy answer? The wave of projects setting up single-sex maths and science classes in schools since the late 1970s clearly has been based on the assumption that it is. Here again, received wisdom that single-sex classes are universally advantageous to girls is a Snark Syndrome over-simplification: it is frequently asserted without a scholarly base. One of the most thorough experiments (funded by the UK's Equal Opportunities Commission) was single-sex setting in mathematics classes in Tameside, England, in the early 1980s (Smith, 1986). Despite some detailed evidence of positive gains by girls ('not made at the expense of the boys' — *ibid.*, p. 40), the researcher concludes that 'a school which mounts a sustained and coherent campaign to provide equal opportunities for girls in maths can succeed without using the particular device of single-sex setting' (*ibid.*, p. 41) on the grounds that the gains were relatively negligible, and that the real factors of influence were the recruitment of three female maths teachers, sustained efforts by *all* maths teachers to ensure that girls play an active part in class, and attempts to change the male bias of the syllabus. All of these factors can and should be replicated in coeducation. Smith still cautions against complacency, however; even after what was seen as successful action research, girls' performance in either setting fell short of parity with boys and more Grade 9 and 10 girls than boys still perceived maths as 'difficult' (*ibid.*, pp. 40–41). A later Australian study by Rowe (1988) of Year 7 and Year 8 students allocated to all boys', all girls' and mixed-sex classes set up in mathematics, tested the three groups of students across two school years. The most notable improvement was in girls' single-sex classes, and was associated with confidence levels. But again, this is a single-school result and is not a basis for wider policy.

The Policy Case against Single-sex Education:
Altering the Ecology, not the Girls

While the evidence is contradictory, overall it should be clearly estab-lished that there is no doubt that boys do, in fact, dominate over girls, demanding and receiving more attention and exerting territorial priority over scientific and computing equipment, in at least some coeducational settings. While it is not universal, the evidence, where it does occur, is convincing and serious in its effect and implications.

Where I differ from previous writers is on the policy implications of this. It simply does not fit girls for either the ocker (uncouth, brash, crude) ecology of first-year engineering or physics, or of the motor mechanics' yard, or of the apprenticeship workshop, to shelter them in the relatively more civilized environment of an all-female discourse and behaviour pattern. There is considerable field evidence from Universities that the women who do manage to make it through to graduation when they are in what the Byrne Scale of Non-traditionality terms the 'abnormal' or 'rubric of exceptions' minority below critical mass level, are either exceptionally gifted, unusually motivated and hardworking and, usually, very middle-class (unlike many of their male peers). The girls who transfer over in or after first year to pure (as distinct from applied) maths or science degrees from engineering, surveying, etc. courses are predominantly those who cannot — or will not — cope with the undiluted effects of impact from male students whose single-sex schooling has reinforced their dominance, sheer decibels of voice, territoriality, assumption of automatic male priority, contempt for girls, and sexual crudeness. (Those who doubt this should work in a University department of teacher education and spend part of each year dealing with boys' schools, and with their male teachers.) Putting girls in single-sex classes or schools produces four negative outcomes, lethal to many mainstream unexceptional but bright or able girls when they move on:

1   It cushions them against the real world of training and work in which men remain the powerbrokers, and it does not teach them strategies for coping in the interim until we succeed in changing a masculine learning environment to a gender-neutral user-friendly one.
2   It perpetuates the masculine ecology unmodified, with the result that most male school-leavers from the (parallel) boys' schools and classes are contemptuous of females or underrate them and see no need to change; they are likely, until we reshape the workforce, still to predominate in workforce decision-making later (unmodified).
3   It perpetuates the wrong paradigm of a female deficit model — that it is girls who must be sheltered and helped, instead of boys who need to alter and to learn to share equal discourse; not to interrupt excessively; to work collaboratively and not always competitively; to value human dimensions of science

and technology; and to treat women with intellectual and sexual respect.

4 Most of all, it gives school, college and University teachers (of both sexes) an alibi for avoiding the real problem of classroom and lecture-hall management, which means teaching in a gender-neutral, student-centred and well-controlled learning environment.

It should be noted that the problems of negative peer attitudes, of the poor image of some disciplines, and of presence or lack of esteem and confidence which are centrally authenticated in research, stem from teachers and from the classroom environment: they do not spring unaided from students alone.

Intervention strategies in the 1980s have, as in the role-model issue, focussed on a single issue — single-sex classes — and not on a holistic approach to the learning environment. The reason for the critical filter within maths may well be partly the result of girls in some (not all) classes not receiving enough teacher attention or interaction or help over those mathematical elements which our evidence shows fewer girls pursue. In turn, the lack of such encouragement as early as Grade 10 or 11 will clearly cause more girls to see physics as 'difficult'. If boys are also labelling them peculiar or unfeminine for even wanting to struggle with physics, it is indeed only the rubric of exceptions who will persist.

Instead of the deficit paradigm (whether seen as girls needing protection or boys needing to be filtered out from disruptive patterns), we need a further cluster of strategies (see cluster 5). One without the others simply will not produce a real, long-term return for investment.

Implications for Action?

Relatively few of those who attended the group interviews or who responded to the ten discussion papers saw themselves as having a direct role to play in changing either the attitudinal climate of male-dominated disciplines or that of their institution; or in reviewing the structure, content and marketing of their disciplines. Almost none was able to recognize the impact or influence of groups of factors on outcomes. For example, most simply said that the media and the schools should alter images. They did not recognize an interrelationship between the images of disciplines, their ascription as sex-normal or sex-abnormal and critical mass — a two-way relationship which it is for

Cluster 5

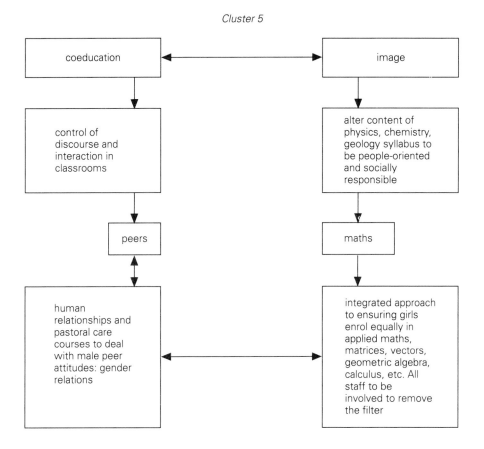

higher education also to address. It was equally difficult for most participants to perceive a direct role for themselves in altering content-orientation of courses or disciplines, or content in texts, to re-establish a positive image of disciplines seen as socially irresponsible. This was summed up by a University engineer who sent in comments from his departmental colleagues as a group: 'They considered there was no need for action as women would increasingly move into the profession of their own volition as was already happening' (lecturer, civil engineering, University).

Equally, the issue of cascading losses (notably at postgraduate level) was generally seen as inevitable and almost irremediable. Yet, like the data on undergraduates in chapter 3, our postgraduate data show major inter-institutional variations. The percentage of women in PhD enrolments across the survey disciplines varied from a mean of 12.5 per cent to 17.7 per cent. Within this, only biochemistry, microbiology and genetics had female enrolments above the gender-neutral critical mass threshold across all the Universities. Mathematics, geology and chemistry, however, showed widely varying percentages for female enrolments at doctoral level among the institutions as a whole. The filter processes to account not only for the cascading losses but also for the wide inter-institutional variations, cannot lie solely with the schooling system; they are substantially the result of the constructed ecology of the discipline in higher education. It is evident that the factors are complex and intermeshed. Where do we go from here?

References

ALBURY, D. and SCHWARTZ, J. (1982) *Partial Progress: The Politics of Science and Technology*, London, Pluto Press.

ALDRICH, M. and HALE, P. (1980) *Programs in Science, Maths & Engineering for Women in the United States: 1966–1978*, American Association for the Advancement of Science.

ARMSTRONG, J. and PRICE, R. (1982) 'Correlates and predictors of women's mathematics participation', *Journal for Research in Mathematics Education*, 13 (2), pp. 99–109.

BECKER, J.R. (1981) 'Differential treatment of females and males in maths classes', *Journal for Research in Maths Education*, 12 (1), pp. 40–53.

BENBOW, C.P. and STANLEY, J.C. (1982a) 'Consequences in high school and college of sex differences in mathematical reasoning ability: a longitudinal perspective', *American Educational Research Journal*, winter, 19 (4), pp. 598–622.

BLOOM, B. (1976) *Human Character and School Learning*, New York, McGraw Hill.

BOARD OF EDUCATION (1923) *Differentiation Between the Sexes in Secondary Schools*, London.

BONE, A. (1983) *Girls and Girls-only Schools: A Review of the Evidence*, Manchester, Equal Opportunities Commission.

BOWLING, J. and MARTIN, B. (1985) 'Science: a masculine disorder', *Science and Public Policy*, December, pp. 308–16.

BROPHY, J. and GOOD, T. (1970) 'Teachers' communication of differential expectations for children's classroom performance', *Journal of Educational Psychology*, 61 (5), pp. 365–74.

BYRNE, E.M. (1985) *Women and Engineering: A Comparative Overview*, Canberra, Bureau of Labour Market Research.

COMMITTEE OF INQUIRY INTO TEACHING OF MATHEMATICS (THE COCKCROFT COMMITTEE) (1982) *Mathematics Counts*, London, HMSO.

DEPARTMENT OF EDUCATION AND SCIENCE (DES) (1975) *Curricular Differences for Boys and Girls*, Education Survey 21, London, HMSO.

DES/HMI (1980) *Girls and Science, Report of HM Inspectorate*, London, HMSO.

DOENAN, S. (1987) *Are Teachers Fair to Girls?* Pennant Hills, NSW, Edvance Publication.

DOLLARD, J. and MILLER, N. (1950) *Personality and Psychotherapy*, New York, McGraw Hill.

DUE-BILLING, Y. and BRUVIK HANSEN, A. (1983) 'Research: women's attitudes to technological studies, especially engineering', *Contributions to Second GASAT Conference*, Oslo.

EBBUTT, D. (1981) 'Girls' science, boys' science revisited' in KELLY, A. (Ed) *The Missing Half: Girls and Science Education*', Manchester, Manchester University Press, pp. 205–15.

FENNEMA, F. (1977) 'Influences of selected cognitive, affective and education variables on sex related differences in mathematics learning and studying' in SHOEMAKER, J.S. (Ed) *Women and Mathematics: Research Perspectives for Change*, Washington, DC, National Institute of Education.

FENNEMA, J. and CARPENTER, T. (1981) 'Sex-related differences in maths achievement' in JACOBS, J. (Ed) *Perspectives on Women and Mathematics*, Ohio, Columbus.

FOX, L.H. (1977) 'The effects of sex role socialisation on maths participation and achievement', in SHOEMAKER, J.S. (Ed) *Women and Mathematics: Research Perspectives for Change*, Washington, DC, National Institute of Education.

GILL, J. (1987) *Which Way to School?* Canberra, Commonwealth Schools Commission,

HARDING, J. (1979) 'Sex differences in examination performance at 16+', *Physics Education* 14, July.

HARDING, J. (1981) 'Sex differences in science examinations' in KELLY, A. (Ed) *The Missing Half: Girls and Science Education*, Manchester, Manchester University press,

HARDING, J. (1983) *Switched off: The Science Education of Girls*, London, Longman, for Schools Council.

HEAD, J. (1984) *The Personal Response to Science*, Cambridge, Cambridge University Press.

HOLDEN, C. (1987) report, *Science*, 8 May, p. 660.

HUEFTLE, S., RAKOW, S. and WELCH, W. (1983) *Images of Science*, Science Assessment Unit, Mineappolis University of Minnesota.

IVES, R. (1984) 'The maleness of science', *Australian Science Teachers Journal*, 30 (1), pp. 15–20.

IVEY, E. (1982) 'Engineering at Smith College', *Engineering Education*, December.

KELLY, A. (1981) (Ed) *The Missing Half: Girls and Science Education*, Manchester, Manchester University Press.

KELLY, A., SMAIL, B. and WHYTE, J. (1983) *Initial GIST Survey: Results and Implications, Manchester*, Manchester Polytechnic.

LEDER, G. (1976) 'Contextual setting and mathematical performance', *The Australian Mathematics Teacher*, pp. 119–27.

MAHONEY, P. (n.d.) *Schools for the Boys? Coeducation Reassessed.*

MEAD, M. and METRAUX, R. (1957) 'Image of the scientist among high school students', *Science*, 126, pp. 384–9.

MICHEL, A. (1986) *Down with Stereotypes! Eliminating Sexism from Children's Literature and School Textbooks*, Paris, UNESCO.

NIELSEN, H. and THOMSEN, P.V. (1985) 'Physics in upper secondary schools in Denmark, *European Journal of Science Education*, 7 (1), pp. 95–106.

ORMEROD, M.B. (1971) 'The social implications factor in attitudes to science', *British Journal of Educational Psychology*, 41 (3), pp. 335–8.

ORMEROD, M.B. (1975) 'Subject preference and choice in coeducational and single sex secondary schools', *British Journal of Educational Psychology*, 45, pp. 257–67.

ORMEROD, M.B. (1979) 'Pupils' attitudes to the social implications of science', *European Journal of Science Education*, 1 (2), pp. 177–90.

ORMEROD, M., BOTTOMLEY, J.M., KEYS, W. and WOOD, C. (1979) 'Girls and physics education', *Physics Education*, 14, pp. 271–7.

ORMEROD, M. and DUCKWORTH, D. (1975) *Pupils' Attitude to Science: A Review of Research, Slough*, NFER-Nelson.

PACEY, A. (1983) *The Culture of Technology*, Oxford, Basil Blackwell.

PHILLIPS, S. (1975) *Young Australians*, Sydney, Harper and Row.

PRATT, H. (1981) 'Science education in the elementary school' in HARMS, N.C. and YAGER, R.E. (Eds) *What Research Says to the Science Teacher*, vol. 3, Washington, DC, National Science Teachers' Association.

RHYDDERCH, G. (1984) 'Half the class: strategies for single sex teaching groups in mixed schools', unpublished paper presented to Girl Friendly Schooling Conference, Manchester Polytechnic.

ROWE, K. (1988) 'Singlesex and mixed-sex classes: the effects of class type on student achievement, confidence and participation in mathematics', *Australian Journal of Education*, 32 (2), pp. 180–202.

SHERMAN, J. and FENNEMA, E. (1977) 'The study of Maths by High School Girls and Boys: Related Variables', in *American Educational Research Journal*, 14, pp. 159–168.

SMITH, S. (1980) 'Should they be kept apart?' *Times Educational Supplement*, 18 July.

SMITH, S. (1986) *Separate Tables? An Investigation into Singlesex Setting in Mathematics*, EOC Research Series, London, HMSO.

SPENDER, D. (1980) *Man-made Language*, London, Routledge and Kegan Paul.

STEEDMAN, J. (1983) *Examination Results in Mixed and Single Sex Schools: Findings from the National Child Development Study*, Manchester, Equal Opportunities Commission.

TOBIAS, S. (1978) *Overcoming Math Anxiety*, New York, W.W. Norton.

TOBIAS, S. and WEISSBROD, C. (1980) 'Anxiety and mathematics: an update', *Harvard Educational Review*, 50 (1), pp. 63–70.

WEINREICH-HASTE, H.E. (1981) 'The image of science' in KELLY, A. (Ed) *The Missing Half: Girls and Science Education*, Manchester, Manchester University Press, pp. 216–29.

WHYTE, J. (1986) *Girls into Science & Technology*, London, Routledge and Kegan Paul.

WINCHEL, R., FENNER, D. and SHAVER, P. (1974) 'Impact of coeducation of "fear and success" imagery expressed by male and female high school students', *Journal of Educational Psychology*, 66 (5), pp. 726–30.

WOOD and FERGUSON, S. (1974) 'The improved case for coeducation', *Times Educational Supplement*, 4 October, p. 22.

Chapter 7

Conclusion: Policies for Change?

The great tragedy of science: the slaying of a beautiful hypothesis by an ugly fact. (Thomas Henry Huxley, *Collected Essays:
Biogenesis and Abiogenesis*, 1894)

Application of detailed scholarly review to Snark Syndrome received
wisdom results in the slaying of a good many faulty hypotheses which
have become embedded in the attitudes and assumptions of the men
who still dominate and administer higher education. (Australia has just
achieved its second female Vice Chancellor in a century of higher education.) Scholarship now establishes without possible doubt that women
have equal intellectual capacity with men in any area of study or work
(out with biological determinism); that women also do, in fact, wish to
participate in all arenas hitherto labelled as territorially 'masculine', and
that some actually do so, and have for centuries (out with sex-role
stereotyping). Within the overall issue of the need for women's voices
to be heard in leadership as elsewhere, assumption after assumption is
biting the dust in the wake of scholarship disproving sexist assumptions and gender-based prejudices. Or are they? Five years on from our
main survey work on the UQ WISTA project, where are we? Whyte
recalls in the British GIST project that 'teachers need to be convinced
of existing bias before they will consider positive action for girls'
(Whyte, 1986, p. 230). By no means all of the Deans, Professors, Heads
of Schools and lecturers we surveyed were convinced even that we
were investigating a 'real' problem:

But Professor Byrne, you are presupposing that women's lesser
enrolment in the physical sciences is a *problem* in the first place.
Why does it matter? If they want to enrol, they will. Why does
it matter who our students are? (group interview, Head of
physics, male, University)

This was by no means untypical, although a majority did see an issue to be investigated and dealt with — preferably, however, by others. Some were actively hostile; others became so committed that they have remained in touch and regularly send us material on female achievements in science to strengthen our argument. In response to the ten discussion papers on which we asked for written feedback, we cite below the two extremes. The following arrived from a University maths department whose Head had circulated the papers:

> This is, of course, exactly the kind of garbage I associate the feminist movement with, and I hope you do not really expect me to waste my time reading it and trying to figure out what all these nonsensical questions mean! It is bad enough that we have to pay tax so that the government can employ people to produce this sort of rubbish; you can't expect me to also spend time on it.
>
> I'll pass it on to the next victim immediately. (lecturer, University)

By contrast, the paper on prerequisites, in particular, produced serious, constructive comment from most: 'Thank you for this Paper. It addresses issues of relevance and poses important questions' (Chairman, academic board, University). Another maths lecturer took a different view on the 'feminist garbage': 'Thank you for the informative and vigorous WISTA Discussion Papers 7–10. I particularly appreciated their minimal use of jargon' (lecturer, University)

One weakness is higher education's lack of a sense of institutional goals as such. The role of key management personnel (Deans, Professors, Heads of Schools in higher education) in policy issues relating to this area is confused, ambiguous, highly varied and extremely idiosyncratic in terms of fulfilment of institutional goals (if any), of institutional strategies and of discipline-based responsibilities.

One first task is to persuade the leadership of higher education that single-dimension strategies do not work and that programmes or strategies which use clusters of causally related factors are necessary. This implies some inservice education about cultural and psychological and not just physical or structural aspects of learning environments. The policy process should operate, rationally, as illustrated in Flowchart 6.1. However, in practice, higher education has tended to jump from awareness based on unsupported received wisdom ('Role models are important,' 'Single-sex schools produce more women physicists') straight to new policy strategies with scant time to acquire new knowledge or understanding of the research and new theory available, and without

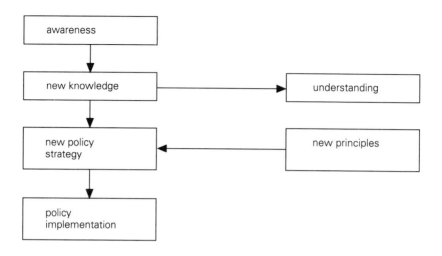

Figure 6.1 Flowchart

seriously debating new principles as institutional goals. The research approach seeks to build new knowledge and increased understanding back in. Management, good management, should be based on both.

If there had been a simple and inexpensive policy or management solution it would have been implemented long ago. We have, however, known for twenty years or more of most of the kinds of issues raised by this study. What we have not known is how much of the received wisdom is either unfounded, or contradictory, or mutually exclusive to other received wisdom. In the impossible task of trying to keep up with escalating research and evaluation, the Snark Syndrome ('What I tell you three times is true') has sprung up and spread like mint in a herb garden or couch grass in the rosebed.

The arguments advanced in this book are no more susceptible to irrefutable proof than the theories we have criticized. It is for the reader to set them against the available data, against reputable substantive theory and against her or his own real-life experiences. We believe they provide improved explanatory theory. They do, we argue, ring true at the level of grounded theory.

What, then, are we saying?

Managing Policy Change

In fact, we are not yet at the point where there is sufficient agreement on the diagnosis simply to embark on one curative course. Let us, therefore, first take stock of the general issues:

1   We have argued for a paradigm shift away from projects without roots focussing on women as a deficit model, and towards an institutional ecology approach where powerful men take responsibility for changing both male and female attitudes and do not leave it to powerless women in the system.

2   We have argued for a new conceptual framework centring on critical mass and on image concepts of non-traditionality, sex-normality and gender-neutrality as environmental explanations of disciplines as an ecological niche. Not until male staff and students alike cease to transmit concepts of the non-traditionality and sex-abnormality of those (of either sex) enrolled in a discipline where they do not reach the level of a critical mass, will we make organic, sustained progress.

3   We have argued that further research should focus on interdisciplinary and inter-institutional differences, and that the blanket terms 'science' and 'technology' are unhelpful generalizations. We postulate that some disciplines are more susceptible than others to institutional influences within their own ecology. We need to know why. Professional institutions and associations need to face these issues as well as higher education.

4   Finally, we have argued for a holistic or cluster approach in policy projects. To continue to invest millions of dollars in single-factor or dyadic one-off models is a poor return for investment, and wasteful and ineffective. We need institutional change to counteract 'genesis amnesia'.

Within the overall picture, there are several specific issues which need to be highlighted.

Progress or Backlash?

There has, of course, been significant progress over the last two decades, and it would be simple, and encouraging, to concentrate only on the undoubted gains in women's access to and progression in the different disciplines and arenas during this time, including since the mid-1980s. But this would be deceptive. The real picture is very mixed, and more complex.

For example, in several states in Australia, curriculum development has created a new multistrand science, the original purpose of which was precisely to break down the historically inherited and abstract theoretical straitjacket of separate physics and chemistry and natural science and deal with scientific problems in an integrate and more socially relevant way. But the inflexibility of tertiary institutions and the general inertia of the schoolteaching force (innovators are, by definition, never a critical mass!) have combined with parental ignorance and prejudice to relegate multistrand science to the same status as 'maths in society': the fail-safe for the less able. Competition for scarce higher education places, with expanding demand, has cast a dead shadow over creative curriculum design.

Similarly, Snark assertions repeated three (or thirty) times — for instance, that we have eliminated the gender gap because, overall, women form half of all undergraduates in many countries; or because girls average half of all maths candidates (if we include 'maths in society' figures); or because we have a few more women Professors (I am still one of Australia's mere 5 per cent of the professoriate who are female: 9 per cent of Professors in my University are women) — are as unscholarly, unselective and unsound as the received wisdom on role models or single-sex education. For while Grade 12 figures since 1985 and 1986 show some continuing small narrowing of the sex gap in one or two sciences, and notably in geology, relatively fewer girls as a whole are studying science or technology at all at Grade 12. In Queensland, the proportion of females as a percentage of all candidates actually fell between 1980 and 1988 in maths I and II, chemistry, physics and earth science. Female enrolments in biology were down 14 per cent over that period. The pattern is replicated in several other states. And the sex gap, while narrower, remains significant. In Queensland in the late 1980s, some 37 per cent of boys but only 13 per cent of girls took physics, and 39 per cent of boys but 24 per cent of girls studied chemistry at Grade 12. Clearly, one overriding issue may be the students' perceptions of the future career outlets from different disciplines. The now dramatically higher financial rewards that may accrue from studying law, medicine, dentistry or computing in Australia filter many able young people out of pure and applied science, or engineering, surveying and mining, into these areas. Yet in Australia, female veterinary science enrolments at Universities have moved from 3 per cent of the total in 1940, through the untypicality band (about 20 per cent) in the early 1970s, to complete gender-neutrality (49 per cent women) in the late 1980s. What changed its image? Was it when engineering and physics lost ground? The answers are important for economic reasons as well as for equity.

Another backlash area is in computing and computer literacy. Unlike mining, which goes back to the Iron Age as a 'masculine domain', and engineering, whose male-domination predates the Pyramids, computing as a discipline is less than three decades old. The participants in the UQ WISTA surveys tended to describe it as gender-neutral but this is incorrect and wishful thinking when set against the statistical data. The most serious and widespread evidence is of growing gender differentiation in access to computers and in perceptions of computing as user-friendly. The now considerable research literature on computing in education shows that:

- Parents still buy computers more readily for sons than for daughters; sons also dominate computer use in the home.
- Boys acquire territorial priority for hands-on work on scarce computers when student numbers exceed available computer hours in school situations.
- Girls are arriving at tertiary level with a narrower (and mainly reproductive) range of computer skills than boys.
- Boys are less willing to work cooperatively on computers than girls: an essential learning process unless and until every student has her or his own microcomputer.

A very recent British study reports that

girls tend to be dominated by boys in computer-based tasks which require cooperative work, even though girls have no disadvantages in these tasks when tested individually or in single gender groups . . . [in measuring] tasks which required the cooperative use of the computer keyboard, . . . both types of single gender pairs improved in comparison with individuals working alone, but mixed gender pairs did not. (Underwood and McCaffrey, 1990, pp. 44–49)

This issue is, again, really one of ineffective or effective classroom management, principally because schoolteachers still do not see girls' under-achievement as a problem for which they are responsible.

Reconstructing Science

It is also clear from a wide range of research and field evidence that unless and until we reconstruct the content and structure of many scientific and technological disciplines, we will continue to lose not only girls but also creative 'androgynous' boys from these. The resultant implications of a future manipulated by theoretical, dehumanized technology controlled mainly or exclusively by the more instrumental and mentally linear approach of males is horrifying. A recent British study of sixth-formers (Grades 11 and 12) across six schools and colleges confirms the continuing trend that:

> Many students had negative attitudes to school science courses . . . the sterile, impersonal nature of that content in physics and chemistry . . . The negative attitude of girls to much of school sciences was due largely to its impersonal and abstract nature . . . the image of scientists portrayed by the media, either as caricatures of the mad (male) scientist or the expert called in to explain away *another* disaster, also affected student attitudes. (Woolnough, 1990, pp. 3–4)

Above all, these students are put off by the lack of opportunity for self-expression (too much formulae and multiple choice) and the lack of relationship to the 'real human problems of life' (*ibid.*, p. 7).

- We believe that the evidence of this and other recent studies justifies a major curriculum review of school and tertiary physics, chemistry, geology, engineering and mathematics, to include the production of gender-neutral textbooks, and focussing in material and content on the human and social implications of what is to be taught and learned.
- There is at least preliminary evidence to support a hypothesis that overstructured and inflexible degree courses, with little choice, increase overall drop-out rates and discourage female enrolments.

Role Modelling and Mentorship

It is clear from chapters 4 and 5 that we believe that our data and analysis justify a major paradigm shift here, in policy terms. Our detailed recommendations are set out in earlier chapters, and are not repeated here. One must register some incredulity at the ease with which men have (again) persuaded women, even feminists, that all of the extra work needed to help girls and women overcome the barriers that males set in their way, must also be carried out by women personally giving up time to rush around being 'visible' as role models, thus once again letting men off the hook of dealing with male-created problems. Breaking the stereotype must be achieved through systemic means, videos and publishing. Individual help to girls and young women is mentorship, and the case has been made for this to be seen and acknowledged as part of school, college and University ecology and placed in a policy context for monitoring and development.

Single-Sex or Coeducation?

This issue may be summed up in the words of a Canadian Grade 10 student in the context of an evaluation of single-sex maths classes: 'teenagers should be taught to deal responsibly and maturely with problems involving the opposite sex; not removed from them' (quoted in McFarlane and Crawford, 1985). While it would be wrong to under-play or under-report the undoubted problems which ocker (uncouth, contemptuous, arrogant, etc.) male peer behaviour creates for girls in school classrooms, it is clear that the whole single-sex issue is a classic of Snark effect policy. The argument in chapter 6 is to deal with the real problems head on, and not by yet again asking girls to take evasive action, leaving boys to remain unsocialized with impunity.

Maths as a Critical Filter

Similarly, it is pointless to continue simply to blame the schools, however rightly, either for incompetent teaching or for gender-conditioning. Schools are by their nature inertia-prone and systemic change is slow, even if we had the maths teachers to remedy the deficiencies. While we continue to research at school level to unravel the processes that filter girls out from applied maths and pre-technology maths, we need tertiary bridging programmes funded by governments (in Australia, by the federal government) to provide the missing maths either in one-semester bridging courses or in the first year of higher education. And not in single-sex classes!

Let me end by telling the story of one of the group interviews in 1986. After having read the first four discussion papers in advance, and listening to the group discussion of the issues raised, a Professor from a discipline in which girls were well into the 'abnormal/rubric of exceptions' minority, said: 'Professor Byrne, I have a problem. You are two women directing this project. Do you not think this invalidates the results?'

After a moment's stunned silence, I replied, 'Professor X, let me be clear what question you are asking. You are saying that because we do not have a mixed-sex research team, our research into these issues is invalid? Presumably you will accept that, then, 90 per cent of scientific research so far is invalid because it has been conducted exclusively by men?'

He shook his head uncertainly.

'I'm sorry. You are saying that because we are women, we are less able or well qualified and need what Simone de Beauvoir termed "a male mediator between us and the Universe"?

He hastily protested that our qualifications and experience were impressive.

'I am sorry to have misunderstood again. You are saying that because we are women, even if our research is in fact sound, no one will listen to us, simply because we are women?'

As the Professor struggled to come to terms with that, a colleague came to his rescue. 'I think what my colleague is saying, Professor Byrne, is that it would be a pity if so much wide-ranging and substantially funded research on so important an issue, were not influential because . . .' His voice died away.

I said quietly, 'So you *are* in fact saying that he believes that however right women are, they cannot be listened to with the same scholarly clout as men?'

The academic asked curiously, 'What will you do, if that happens?'

I answered promptly, 'Go on television and radio, since I do a good deal of media work already, and recount this conversation as representing the essence of the central and real cause of the whole problem we have been investigating.'

He looked at me thoughtfully. 'Professor, five minutes ago, I would have said that I would be up there with you — but let me not suggest that you need a male mediator! So I will rephrase it and say that I will be there supporting you from the wings . . . You should do just that.'

Australia has just published a Report of the Inquiry into Equal Opportunity for Women in Australia, which is rightly entitled *Halfway to Equal*. Recommendation 48 proposes the development of national strategies to address the need for pre-service and inservice education of teachers 'to give them appropriate skills to develop more positive learning environments for girls'.

We know the strategies needed. What we do not have is the federal funds for retraining, nor the commitment to long-term action of the 95 per cent of administrators and government of education who are still male. Until we have a national policy on the education of boys (about the education of girls) to match all the effort to change girls and women, the Snark Syndrome will flourish and change will remain cosmetic. For the sake of the economic and social future of our countries, we cannot afford to let this be so.

References

McFARLANE, S. and CRAWFORD, P. (1985) 'Effect of sex-segregated maths on student attitudes and achievement in mathematics', Research Report, ERIC ED 276 734.

UNDERWOOD, G. and McCAFFREY, M. (1990) 'Gender differences in a co-operative computer-based language task', *Educational Research*, 32 (1), Spring, pp. 44–49

WOOLNOUGH, B. (1990) (Ed) *Making Choices: An Enquiry into the Attitudes of Sixth Formers towards Science and Technology*, Oxford, Department of Education.

WHYTE, J. (1986) *Girls into Science and Technology*, London, Routledge and Kegan Paul.

Index